Music, Archetype, and the Writer:
A Jungian View

MUSIC, ARCHETYPE, AND THE WRITER:
A Jungian View

BETTINA L. KNAPP

The Pennsylvania State University Press
University Park and London

Ad Alba Amica/Sorella

Library of Congress Cataloging-in-Publication Data

Knapp, Bettina Liebowitz, 1926–
    Music, archetype, and the writer.

    Bibliography: p.
    Includes index.
    1. Music and literature.   2. Music in literature.
3. Jung, C. G. (Carl Gustav), 1875–1961.   4. Creative
writing.   5. Creation (Literary, artistic, etc.)
I. Title.
PN56.M87K6   1988   809′.93357   87-43122
ISBN 0-271-00624-2

Contents

Introduction

"... Music should be an essential part of every analysis," C. G. Jung wrote. It "reaches deep archetypal material that we can only sometimes reach in our analytical work with patients."[1] So profoundly imbedded is music in the unconscious and in the dreams emerging from it that most people are unaware of its presence as image, tone, and cadence. "The musical movement of the unconscious" Jung compared to "a sort of symphony" whose dynamics are still a mystery.[2]

Indeed, the interaction between musical motifs, systems of intensity, patterns of tonality, contrapuntal schemes, multiple rhythms, and the writing process is obscure but fascinating. For some writers, sonorities flow archetypally from the unconscious, producing a nearly endless variety of resonant images and pulsations. As an author becomes aware of unknown elements infiltrating his body and psyche, he may become affected by stirrings and inner meanderings. Fresh feelings and innovative ideas are born. The creative writer uses to his advantage these paradoxically soundless and immobile rhythms, transliterating them into the written word. Like the poet Arthur Rimbaud, he, too, will be able to say: "And I sometimes saw what man believed he had seen!"

Archetypal music arises from the collective unconscious—the deepest of subliminal levels within the psyche, which is for the most part inaccessible to the conscious mind. In this suprapersonal sphere, where the *great* artist descends for inspiration, he is exposed to "a living system of reactions and aptitudes" that determine the path his work will take.[3] Tonal sequences, pitches, amplitudes, and movement catalyze him, begetting moods and arousing unsuspected contents within the folds of his unconscious. Like

Orpheus, whose lyre mesmerized animals and minerals by the beauty of its modulations, so the sensitive writer, endowed with an Orphic faculty to charm impulses and instincts, activates unknown and amorphous forces and their accompanying tonal waves. They are then transmuted by the novelist, poet, or dramatist into the *Word*, imbued with endlessly resounding harmonies and cacophonies.

Archetypal music expands consciousness in that it reveals the psyche's potential in distilled, proportioned, and measured tonal messages, disclosing to the creative artist ways of using energies which might otherwise have been diffused into oblivion.[4] Archetypes—and archetypal music as well—

> exist preconsciously, and presumably they form the structural dominants of the psyche in general. . . . As *a priori* conditioning factors they represent a special psychological instance of the biological "pattern of behavior," which gives all things their specific qualities. Just as the manifestations of this biological ground plan may change in the course of development, so also can those of the archetype.[5]

Energy charges are inherent in archetypal music, as they are in archetypes in general. Their impact on an author may determine the structure in which he places the creatures of his fantasy and the intensity which marks their interrelationships; they may help trace the course of the plot or antiplot and the governing rhythmic qualities of his fugal or orchestrated verbal patterns, regulating as well their intonations and cadences.

An archetype is an elusive concept that cannot really be fully defined. Jung, the creator of this seminal psychological notion, suggested that archetypes, perceived in the form of primordial images, are present in dreams, legends, fairy tales, myths, religious and cultural notions, and modes of behavior the world over.[6] They are elements in perpetually mobile psychic structures and, until manifested in events, patternings, and configurations, are nonperceptible, existing as potential energy in their dormant state in the depths of the collective unconscious. As distinguished from the personal unconscious, defined as containing "personal contents belonging to the individual himself which can and properly should be made conscious and integrated into the conscious personality or ego," the collective unconscious "is composed of transpersonal, universal contents which cannot be assimilated by the ego."[7]

Archetypal images, which arise spontaneously from the collective unconscious, are mysterious and undefinable; they are "energy centers," "magnetic fields," which not only influence but frequently dominate an individual's thoughts, feelings, and behavioral patterns. They fascinate and frequently overpower the individual if they are not—and sometimes even if they are—consciously understood and integrated into the psyche or channeled into the work of art.[8]

Arche means "beginning, origin, cause, primal source and principle." The word is also defined as "position of a leader, supreme rule and government." *Type* is interpreted as a "blow and what is produced by a blow, the imprint of a coin . . . form, image, copy, prototype, model, order, and norm": a primordial or underlying form.[9] Jung elucidates:

> The term [archetype] is not meant to denote an inherited idea, but rather an inherited mode of psychic functioning, corresponding to the inborn way in which the chick emerges from the egg, the bird builds its nest, a certain kind of wasp stings the motor ganglion of the caterpillar, and eels find their way to the Bermudas. In other words, it is a "pattern of behavior." This aspect of the archetype is the biological one. . . . But the picture changes at once when looked at from the inside, that is, from within the realm of the subjective psyche. Here the archetype presents itself as numinous, that is, it appears as an experience of fundamental importance.[10]

Archetypes may also be related to the notion of instincts. Edward Edinger writes in this regard:

> An archetype is to the psyche what an instinct is to the body. The existence of archetypes is inferred by the same process as that by which we infer the existence of instincts. Just as instincts common to a species are postulated by observing the uniformities in biological behavior, so archetypes are inferred by observing the uniformities in psychic phenomena. Just as instincts are unknown motivating dynamisms of biological behavior, archetypes are unknown motivating dynamisms of the psyche.[11]

Like the archetype, archetypal music is endowed with energy tones which decide repetitions, modulations, leitmotifs, associations, multiple variants, and combinations that underscore the emotional values or conditions of the novel, drama, or poem being composed. Each emanation becomes "an object with a voice of its own, that one does justice to . . . by letting it alone and allowing it to utter its own meaning."[12] In this way, new sources of creativity may be tapped and writing becomes music: the visual becomes a tactile, olfactory, tastable, *audible* experience.

Myths and fairy tales take shape from the *prima materia;* likewise, archetypal music emanates from the "matrix of life experience."[13] A writer's predisposition to a musical archetype may govern the mood patterns of his literary creation and determine the course of certain inborn reactions to a specific unconscious stimulus. As custodians and channelers of creative energy, musical archetypes dictate the creative individual's verbal composition: the manner in which fantasy images are conveyed and laid out acoustically, the intensity of the feelings expressed, the sensations and behavioral trajectories of the characters, and the linguistical schemes of the prose or poetry used.

Archetypal music may be looked upon as a data processor—a way of coding and decoding what exists inchoate in a space-time continuum, or the fourth dimension, which is the collective unconscious. The writer, like the data processor, transforms the sound waves leaping up from within his collective unconscious into words endowed with their own auditory, rhythmical, and sensory motifs. If music is archetypal for the author, it is manifested as a complex of opposites: it is both concrete and abstract, causal and acausal, linear and mythical, visual and audible, alive in an *eternal present*, the now, the future, and an inherited past.[14]

Archetypal music reveals "inherited *possibilities* of presentation" while also exploring certain predispositions, potentials, and prefigurations— what Henri Bergson called the *éternels incrées*.[15] It embodies not only such figures as the Wise Old Man, the Child, the Great Mother, the Animus/ Anima, the Shadow, and the Ego but situations as well: sacrifice, initiation, ascent, descent, contest, heroism, quest, rites of passage, and so forth.[16]

Just as the author responds to the sensations he experiences from within his depths, then mediates them by cognition, likewise the reader hears, sees, senses, feels, and intuits the drama or poem he is in the process of experiencing. If the reader is affected by the archetypal music picked up by his inner ear, whose rhythms are scanned by his senses, his heartbeat might accelerate, his muscles tense, his blood pressure increase, and his entire emotional system marvel at this collective power alive within him. As a suggestive power, archetypal music may summon up infinite musical resonances within the reader; sound waves of different lengths and traveling at a variety of speeds open up fresh causeways of feelings. Love, rage, hatred, violence, passivity, serenity, may be regarded as cathartic or abreactive, may stir, build, beguile, or repel a whole panoply of affinities within the reader, as archetypal music had done within the author when he was the recipient of this spellbinding force.[17]

The numinosity of archetypal music is apparent in the great world religions. It is audible as in the Word and the Breath; it is autonomous in that it is a transpersonal force; it is creative when transforming chaos into cosmos. In the *Chandogya Upanishad*, we read:

> Prajapati, the Creator of all, rested in life-giving meditation over the worlds of his creation; and from them came the three *Vedas*. He rested in meditation and from those came the three sounds: BHUR, BHUVAS, SVAR, earth, air, and sky. He rested in meditation and from the three sounds came the sound OM. Even as all leaves come from a stem, all words come from the sound OM. OM is the whole universe. OM is in truth the whole universe.[18]

The OM referred to here is a Cosmic Sound or Primal Vibration—a basic natural force inherent in all phenomena. Because as a creative force it shapes and organizes primordial matter, everything emerges from it.

The Divine Voice is also looked upon as a creative force in Genesis: "And God said, Let there be light: and there was light" (1:3); "And God called the light day, and the darkness he called Night" (1:5). In the Gospel According to John, the Divine Word is also considered a generative power: "In the beginning was the Word, and the Word was with God, and the Word was God" (1:1). The *Popul Vuh*, the sacred book of the Quiché Maya, used audibility as the basis for the birth of the world: "Then came the word. Tepeu and Gucumatz came together in the darkness, in the night, and Tepeu and Gucumatz talked together. They talked then, discussing and deliberating; they agreed, they united their words and their thoughts."[19]

Not only was the primordial Voice identified with the Creation, but its infinite tonalities, rhythms, and volumes worked wonders for heroes and humans in the existential sphere. Because of its vibratory powers, feelings were channeled in such a way as to hurt or heal individuals, responding to their energy charges. Indeed, sonorities encoded entire movements in human life. In *The Iliad*, for example, Apollo stops a deadly plague from further ravaging the land when he hears the nation's youth sing sacred hymns and songs so sweetly. As recorded in *The Odyssey*, the pain Ulysses suffers from the wound in his knee is diminished by the chanting of certain lays. When, during the siege of Jericho, Joshua sounds his trumpet and all the people shout "with a great shout," the walls of the city come tumbling down (Josh. 6:5). David drives evil spirits from Saul as he plays his harp (1 Sam. 16:23). In the Finnish national epic, *The Kalevala*, the sage Vainamöinen sends a furious mob into a sleeplike trance by playing his kantela.

Pythagoras reduced the entire phenomenological sphere to numbers, mathematical ratios, and vibrations. For Pythagoras, music consisted in combining proper ratios and their corresponding pure intervals. Such tonal arrangements created perfect harmony. He posited that certain melodies and rhythms had a healing and purifying effect on animate and inanimate bodies, thereby uniting what had been divided and cleansing what had turned putrescent. Music also received a high priority in Plato's *Republic:*

> . . . musical training is a more potent instrument than any other, because rhythm and harmony find their way into the inward places of the soul, on which they mightily fasten, imparting grace, and making the soul of him who is rightly educated graceful, or of him who is ill-educated ungraceful; and also because he who has received this true education of the inner being will most shrewdly perceive omissions or faults in art and in nature. . . .[20]

Although scale, tone, and word are individual entities for Plato, they are indissolubly linked. As conveyers of ideas, they are important in molding people's characters, in conditioning their lives, and in revealing ultimate truths. Aristotle, differing from Pythagoras and Plato, did not look upon music as the organizing force of the universe, but rather as an imitative art imbued with emotional value, which manifested itself in people's actions.

In China, music was perceived as a cosmic force which replicated and prolonged harmony between heaven and earth, thereby balancing the dual forces of Yin and Yang. The foundation note, based on mathematical coordinates involved in the Chinese twelve-note musical system, was supposed to have mystical powers: it revealed the illness or well-being of the state. Each dynasty had its fundamental note and its absolute pitch. When the Emperor Chin-shish Huang-ti (Qin shiu Huang di, 221–210 B.C.), for example, surveyed his kingdom, he did not interview regional officials. Instead, he tested the pitches of the notes in the areas where he traveled. If they were in perfect correspondence, he knew the village was in tune with the kingdom. In *The Analects*, Confucius states that music has the power to alter affairs of state, that it can provoke good or evil, and that it is a tangible force which arouses human potential.

In revealing itself to the writer, archetypal music conveys vibratory activity and frequencies in audible mental sounds, words, images, and colorations, variously paced and pitched. As organized sequences which release their energy charges, archetypal music affects blood vessels, stimulating the writer internally and externally, consciously and unconsciously, individually and collectively. Mirroring an inner climate, it discloses a world replete with shadowy contents: concord or discord, depression or joy, fervor or despondency, strength or weakness. As Boethius wrote in *De*

Institutione Musica (sixth century): "Music is a part of us, and either ennobles or degrades our behavior." Shakespeare's characters are disturbed or elated by archetypal music, depending upon how the tone presents itself to them. Music, for Caliban, is a healing device:

> The isle is full of noises,
> Sounds and sweet airs, that give delight, and hurt not.
> Sometimes a thousand twangling instruments
> Will hum about mine ears; and sometimes voices,
> That, if I had then wak'd after long sleep,
> Will hum about mine ears; and sometimes voices,
> That, if I had then wak'd after long sleep,
> Will make me sleep again: and then, in dreaming,
> The clouds me thought would open and show riches
> Ready to drop upon me; that when I wak'd
> I cried to dream again. (*The Tempest*, III, 2)

Etienne Dolet, the sixteenth-century humanist who was burned at the stake, confessed to the importance of music in his writings: "To music I owe my life and the whole success of my literary labors. . . . I should never have been able to endure my gigantic, unremitting exertions, if music had not refreshed me."[21]

In *The Anatomy of Melancholy* (1621), Robert Burton attributes moods to melody and timbrel: "Many men are melancholy by hearing music, but it is a pleasing melancholy that it causeth; and therefore to such as are discontent, in woe, fear, sorrow, or dejected, it is a most present remedy." So, too, is morality affected by music. In *Don Quixote* (1605), Cervantes writes: "Where there's music there can be no evil." William Congreve, in *The Mourning Bride* (1697), suggests that "Music hath charms to soothe the savage breast, / To soften rocks, or bend a knotted oak."

Basho, the seventeenth-century Japanese writer of haiku, opened himself up to the dominant quality of music in his verses:

> Has the cascade shaken with rushing sound?
> These yellow kerria petals toward the ground?

Another writer of haiku, Kokaku, cleansed and broadened by nature's musicalities and structured forms, conveyed his feelings as follows:

> The little nightingale of buff and brown
> Singing its first spring quaver—upside down!

Carlyle maintained that if you "see deep enough . . . you see musically; the heart of nature being everywhere musical, if you can only reach it."[22] In *Hero-Worship and the Heroic in History*, Carlyle wrote: "Who is there that, in logical words, can express the effect music has on us? A kind of inarticulate, unfathomable speech, which leads us to the edge of the Infinite, and lets us for moments gaze into that!"

Words for Heinrich von Kleist were tones. His short stories are comparable to orchestrated compositions. "Saint Cecilia," or "The Power of Music," tells of four young men who break into a convent at Aachen. No sooner do they hear the nun, Saint Cecilia, play an ancient hymn on the church organ than they are transfixed, completely won over; but in the process, they become insane. As religious fanatics, they are forced to live out the remainder of their lives in a mental institution.

Emerson tells us in his *Journals* (1836) that music "takes us out of the actual and whispers to us dim secrets that startle our wonders as to who we are, and for what, whence, and whereto." In *Balaustion's Adventure* (1871), Robert Browning remarked: "Who hears music, feels his solitude / Peopled at once."

For the French symbolist poets, among them Baudelaire, Verlaine, and Mallarmé, archetypal music played a key role in the creative process. Tone, melody, diapason, and rhythm triggered Baudelaire's creative impulses and opened up his imagination to infinite analogies, dreams, and the synesthetic experience. He likened tonal sequences to the sea in his poem "Music"; and in "Correspondances," he wrote that "Perfumes, colors, and sounds respond to each other." In Verlaine's "Formerly and Not Long Ago," he placed "Music before all else . . . / Music again and always!" His special use of meter, feminine rhyme, assonance, alliteration, repetition, and enjambement, which prolonged and unified the melodic line, attests to the profound influence music had on his work. Mallarmé considered music the most abstract of presences. In a letter to Charles Morice (1893), he wrote that "Song bursts forth from an innate source, anterior to concept." In *Divagations*, he noted that "Soul is melody." Music haunted him; it spoke to him as if through transparent antennae; it helped him bring forth his verses, with their complex and innovative syntactical and rhythmic devices, lending a musical framework to such poems as "Afternoon of a Faun." For Mallarmé, the old distinction between Music and Letters no longer existed.

Nietzsche remarked, in "Maxims and Missiles," that "[w]ithout music, life would be an error. The German imagines even God singing songs." In George Santayana's *Little Essays* (1920), "music is a means of giving form to our inner feelings without attaching them to events or objects in the world." In *The Magic Mountain* (1924), Thomas Mann wrote: "Music quickens time, she quickens us to the finest enjoyment of time."

The list of writers whose works were written under the influence of archetypal music is extensive. In *Music, Archetype, and the Writer*, I limit my analyses to twelve authors (others could have been chosen), studying their reactions to personal and transpersonal voices emanating from their collective unconscious, and to the manner in which they used choric and rhythmic sequences to heighten their art. Drawn from ancient and contemporary Western and Eastern literatures, the works included here have one element in common: the musical archetype governs the attitude and approach of each author to his literary work and is the prime mover of its syntax, speech, pace, pitch, and diapasons.

It is hoped that the readers of this book will also be affected by these analyses—emotionally and intellectually, consciously and unconsciously—that the tones, rhythms, and diapasons will work on their soma and psyche; that infinite reverberations will not only expand their understanding and enjoyment of the verbal experience but will stimulate their own creative urge, encouraging them to peruse the work in question directly or listen to their own inner soundings and pulsations. Then the reader becomes a musician, a producer.

The works analyzed here are purposely varied in an attempt to reveal the universality and timelessness of the interaction between archetypal music and the written word.

Archetypal music is the prime mover in E. T. A. Hoffmann's "Kreisleriana" (1814–15). A composite work made up of memoirs, letters, vignettes, and analyses of symphonic and lyrical outpourings, "Kreisleriana" is one of the earliest examples of the *synesthetic* experience in literature. The simultaneity of sense impressions experienced by Hoffmann's protagonist, Kreisler, when under the spell of the musical archetype, enables him to articulate his thoughts and feelings in a new language replete with preformal tonalities and archaic rhythms. The manner in which Hoffmann performed such a feat will be examined.

Archetypal music is also the key to Balzac's short story "Gambara" (1837). Because music is both a science and an art, obeying the laws of physics and mathematics, it was, for this nineteenth-century French writer, the highest form of creative expression. For Balzac, music also nourished the imagination, stimulated memories and feelings, and thereby expanded consciousness. The value of dissonance and the broadening of the notions of polyphony and the interrelationships between minor and major modes are also explored in "Gambara," at a time when harmonious interludes were highly esteemed. The reader is thereby made aware of new sounds, amplitudes, and frequencies, which foreshadow contemporary atonal and concrete music.

Baudelaire was electrified by Wagner's *Flying Dutchman*, *Tannhäuser*, and *Lohengrin*. The amplitude and dynamic nature of these operas swept him into spaceless and timeless dimensions and into the voluptuous but harrowing world of the dream. In Baudelaire's essay "Richard Wagner and *Tannhäuser*" (1861), archetypal music is characterized as that force which led the French poet to express feelings and sensations aroused by the pace, volume, and pitch of Wagner's primordial sounds. So powerful was their impact upon him that music not only acquired color, shape, taste, and scent but also generated subliminal levels of emotional intensity, leading directly to the religious experience of *redemption*.

Tolstoy's short novel *The Kreutzer Sonata* (1891), named after Beethoven's violin sonata (opus 47), dramatizes the destructive influence of archetypal music. Working subliminally on Tolstoy's protagonist, its melody, amplitude, and rhythms unleash repressed instincts, opening the floodgates of the irrational sphere and leading him to the shadow world, which, for the author of this strange tale, represents carnal love—his nemesis. The protagonist, who longs to remain chaste and yearns for rejection of all physical contact, fails in his endeavor, because archetypal music, for him, is a tantalizing and overwhelming *demonic* power.

Kandinsky's *Sounds* (1912), a volume containing thirty-eight poems and fifty-six woodcuts, fuses various art forms: written, pictorial, and aural. By uniting different disciplines, Kandinsky believed he not only enhanced and deepened the creative experience but reached that *soul force* alluded to by mystics as the *Creative Point*: that space from which all life emanates. What is considered as empty space—void—is in reality filled with waves, signals, auditory intensities, and shapes, each generating new life and unknown potential. "Music," Kandinsky wrote, is "the best Teacher." It is archetypal—that is, both objective and subjective—and is a conveyor of spiritual essences through vibrating and alternating rhythmic patterns and frequencies.

"Eveline," one of the tales from Joyce's *Dubliners* (1914), reveals both structurally and thematically this Irishman's early use of music as metaphor and as organizing agent. The auditory experience contained in "Eveline" is accentuated by Joyce's complex figures of speech and by his system of stressed and unstressed phonemes, which are beguiling because of their sonorities, choric elements, intonations, meters, resolutions, and harmonic progressions. Archetypal music, as used by Joyce in his linguistic structures, helps convey feeling, mood, drama, and character.

Marcel Proust used archetypal music as a literary device throughout *Remembrance of Things Past*. An autonomous power, it acted as a stimulant arousing involuntary recall, a vehicle to provoke interludes of active imagination, and a power capable of paving the way for periods of transcendence. The musical interludes transliterated by Proust into verbal and, paradoxically, auditive images and motifs sweep readers into new dimensions, inviting them to experience deeper levels of reality and altered states of consciousness.

The protagonist in Jean-Paul Sartre's novel *Nausea* (1938) reacts so powerfully to the jazz song "Some of These Days" that it takes on archetypal dimension in his psyche. The energy contained in the commanding voice intoning this song is instrumental in awakening him to *existence*, thereby enabling him to discover the source of his creative élan.

The violin in Yizhar Smilansky's short story "Habakuk" (1960) is the medium used to create the archetypal music which transmutes a literary work into an emotionally charged event. The biblical Habakkuk, after whom Yizhar named his protagonist, was a prophet who attempted to understand the mysteries behind God's acts by intoning his anguish in melodious incantations that reverberated throughout the cosmos. Yizhar's Habakuk likewise relates his poignant story in archetypal musical language, which, like a mantra, overflows its human limitations in preparation for the prophetic experience.

The last three chapters deal with Indian, Chinese, and Japanese archetypal musical concepts in the written work. In Bhasa's play *The Dream of Vasavadatta* (c. first century B.C.), a convention in Sanskrit drama, the union of music, song, dance, iconography, and the spoken word becomes an earthly replica for spiritual Oneness. Archetypal music is one aspect of a whole gestic, visual, and rhythmic language aimed at arousing feelings of aesthetic delight (*rasa*), which is the goal of Sanskrit theatre.

Archetypal music in the Chinese play *The Jade Mirror-Stand*, by Guan Hanqing (1280–1368), also illustrates a metaphysical concept: multiplicity in Oneness. In that tones, frequencies, vibrations, and acoustical qualities are considered as crystallized emotions and distilled feelings, they are knit together in thoughtfully coordinated and rigorously disciplined sequences, accounting to a great extent for the infinite reverberations they create in the reader and critic.

Yukio Mishima's Noh drama *The Damask Drum* (1955) reveals how non-sound is conveyed onstage by a mysterious drum, how tones issuing forth from this theatrical accessory during the ritualistic beatings create a network of silent as well as rhythmified patterns, leading protagonists and viewers into a fourth dimension: an undifferentiated aesthetic continuum. The archetypal drum beat in Mishima's play *is* power and energy. It *is* concrete phenomenon. As such, it shapes events and fantasy images, while also removing the veil which separates visible from invisible domains.

In the twelve works examined in *Music, Archetype, and the Writer*, tone, rhythm, amplitude, and melody fulfill a different function for each writer, both aesthetically and psychologically. Activating feeling, thinking, intuition, or sensation, they may produce a mystical, prophetic, scientific, philosophical, or literary episode. During their trajectory through soma and psyche, they may arouse disturbing, upsetting, or joyful moods in the reader, elevating him to rapturous heights or plunging him into dismal depths. The incantatory quality of archetypal music restores to language one of its earliest functions: to link humans with the cosmos and, most important, with their own inner being. As Schopenhauer wrote:

> [Music] never expresses the phenomenon, but only the inner na-
> ture, the in-itself, of every phenomenon, the will itself. Therefore
> music does not express this or that particular and definite pleasure,
> this or that affliction, pain, sorrow, horror, gaiety . . . but joy, sor-
> row, horror, gaiety . . . peace of mind *themselves*, to a certain extent
> in the abstract; their essential nature . . . we understand them per-
> fectly in this extracted quintessence.[23]

Archetypal music exists in the psyche, as do harmonic series, underscoring the fundaments of a personality and personifying the dominant elements within it. It *deconcretizes* and thereby *remythologizes* a literary work, taking it out of its individual and conventional context and relating it to humankind in general. It lifts readers out of their specific and, perhaps, isolated worlds, allowing them to expand their vision and thus to relate more easily to events and to understand them as part of an ongoing and cyclical reality.

Music is that autonomous power and that generative force which streams out of the collective unconscious into the work of art. It is that element that gives it both its specific and its cultural stamp, its fundamental frequency, and its audible and mental sound pattern. As Jung remarked to the concert pianist Margaret Tilly, who was experimenting with the therapeutic value of music: "Don't just tell me, *show* me—*show* me. . . . I begin to see what you are doing—show me more. . . . This opens up whole new avenues of research I'd never even dreamed of. . . . This is most remarkable."[24]

1 E. T. A. Hoffmann's "Kreisleriana": Archetypal Music and Active Imagination

E. T. A. Hoffmann (1776–1822), composer, pianist, writer, critic, painter, set designer, director, jurist, teacher, and civil servant, was one of the earliest authors to use the *synesthetic* experience in his writings. Ushered into existence by archetypal music in compositions, improvisations on the piano and other instruments, and in song, synesthesia encouraged Hoffmann to explore new levels of consciousness. The perceptual images he apprehended during these moments of heightened awareness led to a psychological operation which today we call *active imagination*. Hoffmann's literary and musical exploratory forays nourished his creative spirit and disclosed insights into his psychological condition as well.

"Kreisleriana" (1814–15), made up of memoirs, letters, vignettes, confidences, and analyses of symphonic and lyrical works, was written to a great extent by the music master Johannes Kreisler, who was none other than Hoffmann. Kreisler/Hoffmann's goal was to impose a new poetico-musical language on an unfeeling society, to which his sensitivity, imagination, and values were foreign.

The synesthetic technique Hoffmann articulated in "Kreisleriana" was so innovative that it influenced the course of much of nineteenth- and twentieth-century writing. The notion of synesthesia stems from a metaphysical concept: a monistic condition which existed in the universe prior to the Fall from the Garden of Eden. The Romantics named this paradisiacal, undifferentiated realm the *All*. As a literary device, synesthesia attempts a reunification of primordial oneness by fusing the senses, which had become divided on earth. The synesthetic experience in music, a poem, a painting, or any other art form sweeps into being an image, sound, texture, or palpable entity that may be heard, smelled, touched, or tasted; or a taste that may be heard, seen, smelled, felt; and so on. Synesthesia, psychologically speaking, may be looked upon as a giant awakening, a psychic happening, a flaring up of unconscious contents within consciousness. The simultaneity of sense impressions experienced by Hoffmann during such periods enabled him to distill new languages, preformal tonalities, and archaic rhythms through the action of a catalyst: archetypal music. Such happenings bore full fruit because they nourished his creative élan; they also took their toll on him, since each foray into subliminal spheres (required by the synesthetic experience) caused a momentary eclipse of his conscious personality, or ego.

Baudelaire was so deeply impressed by Hoffmann's synesthetic experiences that he included this extract from "Kreisleriana" in his *Salon of 1846:*

> I not only find an analogy and an intimate reunion between colors, sounds, and perfumes when I dream or during that slightly entrancing period preceding sleep, but also while I am still awake, when I listen to music. It seems to me that all these things were engendered by the same ray of light and must reunite in a single marvelous concert. The brown and red odor of worry produces an especially magic effect on my person. It makes me succumb to profound reverie; and then, as if from a distance, I hear the grave and profound sounds of the oboe.[1]

Active imagination, another device used by Hoffmann to promulgate ideas and sensations, was described by C. G. Jung as "the only way toward a direct encounter with the reality of the unconscious without the intermediary use of tests or dream interpretations."[2] Unlike a passive state, which simply allows subliminal contents to emerge into consciousness, active imagination requires catalyzation by some inner or outer pulsion. It enables one to personify complexes through visual and verbal images. For Hoffmann, of course, music was the agitator: melody offered him the necessary dynamism to force abstract and sensuous shapes to flow through his whole person, energetically.

Neither synesthesia nor active imagination was invented by Hoffmann or anyone else. They were discovered and used by those who may have unconsciously felt compelled *to enter into themselves* so as to better relate to their component parts and to the world at large. They perhaps believed that these techniques would help them integrate what was disparate within their psyches and heal the birth wound as well as the lacerations inflicted in later years.

Hoffmann was, for many, the prototype of the suffering, tortured, lovesick visionary: the creative romantic. Sainte-Beuve remarked that no one, be it critic or poet, had been able to describe better than Hoffmann "how it feels to be an artist." His disclosures about the inner climate of "those disquieted, perpetually anguished geniuses—mystics without faith, geniuses without work, souls without organs," are unparalleled.[3]

In Offenbach's *Tales of Hoffmann* (1881), the composer-writer is portrayed as being constantly in love, surrounded by ill-wishers, forever inebriated and on the verge of madness. Although this description may be tinged with some truth, it is, nevertheless, an exaggeration. Hoffmann did experience sorrow when he learned of the tragic death of his only child; he did know hunger and hardship. But in 1809 he finally obtained a post as musical director for the Bamberg theatre, and three years later he became director of the Dresden opera house. He composed choruses, a mass, a symphony, piano sonatas, a harp quintet, and operettas, as well as an opera, *Undine*, based on the work of Baron La Motte Fouqué. Its performance marked the birth of romantic opera. Hoffmann also became a music reviewer, gave private lessons, and fell in love with one of his pupils, Julia Mark—an unrequited passion which haunted him for the rest of his life. He also wrote short stories and fantasies: *The Devil's Elixir*, *Don Juan*, *Kater Murr*, *The Educated Cat*, *Princess Brambilla*, and others. Hoffmann's difficult and dissipated life made serious inroads into his health. He died in Berlin from spinal paralysis.

Hoffmann was certainly misunderstood by most of his contemporaries, but not by such great figures as Schumann, whose *Eight Piano Fantasies* (opus 16, 1838) was inspired by "Kreisleriana." Hoffmann's enemies, nevertheless, were many. There were those who took umbrage at his caustic and wry humor, and others who decried what they considered indistinct and blurred musical cacophonies. Hoffmann suffered deeply from their rejection. Yet, he persevered, continuing to compose, write, and paint for a world not yet ready to receive the products of his imagination.

Archetypal music actuated the synesthetic experience and episodes of active imagination depicted in "Kreisleriana." Sound, for Hoffmann, lived in the mind's eye, the inner ear, the taste buds, in touch sensations, and the olfactory nerves. Tonality, rhythm, pitch, and amplitude were forever being distilled by his sensitized system in patterned series and modulations, in colored shapes bearing their emotional impact on him. Each sensation was cast into form: "Man hört besser, wenn man sieht die geheime Verwandschaft von Licht und Ton ofenbart sich deutlich; beides, Licht un Ton, gestaltet sich in individueller Form, und so wird der Solospieler, die Sangerin, selbst die ertönende Melodie."[4]

Dark chords, associated with lower registers, awakened feelings of fright; C-major and minor chords, identified with demons, ghosts, and death, as well as with insanity, produced trembling and terror. Higher pitches—with their velvety and mellifluous textures—inspired feelings of godliness, purity, sublimation, freedom, and expansiveness. Sensations of floating, accompanied by graying, blue, and sunlit colorations, left him warmed and cleansed. Melody in particular exerted magic power over his soul; its amplitudes, hues, and paces fostered a panoply of moods ranging from serenity to acute tension.

Kreisler relates his thoughts, dreams, and pain in confessional style in "Kreisleriana" and tells us from the very outset that he was aware of his "excessively sensitive" nature. Certainly his depth of feeling was instrumental in triggering flamboyant reactions to the hostility of bourgeois society; and his fiery imagination, described as a "devouring flame," swept everything within range into its orbit, adding fuel to an already high degree of volatility (p. 881). But why do the bourgeois castigate him for inhabiting a dream world? for not being of this earth? he questions time and time again. He finally understands that he can appeal only to an elite. Only those whose minds are as developed as his can respond to his new musical style and the verbalizations emanating from his creative interludes. The others, unaccustomed to viewing textured, perfumed, and colored tonal patterns, turn away. Were a common denominator to be found between himself and the world at large, he would, he thought, be able to endow the blind with sight! Forced as he was to earn a living, however, Kreisler found himself in the absurd situation of being compelled to perform before hard-hearted audiences. Increasingly irate, he withdrew into his own inner world, where fantasy took over. The breach between the empirical sphere and his own highly charged unconscious domain grew. His increasing alienation from society and his struggle to engender new ideas in his musical compositions left him virtually helpless, as though he had been caught in a tightening vise.

Kreisler is a *feeling* type, sensitive to human needs and moods, to acceptance and rejection. He judges the world according to his own criteria, largely based on the reactions of others toward him. "The valuation by feeling extends to *every* content of consciousness," Jung wrote. "When the intensity of feeling is increased an affect results, which is a state of feeling accompanied by appreciable bodily innervations."[5]

Psychologically, society had, for Hoffmann, taken on the allure of a Negative Mother archetype: a devouring aspect of the feminine principle. She (society) was that powerfully threatening force ready to crush and masticate the helpless artist, to pounce on him and those who sought to go their own way, refusing to follow society's course. Ruthless and stonelike, she did not react to beauty, to the sustained magnificence of sublime works, be they those of Bach, Haydn, Mozart, Beethoven, or other giants—including Hoffmann himself.

That Kreisler's inspirational powers take hold most forcefully at night is understandable. During these sunless hours, the rational sphere recedes, while the subliminal world gains in dominion. It is then that the dream takes hold and Kreisler feels liberated, free to experience the state of *overexcitation* which he considers the *sine qua non* for his creative élan. His enthusiasm drives him to the piano, where he sings and plays his modulations with such gusto that they can be tasted by him, smelled, heard, touched, and envisioned. Tears pour down his cheeks—not from pain or sorrow, but from sheer passion! As he strikes chord upon chord, pursuing his variations and phrasings with increasing frenzy, his arpeggios, scales, and glissandos ripple forth in amplitudes ranging from fortes to pianissimos. His soul soars, unleashing in its wake prodigious flamelike sensations which both warm and burn his flesh, nourish and sear his being.

Since song catalyzes Kreisler's already volatile emotions, transforming them into burning volcanic forces, he realizes that this art has a particularly deleterious effect upon him and, perhaps, on those who listen to him vocalize. Singing, unlike the recitation of the actor or the music-making of the instrumentalist, has no intercessor, either mechanical or verbal, no force that intervenes between the performer and the tones emanating from him. He may be, as Kreisler was, carried away on the proverbial wings of song.

Mystically speaking, *voice* combines the collective creative breath of spirit (*pneuma*) with the individual breath of the performer. The whole emotional world which Kreisler decanted through song seemed devoid of stops and restraints. When Kreisler accompanied himself on the piano, tones simply filtered through the air, effortlessly, his fingers guided by an unknown mind and an automatic inner discipline. What Arthur Schopenhauer wrote about music in general is applicable to Hoffmann's approach to this art: "[Music] never expresses the phenomenon, but only the inner nature, the in-itself, of every phenomenon, the will itself."[6]

Song so stimulated Kreisler's imagination that he became not only oblivious to his whereabouts but *detached* from the very piece of music he was playing. Two personalities emerged at this juncture. Only when reason returned sometime later did he realize he had been on a prodigious journey. We may say, psychologically speaking, that under these circumstances Kreisler's ego had been overwhelmed by the powerful waters of his collective unconscious (the deepest subliminal layers within the psyche, usually inaccessible to consciousness). A drowning of the ego, or center of consciousness, led Kreisler, at least at the outset of his verbal and melodic peregrinations, to experience a new musical awareness. A superior language was being distilled in these spheres: the silent became audible; the unfelt, felt. As he learned to speak nature's sacred glyphs, conveying its arcana in tone and pace, his heart became filled with "an infinite aspiration." Then, mysteriously, he was accorded the power to transliterate the vibrations, sonorities, pitches, and amplitudes of trees, flowers, stones, and water into verbal sequences. Like Orpheus, Kreisler understood the secret and disquieting combinations of nature's designs, as well as those organic and inorganic entities that unfolded within his subliminal world, which he then brought into consciousness (p. 896).

During Kreisler's ascents/descents, prodded always by the archetypal music he played or heard in his mind's eye, his whole being seemed to participate fully in multidimensional experiences, which he alluded to as *semi-ecstatic* states. When floating heavenward and drifting about in aerated realms, he felt safe from the clutches of the Devouring Mother archetype. His sense of liberation from the earth domain and the ensuing feelings of rapturous bliss bathed him in pure tonality, combining sparkling sounds and diamondlike illuminations with sonorous verbalized sequences.

The Concert Hall

The concert halls and homes in which Kreisler was forced to perform to earn his bread actuated episodes of synesthesia and sequences of active imagination. On one occasion, early in "Kreisleriana," he describes his entrée into a large performing area. Weighted down at first by worldly matters, his sensations began to change. His body feels as if it were being lacerated by stinging insects, each injecting poisons into him. As Christ was pierced by the crown of thorns and the nails driven into his flesh during the crucifixion, so Kreisler considers himself a martyr and sacrificial agent, mortified because he, too, had a new message to impart to humanity. As he sits at his piano and begins his performance, an otherworldly power seems to take hold of him:

> Yes, a divine force invaded him; and yielding with childlike faith to what the spirit arouses in him, he begins speaking the language of this mysterious kingdom. Similar to an apprentice who reads his master's book on magic aloud and without realizing it, he conjures forth from the depths of himself a thousand marvelous apparitions which infiltrate life, fly about in radiant rounds, and fill whomever sees them with infinite nostalgia. (p. 890)

The ascensional images described above, containing both idea and melody, infuse Kreisler with zest and impressions of power. In these rarefied climes, he experiences heightened states of consciousness. What he also encounters, but as yet does not understand, is the Great Father archetype in its most positive form for him: as representative of spirituality, wisdom, and mana. This powerful masculine principle stands in opposition to the negative Great Mother Earth: the vale of tears. Kreisler envisages himself embracing the sky as he floats within its stimulating and cleansing hues. His imagination glows, inviting him to penetrate spectacular forms, shadowy shapes, and brilliantly incarnated tones that fly about, bubbling in exciting verbal arrays. Words, in these atomized scapes, are transformed into chromatic and enharmonic interludes, filling him with a sense of accomplishment. He sees himself as having transcended the humdrum world, as having stepped out of the mediocre frame of existence, passing through those "ivory gates" into a domain that spells light and purity in ringing and pulsating meteoric beats. As the magnificent spectacle of nature unfolds before his eyes, he resists the thought of being pulled back down to reality and clings, paradoxically, to the heights—to those fiery and energetic particles exploding about him in archetypal melodic sequences:

> Then, a never before feeling of exaltation took hold of me, and I rose, expanding fully above the terrestrial mire; all the sounds, iced in my heart by bloodied pain, will live again, burst out tremulously, sparkling like brilliant salamanders; and I will have the strength to seize them, bind them so that once assembled by a sheaf of fire, they will be transformed into a flamboyant image which will transfigure, magnify your song! (p. 892)

In these aerated yet flaming regions, Kreisler finds that he can speak multiple tongues. Let us recall that speech has frequently been equated with flame because of its motility as well as its creative and destructive force. In Isaiah, God's tongue is compared to "devouring fire" (30:27). In Acts, we read: "suddenly there came a sound from heaven as of a rushing mighty wind, and it filled all the house where they were sitting. And there appeared unto them cloven tongues like as of fire, and it sat upon each of them" (2:2–3).

Reaching such heights may expand consciousness, but it may also have deleterious effects, as in the Icarus myth, in which *inflation* (*hybris*) wreaks destruction. As Kreisler hovers over the "terrestrial mire," he sees fungal beings anchored to base matter. He looks upon himself as superior to the madding crowd below, which could prelude an unbearable tension of opposites: a future split within the psyche that would take hold not merely during musical interludes but in the real world as well. That the image of the "salamander" is added to the picture further supports this possibility. In ancient times, the salamander, a type of triton, was believed to be able to live in fire without being consumed; thus, it represented eternality, a never-to-be-extinguished flame. The reverse was also true: in an Egyptian hieroglyph, the salamander represented a man dying from cold. In this instance, it is identified with an "iced" condition, with death, and with creative sterility. Questions arise. How can an artist survive if caught in the world of contingencies? in earthly linearity? Which would be Kreisler's path?

Kreisler, the Music Teacher

Containing his indignation, Kreisler describes his life as music teacher to the daughters of the well-to-do and socially elite Roederlein family. Miss Nanette has made extraordinary progress, he confesses wryly. After three and a half years, she can sing a tune she has heard ten times and studied another ten times on the piano. As for Miss Marie, she can sing her song after having heard it only eight times. She, however, always sings a quarter of a tone off key, but it really does not matter, since she is so cute that anything emerging from her lips is endurable. Still, a satanic spirit enters her throat every now and then, "gnawing, torturing, wringing out all sounds," which, Kreisler confesses, bruise his ears and sear his nerves (p. 895).

Kreisler, frequently asked to play the piano at the Roederlein dinner parties, describes one of these séances with point and irony. After the finest of dishes had been offered and the most exquisite of wines decanted, the guests were "served a little music which high society absorbed with as much pleasure as the rest" of the fare (p. 884). On one occasion, after Kreisler had finished his performance and thought he could retire for the night, one of the guests asked him to improvise. Kreisler declined, but the guest insisted. Kreisler chose Bach's *Well-Tempered Clavier*, in the certainty that his audience would be bored in no time. The young ladies left after the first twelve variations; by the fifteenth, the hall began emptying. Incredibly enough, it was at this very moment that something strange—inexplicable and frightening—took hold of Kreisler. The sequences of notes he had been playing suddenly seemed to materialize before his very eyes. They forced themselves upon him, radiating a thousand imitations and developments of the very themes he was to play:

> The notes took on life, sparkled and hopped around me; an electric fire passed from the extremity of my fingers onto the keys; the spirit from which this torrent flowed endowed ideas with wings; a thick vapor floated into the entire room, and the brilliance of the candles diminished ever so slowly. At times a nose could be

spotted, a pair of eyes, but they disappeared immediately. So completely, that I finally was alone, seated at my piano, with my Sebastian Bach. (p. 887)

During this interlude, Kreisler seemed to have been physically and spiritually extracted from the terrestrial sphere. No longer was he dominated by the Terrible Mother archetype, which he identified with containment and imprisonment. Everything that had held him down to a bleak and banal life now seemed to have been uprooted. Freed from the vise that bound them, his fingers worked their way over the piano keys as if mobilized and energized by a force outside himself. A transpersonal fire spirit emerged in his vision, guiding him through the maze of black and white keys.

Such a vision might be described as schizophrenic: Kreisler's ego had been eclipsed from consciousness and allowed to float around as if suspended in some heady dimension. Unprotected, it fell prey to the fiery emanations inhabiting unconfined, infinite space. Flaming archetypal images, currents of energy, and electrical fields endowed with concretized notes came into Kreisler's grasp, their multiple colorations and shapes catalyzing his musical performance. Virtually personified, each tone and semitone worked on his soma and psyche, affecting each with the intensity of its individual vibrations. Jolted, galvanized, and thrilled, Kreisler became increasingly excited by the brilliance of the spectacular electromagnetic radiation he not only saw but apprehended in his tonal combinations and his verbal transliteration of these. Having experienced a willed dissociation of the ego, Kreisler could return to earth, not broken in soul or in limb, but strengthened by his exposure to the Father archetype.

Tone and color are measured today by auditory and visible waves or vibrations and translated into their mathematical components. In Kreisler's vision, the huge concentrations of vibrating waves with their multiple frequencies or pulsations shooting into him activated his every nerve and distended his muscles, transposing their power into moral and emotional effects. Boethius's statement that "the soul of the universe is united by musical concord" is applicable to Kreisler.[7] He had become the bridge through whom the infinite poured its libations in particles, sound waves, and distilled visualizations. Divested of his ego, Kreisler was flooded by archetypal music in all forms and shapes—emanating from archaic spaceless and timeless regions. Unheard-of and unthinkable modalities unleashed themselves in new pitches and tones; so powerful was their impact upon Kreisler that whatever had been repressed, corroded, and iced within him yielded to the warmth and joy equated with complete freedom.

Psychologically, the sparks in Kreisler's hallucinatory image indicate contents from his unconscious bursting into consciousness. These power-ful forces have been identified by Gnostic thinkers with "tiny soul-sparks"—light imprisoned in *physis* (matter), in the divine, and in the profane. That these emanations glowed and radiated, bombarding him as he performed, indicates that high dosages of *libido* (psychic energy) were being spent in determining his course of behavior as well as his creative urge.

That "ideas" are endowed with "wings," as mentioned in the Bach episode, is Platonic in origin. Wings endow humans with feelings of power and beatitude (Plato, *Phaedrus*); they help us attain celestial spheres (Psalms 54:7). In the *Rig-Veda*, intelligence is associated with the world of air and travels more rapidly than birds. The Church Fathers believed that when humans were far from God they lost their wings. Kreisler's ascen-sions and displacements indicate a sublimation of human talent, a condi-tion of inflation, and an unconscious belief that he possessed superhuman capacities. A fall from such heights must eventually come to pass.

The very concepts of *aspiring, aspirate, aspiration*, inherent in Kreisler's flight images, may also be related to breathing. The taking in and expel-ling of breath may be viewed in terms of a power drive which enables human beings to live on, to seek, to rise, and to acquire. "Thick" vapor, referred to in the Bach episode as assuming the form of gigantic, shape-less, indistinct masses diffused throughout the atmosphere, may also be perceived as nebulous, unconscious contents and scattered, directionless quantities of bolts of energy. Now, however, these amorphous shapes act as a screening device, protecting Kreisler from the destructive Earth Mother. As long as he remains in these upper spheres and the world remains out of sight, he need answer to no one. The dimming of the lights at the conclusion of the same passage indicates a further need to flow more deeply into the collective sphere, for there he feels nourished and cared for by energy pockets, even though they further fragment an already weakened center of consciousness.[8]

Number interpretations are also involved in Kreisler's vision. Prior to his inspirational interlude, he had completed thirty of Bach's variations for the clavichord. Thirty, for Kreisler, so well versed in the occult, has great significance. The 3 in the 30 indicates a third, an interval measuring three diatonic degrees, and a triad consisting of a root with its third and fifth above. Three is also significant in world religions: for the Christian, it represents the Father, Son, and Holy Ghost; for the Hindu, Brahma, Shiva, and Vishnu; for the Hebrew Kabbalist, the first three Sefiroth, or Divine Emanations (Kether, Bina, Chochma). The Taoist believes it marks time: past, present, and future. The alchemist looks upon it as the number of elements necessary for the completion of the philosophers' stone: sulfur, mercury, and salt. The *0* in 30 signifies infinity and oneness—the condition for which the Romantics longed. The combination of 3 and 0, we may suggest, indicates an ability on Kreisler's part to participate in a transpersonal sphere, in a fourth dimension. Such is the prerogative of artists who seek to divest themselves of a logical frame of reference which roots them to conventional ways.

Not only had Bach been the vehicle for Kreisler's foray into spiritual colorations and heady perfumes, but the mathematical and ordered nature of Bach's compositions also had a grounding influence upon him. Bach's *Well-Tempered Clavier*, sometimes referred to as the "Forty-Eight," includes preludes and fugues in all the major and minor keys. Its contrapuntal music is so rich that it was regarded by Kreisler—and by composers and performers in general—as the *summum bonum* of musical composition. As a classicist who worked along structured and patterned lines, Bach may be regarded as a steadying force in Kreisler's world. Identified with method and discipline, he built his sequenced, multileveled units with the solidity of a cathedral. In awe of Bach's ability to alter dynamics, Kreisler used his internally and externally balanced variations as a base upon which to add his own melodic configurations and climaxes. Bach fed Kreisler's power drive and strengthened and guided him in his search for beauty and perfectibility. Bach encouraged him to combine intuition with method, the innovative with the noble.

That Kreisler chose *The Well-Tempered Clavier* to perform is significant for other reasons as well. Bach's cycle of pieces had put the stamp of approval on the entire concept of "equal tempered tuning," which was so important in the eighteenth century. *Tempered*, associated with *temperament*, referred to the practice of tuning notes of the chromatic scale according to semitones rather than in keeping with the laws of nature, since these varied slightly, acoustically speaking (C-sharp and D-flat were regarded as the same). Differences, therefore, were modified or tempered so that a single note on the keyboard could adjust or conform to a variety of pitches. Although the standardization of keyboard instruments was inaccurate, it made modulation and tuning far easier.[9] By performing Bach's *Well-Tempered Clavier*, Kreisler, who had perfect pitch and an understanding of numerical ratios and their vibratory power, not only followed an order and a system but also opted for the artificial—yielding thereby to convenience.

Bach's preludes and fugues also enabled Kreisler to reveal his dexterity on the piano. As his fingers flew over the keyboard, rich sensuality emerged into being, pulsating in accord with the dynamics of the melodies intoned. The articulation of this physical and vibratory process in "Kreisleriana" brings today's *oscilloscope* to mind—an instrument able to measure the amplitudes and frequencies of electric waves passing through the air as vibrations and make them visible in a picture that appears on an illuminated screen.[10]

Music for Kreisler was not something to be taken lightly. It was a divine force, distilled and diffused by the cosmos through organic and inorganic nature. Hoffman, like Friedrich Schelling, believed that nature and spirit could not be separated, that together they arose from the world of the *absolute*. As such, "Nature is visible Spirit, Spirit is invisible Nature."[11] Kreisler's creative interludes, then, may be viewed as a means of reentering *primal oneness* and experiencing an undifferentiated state. Psychologically, such a need for oneness is comparable to a reentry into the birth canal and a concomitant divestiture of conflict. To make music offered Kreisler this possibility. It allowed him to *blend* into universal forces, to be welcomed, and to feel warmed and fulfilled by the embrace of collective movement. While he played and composed he could step out of the hard crust of earthly commitment and flow into the perpetually swirling domain of *eternal becoming*, with its never-ending assimilations and dissolutions.

Through this new emphasis on the cosmic realm, and a concomitant devaluation of the world of reality and appearances, Kreisler's corrosive sense of rejection seemed attenuated. He felt he belonged to the world, permitting him to gain access to infinite spheres. His imagination, therefore, looked beyond the illusory world of the Negative Mother archetype, with its concerns over earning a livelihood and other mundane details, to the positive Father principle, with all of its tremulously exciting dreams of escape and flights of fancy. Even while modulating from tonic to dominant—certainly a basic keyboard scheme—the tonalities which came into existence appeared new and fresh to him. They were archetypal in breadth, since they included the beautiful and the odious, the lovable and the hateful, as well as harmonic and enharmonic tones. Each nuance, inviting him to venture into unknown domains, provoked special movements of the soul. The melodies he played spoke to him, awakened particles and eidola endowed with mysterious vibrations and secret relations which forever flowed together and apart again in flamelike magnetic strains.

Haydn (1732–1809)

A change of mood occurs and a new cognitive scheme presents itself when Kreisler strikes deep into the philosophy, aesthetics, and psychology of the music of Haydn, Mozart, and Beethoven. Kreisler identifies Haydn's tonal patterns and rhythmic interludes with "childlike serenity," verdant plains, burgeoning flowers and bushes, and happy young people at play. The season is spring—the *renovatio*—when the human spirit, no longer suffering impulses of defeat or sensations of being torn apart, seeks to realize itself. Haydn's creations reveal inner strength and balance; their formal elegance invites Kreisler, so fascinated with nature's rhythms and periodicity, to keep in tune with its dynamisms and fluctuations. Even when sadness intrudes, it is toned down and appears as "gentle melancholy" floating about in some distant sphere, but warmed by a radiant sun (p. 900). Kreisler blends into the natural surroundings which Haydn's tones stimulate within him, and by the same token, he discharges the insalubrious contents which had caused him such turmoil. Painful encounters are thereby transformed into titillating, sense-provoking, and perfumed textures.

Certainly, Kreisler's approach to Haydn's music is infantile or adolescent—a kind of sinking back into Mother Nature's embrace. Such a need for immediate expression and gratification, psychologically speaking, destroys the possibility of further development on his part. *Feeling*, not thinking, as had been the case to a certain extent during Kreisler's playing of Bach's *Well-Tempered Clavier*, is uppermost once again. But each foray into the world of nature or celestial spheres takes its toll on him, thrusting him back more deeply into the womb, into childhood, uniformity, and union—into round upon round of continuously circular movements.

The rounds and circles emerging from Kreisler's active imagination are comparable to rungs of a ladder leading outward or inward, cutting through levels of consciousness. These circular trajectories or paradigms of crystallized energy are catalysts, pushing Kreisler to act, perform, and exteriorize his inner feelings. Circles here represent wholeness, the condition for which his psyche so desperately longs. Reminiscent of the Gnostic symbol of the *ouroborus*—the snake eating its own tail—circles may be identified with eternity. Repeating *ad infinitum* the same acts and reiterating the same yearnings and longings can easily lead one to vertigo or narcosis: the possibility of becoming imprisoned in self-perpetuating repetitiveness, in a constantly unfolding escape mechanism. Unlike Faust, who left the realm of the personal unconscious and entered the transpersonal domain—the world of the Mothers, as he called it—finding sufficient nourishment in this sphere to emerge from it redeemed, Kreisler becomes the instrument of an aggressive intent, a force within him which he can neither regulate nor direct.

Mozart (1756–1791)

Kreisler's evaluation of Mozart's music is equally revealing. Darker and increasingly mysterious abysses open up as he listens to the *Symphony in E-Flat Major*. All is not sunlight and verdant, as it had been under Haydn's baton. Fear, but not pain, is called into existence. Feelings of "infinitude," along with love, sadness, and spirituality, float into view. Cloud formations waft him along; rounded spheres beckon to him, enticing him to follow them in their dazzling array and then leading him back into unformed, unstructured domains.

Mozart is "master of the superhuman, the marvelous which inhabits the depths of our mind," Kreisler remarks (p. 901). He conjures up a strongly lyrical world, while still maintaining a harmony of delicate hues. Free from excesses and flourishes which might otherwise have weighted down his tonalities, binding them to a particular period or environment, Mozart's archetypal music is both shadow and sun. As such, it draws Kreisler into unknown and untried areas, into the heart of the life force: the divine and the satanic.

Shadowy realms, as personified in Satan, were to preoccupy Kreisler increasingly. As an archetypal principle, Satan represented the Adversary, the Light-Bringer (Lucifer), the one who forced open the doors of the instinctual world. He was the revolutionary, the rebellious one. Many writers and composers in the nineteenth century identified with him, as they did with Cain: the one whom God would not destroy; the one who suffered throughout his life for his crime.

Psychology teaches that the Devil/shadow exists in each being. As defined by Jung, the *shadow* is the unconscious part of the personality. When confronted and understood, aspects of the shadow may be looked upon by the ego as containing inferior characteristics that remain unacceptable to the individual or positive forces that work in harmony with the personality as a whole. To transform the negative qualities into their opposite, however, requires delving into one's own mephitic regions and dealing overtly with dangerous and wildly frenetic impulses—those hidden suns within the psyche that have not been redeemed and those lurid lights and livid moons that have not been retrieved. If Kreisler were capable of plunging into the insalubrious spheres within his psyche, he would be able to confront the adversary within him. His unchanneled and unregenerate drives could then be siphoned off in ordered ways so that, during moments of intense creativity, unformulated amplitudes, arcane melodies, and mysteriously silenced sounds and undifferentiated unities could flow forth.

Beethoven (1770–1827)

Kreisler's fears and joys found their resolution in Beethoven's works, which he understood as an "aspiration toward the infinite." The echoing bass sonorities evoked darkened pitlike vortices and maelstroms within him, while the lighter tones took on the contours of sanctuaries (p. 901).

Kreisler singles out Beethoven's *Symphony in C Minor* for his aesthetic and psychological evaluation. The incommensurability of this work is evident from the very first allegro, he writes, which is only two measures long. Its "anxious disquietude" leads into the secondary theme, in which tension-filled clarities burst forth, ushering in a mood of extreme torment. In previous images, Kreisler had felt compelled to *aspire*, to *aspirate*— terrified at the thought of being stifled by destructive earth forces. His spirit then was not in tune with the systole and diastole of universal rhythms. Despair is now suddenly cast aside as smiling faces parade before him, dissipating the frightening shadows. The sound of G major, already touched upon by the horn in E-flat major, reminds Kreisler of a "non material pure voice," striking two vitally crucial areas within him— his heart and lungs.

The utter beauty of Beethoven's rhythmic proportionings, their exciting tempi, order, and phrasings, and their short and prolonged chords and harmonies seem to heal Kreisler's recurring corrosive pain. Instrumentation, themes, and inner phrasing in the *Symphony in C Minor* are experienced as related, continuous, contiguous tone, built in tapestried compositional sequences. When the short allegro (only two or three measures long) makes its presence known, its beats are so deftly partitioned between the wind and string instruments that the effect, instead of being choppy, breathes symmetry and exudes inflections that create correspondences between them. The counterpoint, variations, and incidental measures are all centered on the main theme, revealing the incredibly solid structure of this master's work—he who knows how to "pour out hope and consolation into our heart" (p. 903): "If the master's imagination has conceived an entire musical tableau, with colored groups, lively lights and profound gradations of shadow, he can make it erupt from the inner world on the piano, with all of its colorations and brilliance" (p. 904).

Kreisler compares Beethoven's orchestral arrangements to iconographic symbols imprinted in books of magic, to ciphers passing from an inanimate to an animate state, to engravings copied from a master drawing. That he makes an analogy between Beethoven's *Symphony in C Minor* and an engraving indicates the power and pain associated with this musical work. Engraving requires incising lines into wood, metal, glass, or some other hard object, then covering the plate with a chemical that eats into the indented lines, after which a print or impression is made in intaglio. Beethoven's music, then, is biting, cutting, and wounding. It is also sublimely joyous and never to be forgotten, carved into the very fabric of being.

Shafts of color also inundate Kreisler's mind's eye as he listens to Beethoven's symphony: volcanic flames and sparks explode, burn, and sear. They also inspire. Multiple sun images come to the fore as Kreisler listens to the orchestrated sequences. Within Beethoven's music there exists a "profound night," he adds, as well as "jubilant clarities," pierced every now and then by "gigantic shadows" flying about (p. 901). As for Beethoven's instrumentation and thematic encounters, they reveal a music of ideas—strongly programmatic and disclosing great feeling for humanity.

Colors, which Kreisler uses throughout his narrative, represent emotional climates. Greens, yellows, reds, blacks, grays, blues—each reflects a mood, a feeling, and tremulous activity. Numerical relations, as in the Bach episode, are concealed in both notes and colors. The a, for example, has the lowest vibrations per second (28); the c, the highest (8,192). If a string is tuned down, its pitch becomes lower and lower, eventually becoming inaudible: the string is vibrating too slowly for our ears to catch the sound. High-pitched squeaks may also be inaudible, for their vibrations per second are too rapid to be heard. Just as tonal vibrations may be measured, so may colors be marked in light waves. Red, for example, measures 400 million million vibrations per second; violet, twice as many.[12]

As Kreisler listens to Beethoven's music, he is constantly being bombarded by oscillating vibrations which impress their richness or paucity into his psyche and flesh, arousing within him parallel rhythmical patterns which elicit instinct or spirit, fear or joy, activity or passivity. The seven colors of the rainbow which Kreisler envisages correspond to the seven notes of the musical scale, each making its emotional inroad upon him. The most important colors with regard to Beethoven's symphony are fiery reds (such sparkling luminosities have a high vibration count per second) and blues of all grades and shades, ranging from the lightest to the blackest (their decreasing vibrations per second arouse in Kreisler regular, recurring sympathetic movements).

The Poetico-Musical Club Episode

One of Kreisler's most spectacular episodes of synesthesia and active imagination occurred at eight o'clock in the evening in the "Poetico-Musical Club." He had previously described concert halls as small or large, confining and restrictive, in which he was bait for hostile audiences. This night, however, was different.

As Kreisler sat down at the piano, a friend, who wanted to make sure that its broken hammer had been repaired, brought a candelabrum over to the instrument. While he was peering into the piano, the candlesnuffer fell onto the strings, breaking twelve to fifteen of them. Kreisler, though he made a wry face, was not to be stopped. He would improvise, he thought.

(Let us not forget in this regard that Haydn, Mozart, and Beethoven had encouraged improvisation. Cadenzas—passages in a concerto in which the solo instrument performs without orchestra—stimulate the development of thematic material and flesh out structural qualities within a work, while also permitting the performer to display his technical mastery.)[13]

Since Kreisler could not use the upper registers of the keyboard because of the broken strings, he used the lower tones, which were intact. To dramatize the very special atmosphere bass notes conveyed for him, he asked that all the candles in the hall be extinguished. Light, representing spirituality and salvation, had been eradicated; the path leading to celestial spheres was barred. Only through the lower registers—the darker, irrational world where vibrations were toned down in intensity and coloration—would redemption be accessible. The shadow was to prevail. Negativity and destruction were to be encountered.

Kreisler struck his first chords: pianissimo bass notes, but no treble. Then he chanted his narration, supplementing in this way the missing pitches. A kind of polyphonic technique added drama to the piano piece. Mellifluous and velvety timbres rang alongside hard, metallic, choppy, and sometimes dirgelike intonations. Strong, stark, idyllic fantasy figures imbricated themselves into his tonal and verbal configurations, as if blending "an individualized language with the universal language of music" (p. 960). A spell had been cast on those present. A *Geistersprache* had invaded the surroundings!

> What are these strange and marvelous murmurings around me? Invisible wings beating, ascending, and descending. . . . I am swimming in vaporous ether . . . but mysterious intertwined flaming circles illuminate the vapor. They are gracious spirits fluttering about, their golden wings producing infinitely splendid chords and harmonies. (p. 937)

Minor and major chords followed in swift succession, in mezzo fortes, sixths, and thirds, each depicting his trajectory into the land of "eternal desire," evoking the pleasurable feelings accompanying flight into aerated spheres. As Kreisler personified the fantasy image of his beloved, whom he held close to his heart, a "splendid crown" came into view. Its diamonds scintillated with such sparkle that they resembled human tears. Golden tones shimmered; their flames consumed. A supernatural world called upon mobile forces to assuage his yearnings and to diminish his sense of inadequacy and despair.

In this example of active imagination, the reader is introduced to the murmurings of angelic beings—evanescent creatures fluttering about in the air. They, too, along with Kreisler, fear being caught up in earthly matters. Semidivine creatures, angels are composed of fire and water, and sometimes both. They are looked upon as agents capable of traveling from the heights to the depths—messengers, as the Greek word *angelos* indicates. There are many types of angels: destroyers (2 Sam. 24:16); interpreters of God's message (Job 32:23); protectors (Gen. 19); and prognosticators, as described in the Gospels. Serving as intermediary forces, angels allow Kreisler to feel related to celestial and earthly spheres; they may therefore be looked upon as invisible transformative principles.

Kreisler's angelic images may also be considered as birds—symbols of the archetypal Great Father. As spiritual and sacred forces, they are also numinous entities, animating unconscious energetic factors within Kreisler. Their linguistic messages, voiced in brilliantly irradiating visions, are energetic forces carrying out dictates from on high.

The murmurings of these angels or birds are graphically and semantically studied by Kreisler, who seeks to penetrate the hidden meanings of their utterances. According to mystics, human beings could—at some archaic period—decipher all forms and manner of communication in nature through music. So, too, does Kreisler feel it possible to experience the message of the angels/birds met during his ascension. The beating of their wings and the pace of the emotional waves they create by their vocalizations replicate microcosmically the giant inhaling and exhaling of the universe itself. He experiences the buzzing and beating around him in terms of waves and particles—as pockets of energy falling toward him in sheets and burning droves. These primordial revelations help him pierce the cloud formations which dull or hide further hallucinatory experiences; they also energize him telepathically and magnetically. As Kreisler listens more attentively to the utterings of these strange beings, he feels as if he had been transformed into a soul and allowed to peer into a cosmic stream. Overtones ring out; pulsations cast him here and there as vibrations disclose their multidimensional messages in "the vaporous sphere about him." No longer rooted to the earth, Kreisler pursues his directionless motions, losing himself in the endless dynamism of the particles that paradoxically close in upon him. In time, he loses all identity; his earthly garb has vanished. He is divested of *concretion* as he ascends still further to the *summum bonum*—that shimmering region where he experiences his beloved in the musical tones he embraces. These audible emanations speak to him from the very depths of his being; and as he listens to their mad, savage, and dark sounds, fearsome overtones crackle about, arousing before him a whole world of specters and demons. The mood has changed. Minor and major chords in C are pounded out in brash fortissimos; the pedal point sustains the bass for several measures, adding a devilish timbre to the already unstable and fearsome atmosphere.

As Kreisler lunges into his Devil incantation in graded fortissimos, he concomitantly sounds out the accompanying bass notes. His voice grows increasingly tremulous, then strident; it screeches and shrieks, and finally becomes staccato, metallic, detached. Has Kreisler gone insane? the audience wonders. Has he penetrated that demonic abyss from which few emerge? Desperate lamentations are heard as Mephistopheles himself seems to have possessed Kreisler's very soul. Terror permeates the concert hall. The lights are lit, and the cognitive side of being emerges, while repressing once again the blackness associated with the irrational sphere. A confrontation with the shadow was not to be.

There is something tragic and fulfilling in Kreisler's explorations into archetypal music. A catalyst enticing him into inner and outer space, it also disclosed some of nature's secrets: its sonorities, rhythms, and amplitudes, in sequences of synesthetic experiences and active imagination. In "Kreisleriana," we follow the composer on his trajectory into superior spheres made accessible to him through archetypal music; we accompany him as he transcends ordinary understanding and experiences the feel, the taste, the perfume of music and all of its associations. No longer does he remain simply a lackey, subservient to empirical rules and strictures. He becomes capable of drinking heavily of the elixir of music and of cohabiting with angels; of distilling his own archetypal music as well as that of the masters: Bach, Haydn, Mozart, and Beethoven. But there is a price to pay for each tonal drop redolent with passion, feeling, and love. The price is sanity. The irrational takes over, the Devil dominates his world now; bass tones accompanied by shadowy and somber glissandos prevail.

Only Hoffmann could have created "Kreisleriana," bringing to life a domain where affinities and correspondences reveal a shimmering World Soul in the form of archetypal music. Like the Romantics, Hoffmann identified with cosmic moods and was enthralled by their infinite riches and sonorities. Archetypal music fed his soul and inspired him to compose interludes which transported him ever deeper into the unlimited magical world of wonderment—which is "Kreisleriana."

2 Balzac's "Gambara": Archetypal Music as Science and Art

Balzac considered music the greatest of the arts because it speaks directly to the soul, fires sensations, and galvanizes ideas. He saw it as both a science and an art in that it obeys the laws of physics and mathematics and it also nourishes the imagination, intensifies fleeting perceptions, and stimulates benumbed or heretofore forgotten memories.

In "Gambara," a short story he wrote in 1837, Balzac fleshed out what was involved in one man's passion for music, a passion so deeply embedded in Gambara's psyche that it devours all other areas of his existence. Everything Gambara feels, thinks, and does, and all of his relationships, are made to serve this fiery force within him.

Psychologically, one may say that Gambara's ego (the center of consciousness, or the factor within the psyche that relates to both outer and inner worlds) was no longer functioning as an independent entity but was dominated by an autonomous complex: an *anima figure* in the form of music. He was like a man possessed—the victim of spontaneous irruptions from his unconscious which took the form of melody, rhythm, and pitch. Like an emotional charge, music drew everything to its nucleus.

Gambara's musical compositions—his opera *Muhammad*, for example, described by Balzac—are archetypal, stemming from the most archaic levels of his psyche. They are universal, encompassing his heritage, culture, imaginative processes, and the hallucinatory fantasies from his inchoate collective unconscious.

Balzac had always been fascinated by the genius. He had written about this kind of "monster" or "aberration" in *The Unknown Masterpiece, Louis Lambert, In Search of the Absolute*, and other works. A genius or *seer*, whose perceptions are far more acute than those of ordinary beings, can pierce through barriers in the empirical world, experience cosmic soundings—the fourth dimension—and know moments of ecstasy. But because of these very capabilities, he may also become a sacrificial agent. Society ridicules the genius for his *outlandish* ideas and his *eccentric* comportment; he is reviled and exiled from the rest of humanity. Different from the average individual, the genius has a *flame* which compels him to forge ahead and also empowers him to defy tradition, rebelling against existing structures, be they musical, as in Gambara's case, or other. The genius does *not submit to destiny*; he carves out his own. Gambara, therefore, is defiant, rebellious, and gigantically ambitious. He is a man whose life revolves around a *musical complex*. So dominated is he by the archetypal music that exists within him that he is unaware of reality, living only for and in his tones, rhythms, pitches, harmonies, and cacophonies. No human being can possibly stand between him and his music: no earthly force may interfere with the message he seeks to impart to humanity.

One of the many innovative musical notions in "Gambara" is that of the *value of dissonance*. At a time in the early nineteenth century when music relied on harmonious interludes to heighten emotion, Balzac's protagonist offered his listeners discords, clashing and conflicting sounds, whole and half tones, even overtones of various duration and timbre. Distinctly ahead of his time, he expanded notions of harmony and polyphony and of relationships between minor and major modes; these made him aware of new sounds, of strange combinations, of pictorial and narrative schemes, and of emotions woven into absolute or abstract resonances, amplitudes, and frequencies. Foreshadowing atonal and concrete music—perhaps even computer and electronic compositions—Gambara has formed a pulsatingly exciting, energetic world of compulsion and contradiction. This world reacts to such stimuli as the dynamic, primitive forces surging raw from his unconscious and finding release in chromaticism, extended tonality, and finally a kind of dissonance in which sonority itself seems to have been annulled.

Balzac's approach to music and to the notion of genius is mystical, stemming from his fascination with the occult, the hermetic, and illuminism. Even as a child he saw the universe as something alive, peopled with invisible souls and secret correspondences. According to his sister, Laure, he had found in his father's library and read the works of Emanuel Swedenborg (1688–1722), Claude de Saint-Martin (1743–1803), and Jacob Boehme (1575–1624).

Swedenborg believed that the invisible domain was merely an extension of the visible world and that interplanetary space was filled with angels living in various spheres depending upon their stages of perfection. In his

Arcana Caelestia, Swedenborg tells us that he was empowered with second sight, that he could contact divine spirits and converse with angels, that secret correspondences existed between himself and the universe. He also believed that light—that is, goodness—would eventually triumph on earth.

Saint-Martin stressed a return to biblical texts. Each person, he wrote in *The Unknown Philosopher*, must build himself from the ground up—as Solomon had constructed his temple, stone by stone—elevating himself strongly and sturdily. Only then can inner growth and spiritual evolution take place.

Boehme, a shoemaker turned mystic and author of *Mysterium Magnum* among other works, greatly influenced the Romantics in general and Balzac in particular. He believed in the fundamental unity of nature as a vehicle for immediate contemplation of divinity. Important, too, was the fact that his views were a direct outgrowth of Hebrew Kabbalistic writings. Unlike Saint Augustine, who envisaged an All-Good and All-Light God, Boehme believed in a *total* God: a composite of Light and Darkness, Good and Evil, Love and Anger. The Church Fathers had always fought what they had considered to be this *dual* principle: they could not accept the fact that an All-Good God could have created evil. For Boehme, however, God was a theogonic process, and the notion of good and evil was an empirical and not a divine concept. Existence, therefore, was to be looked upon as a composite of crosscurrents which brought on both construction and destruction—positive and negative factors, all of which exist in the human soul and in the Godhead.

The Ideologues also influenced Balzac's approach to music and genius. Materialistic and pragmatic philosophers—Condillac, Cabanis, Destutt de Tracy—believed that *ideas* originate in physical sensation. Balzac added the notions of Jean-Philibert Dessaignes to those of the Ideologues, conceiving *thought power* as etheric fluid. It was, therefore, physical in nature: an all-powerful energetic and fiery life force.

Since *thought* for Balzac was *material* and was described in terms of a fluid, which we would refer to today as wave or vibration, it could be transformed into one of the most violent of destructive agents: a "veritable exterminating angel" for humanity because "it kills, but also vivifies," Balzac wrote in *The Ignored Martyrs* (1837). Since thought is concrete and moves about the universe, it is an energetic principle as well, inflaming passions and vices. "Torrents of thoughts" can be as dangerous as numerous stabbings. When thoughts remain unchanneled, they are as harmful as undirected instincts; they must, therefore, be ordered and delimited in structured and positive paths.

Balzac was not the first to believe that thought is fire and combustion and that it can tyrannize a person, as it did so many of his protagonists, and Gambara in particular. Like André-Marie Ampère (1755–1836), physicist, mathematician, and natural philosopher, who had experimented with electricity and magnetism, Balzac believed that human beings were *electrical machines* and that their powers could be measured. (Compare today's electrical and sonar-wave measurements.) Balzac contended that the genius was born with a greater electrical charge (or vital fluid), which determined not only his intellectual operations, will, passions, and thought but his creativity as well.

As *thought* is *fire* and subject to all sorts of waves and sympathetic vibrations, so it is also *sound* for the same reason, infiltrating the entire cosmos in what Pythagoras had called a "music of the spheres." As sound, it produces emotion, color, and form; it awakens sensations and ideas in the listener and composer. Musical language in the differentiated world possesses its own vocabulary and disciplines: melody, tonality, modulation, rhythm, and so forth. Pitch, intensity, color, and volume are properties of tone, which is "prefigured in the physical process, in the length, breadth, and shape of the sound wave."[1] If something alters in tone, the physical process also changes. As melodic energy (fire) stimulates internal momentum, Balzac suggested, it generates finite and infinite relationships and transforms the amorphous into the concrete and the ephemeral into the eternal. "Music alone," Balzac wrote, "has the power to make us penetrate ourselves."[2]

That the story begins on January 1, 1831, is auspicious. The New Year is the time when people look forward to a *renewal* of life and to their own future. This is the anticipation of the young, handsome, elegant Milanese Count Andrea Marcosini. As he walks through the Palais Royal galleries, we learn that he is a political exile and a devotee of music and poetry, and, shortly thereafter, that he is following a beautiful young woman through the labyrinthian streets into a grimy neighborhood. She slips out of sight, and he goes back to his lodgings. But something gnaws at him, and he feels compelled to keep searching for this *anima* figure. He questions the owner of a restaurant in the neighborhood and finally meets the lady and her husband, Signor Gambara, a composer born in Cremona. They make their home on the upper floor of the building that houses the restaurant.

Gambara is described in detail. Balzac accepted the ideas of the phrenologist Franz Joseph Gall (1758–1828), who studied the relationships between the formation of the skull and character traits, as well as the concepts of Johann Kaspar Lavater (1741–1801), who drew analogies between facial structure and personality. There is, then, a correlation between Gambara's character and temperament and his physical traits.

Gambara is forty years of age, "pale and grave." His high forehead, his face etched with deep furrows, his hollow temples, and his deeply set black eyes reveal a powerful inner struggle. In time, we learn that Gambara veers from jubilation to despair in truly romantic style, that he is an instinctive type whose impulses are triggered by outer and inner stimuli. Such a man is dominated by affects. As C. G. Jung wrote, "Psychic processes which, under ordinary circumstances, are functions of the will (thus entirely subject to conscious control), can, in abnormal cases, become instinctive processes through a linking up with unconscious energy."[3]

An amiable and gallant man, he lives a strange existence, spending all of his time composing operas and symphonies and making a great variety of instruments. In some ways, Gambara resembles Beethoven. Both were arrogant and irritable; both were endowed with caustic wit and sharp, biting, obstinate ways. Beethoven had suffered spiritual torture by his overly ambitious father, while Gambara's youth had been transformed by events into a living inferno. After Gambara's father, a successful instrument-maker, had been ruined by the conquering French armies, the young lad left home. Poverty and solitude, and a life of wandering throughout Italy in search of jobs as a musician, became his lot. Unlike Beethoven, Gambara's pain and solitude were not compounded by deafness but were assuaged after his marriage to the angelic, tender, and always giving Marianna. Beethoven *was* the innovator, rebel, and genius that Gambara wanted to be. Although the following statement was made by Beethoven, it could have been spoken by Gambara: "Power is the morality of men who are above the common, and it is mine."[4]

Gambara and the young Count sit down at a table in the restaurant and begin talking about music. Andrea deprecates Italian opera in general and Rossini in particular for their monotonous crescendos and their stylish *rossignolades*, which, like perfume or "chatty females," meander along in a swirl of banalities. Gambara does not wholly agree with his guest. Although such operas as the Count describes do show off a singer's talents, where would French and German composition be today without Scarlatti and Cavalli and others of that ilk? he asks. After other arguments have been aired, Gambara finally begins discoursing on the philosophy of music, while Andrea sits enraptured. During their discussions, Gambara voices the story's main theme, that "music is both a science and an art" (p. 596).

When, in pursuing his conversation with Andrea, Gambara says that sound, being modified air, contains all types of sympathetic vibrations, he is referring to particles of infinite and microscopic dimension that filter through the individual and the cosmos, increasing thought and brain-power. Such sound triggers a need in people to express what lives, breathes, and foments within them. Air contains many different "elastic particles capable of as many vibrations of various duration as there are tones in sonorous bodies" (p. 596). When someone's ear perceives these particles, they affect his thought centers and permeate his nervous system. His mind responds to them ideationally, organizing and hierarchizing them into viable, understandable, and meaningful structures.

The prophetic aspect of Gambara's vision of music is striking. For example, when Gambara states that "sound is light in another form," we think of computer music that is digitally programmed (p. 596). The tonalities emanating from programmers affect filters and oscillators, since each generates electrical signals whose parameters can be received as sound events when transcribed onto magnetic tapes. We also associate electronic music with Gambara's vision because of this music's sonic components, which are produced or modified electronically. The Ondes Martenot, which was invented in 1928 and was designed to produce "pure" sound, freed from overtones and harmonies, is an example of an electronic device that was already described by Gambara in nineteenth-century terms.

Gambara's linking of *physics* and *mathematics* with the art of music not only presages modern musical and acoustical concepts but also makes Gambara a follower of Pythagorean, Platonic, and Aristotelian views. Traditionally, Pythagoras first formulated his ideas on mathematics and music because of the various sounds he heard as he walked past a blacksmith's forge. The blacksmith was using five hammers, four of which sounded in harmony; the fifth, however, made a discordant sound. Later, Pythagoras realized that the first four hammers, weighing twelve, nine, eight, and six pounds each, were measured in terms of whole numbers, but the fifth wasn't. He concluded, first, that harmony arises from a connection with whole numbers, and, second, that sound is a form of vibration and that a tone may be measured by the number of its vibrations per second. Furthermore, he reasoned that the orderly world of numbers, as manifested in digits, underlies musical relationships and that phenomena in general manifest the "all-embracing laws of proportions."[5]

For Plato also, music was an art and a science. Following Pythagorean mathematical laws, music guides the philosopher via its sound, rhythm, amplitude, and its very special language, which trains both body and mind. Presupposing the ultimate unity of all things, Plato's concepts amount to a paradoxical condition of static in motion. Aristotle added the concept of movement when he said that *form* is forever realizing itself in *matter*. By creating an antithesis between form and matter, Aristotle was suggesting that, unless materialized, form has neither function nor meaning. Music is one way of organizing phenomena—one way of bringing into being a chaotic entity.

Like his Greek predecessors, Gambara believes that musical tones can be measured by mathematical proportions. He alludes to such ideations as "geometric constructions" that are implicit in sonorities, volume, chords, dissonances, thirds, fifths, whole and half tones, overtones, and so on (p. 596). Endowed with temporal and nontemporal components, form and matter are forever evolving in rhythmic sound and light waves, each the product of mathematical intervals and sequences.

Mathematical laws pertaining to music are better known, Gambara suggests, than those based on physics. Indeed, as early as the ninth century A.D., single or multiple melodies were combined to sound at the same time, and in so doing gave birth to polyphony. It was not until the seventeenth century that this acoustical phenomenon was altered, with the introduction of harmony, or the simultaneous sounding of various tones. Had Haydn, Mozart, Beethoven, and Rossini known physical as well as mathematical laws, Gambara asserts, they would have gone much further than they did. The aesthetic substances that permeate the atmosphere stimulate phenomena, including vegetal as well as zoological and mineral matter. As these substances infiltrate the composer's soul and mind, they enrich him, empowering him to create superior tonalities and instruments that can shape "grandiose harmonies" (p. 596). The composer, then, becomes the sounding board for celestial and also terrestrial fluidic forces; his response to these powers, measured scientifically and artistically, calls both intellectual and instinctual factors into play. These collective entities he modifies and transposes according to his own subjective and objective vision.

After having expressed some of his notions concerning music, Gambara retires to his room to pursue his work undisturbed. He encourages his wife to remain with Andrea. It is at this point that the reader begins to understand Marianna's role as *anima figure* and how such a force functions in Gambara's world. Anima images have existed from time immemorial and manifest themselves in innumerable avatars: virgin or harlot, saint or sinner, *femme inspiratrice* or destructive force. The anima represents *eros:* love as passion or as relatedness. Psychologically, the anima may be defined as an autonomous psychic content in the male personality—a kind of inner woman. As *eros*, it is the anima figure that establishes for a man what sort of emotional and sexual relationships he will have with the opposite sex. When a man falls in love, for example, he projects his anima onto a real flesh-and-blood woman. In Gambara's case, however, his passion focused on an abstract entity—an autonomous psychic content which he worshipped unreservedly. Having come under the spell of this powerful force, he spends his life as its votary. When the anima is acknowledged consciously, which is not Gambara's case, it may provide the genius with the deepest and finest kind of human inspiration, such as Dante's Beatrice and Petrarch's Laura.

Marianna existed in Gambara's world as an abstract personification of the feminine principle—the Platonic Ideal. As such, she sacrificed not only her person but her individuality and her *livingness*. It was not Marianna that Gambara had loved, not the earthly woman, but rather what she represented in the divine sphere: the perfect essence existing in his unconscious. That Gambara should have felt confident in his wife's fidelity, then, is not surprising. How could she be unfaithful since she existed as an abstraction: his Muse/Music?

The idealization of woman as inspiration for the artist was depicted by Balzac in *The Unknown Masterpiece*, by the Goncourt brothers in *Manette Salomon*, and by Zola in *The Work*. The flesh-and-blood woman in these novels was looked upon as the artist's *rival*, his *enemy*, someone ready to sap his vitality, depotentiate his inspiration, and erode his strength. Although Gambara's wife is a saintly creature who would never hurt her husband, she is nevertheless human and in need of attention and love. To fulfill her needs would deplete his energies, taking his *fire* away from the Ideal woman—Music.

It is Marianna who sees to the couple's food and rent, and who keeps their dingy little room clean and neat. When Andrea visits them, Balzac, drawing analogies between the phenomenological world and the inner climate of his characters, describes the couple's domain as strange, phantomlike, and incredible. The furniture, bed, table, and chair are fashioned from parts of instruments Gambara invented; the "grotesque" bed is made out of an old clavecin. An aura of secrecy and hidden despair—but of creativity—hovers over this bizarre conglomeration of things.

Gambara, who had probed nature's melodies—its "perfect harmonies" and geometric progressions—has completed *Muhammad*, the second opera of his trilogy (the other two are *The Martyrs* and *Jerusalem Delivered*). Although the opera's subject is drawn from history, its music has been subjectively conceived and executed. After sitting down at his piano to explain his opera to Andrea, Gambara becomes consumed by his passion. Like so many romantic performers and composers, he relies on divinely bestowed inspiration to bring on his creative élan. The fiery forces inundate his being and flood his imagination, lending his music archetypal scope—that is, assaulting him in the form of melodies, rhythms, timbres, assonances, and harmonies. Once these forces have materiality, Gambara shows how he develops them. Applying his rational principle, he alters their form and coloration and trims the recitatives, choral and vocal interludes, and the instrumental sequences.

Gambara's *Muhammad*, like Monteverdi's *Orfeo* (1607), has lavish staging instructions and eloquent musicality as well as lyrical tonalities that encourage elevated passion, with heightened dramatic effects. It was intended to be a microcosm of the macrocosm—to frame an entire universe by representing the highest type of life. Its oratorio elements give it a distinct religious quality, so that it blends celestial and terrestrial spheres into one "great human poem" (p. 599).

In three acts, the opera deals with the prophet's youth, his marriage to the rich widow Khadija, his visionary experiences, his exile from Mecca, the flight to Medina, and the wars, followed by Muhammad's proclamation of his new ideas, and, finally, the establishment of his religion. As Gambara, seated at the piano, explains his opera's cadences and its harmonic and chromatic modulations and combinations, the atmosphere in the small room vibrates with resonant and oscillating emotions. The rich bass tones that dominate the opera fill the air, imparting majesty and a sense of nobility. One feels Muhammad's frenzy mounting, and Gambara's as well, since the composer's identification with his protagonist is complete. Gambara takes on the spectacular personality of a Liszt—and, like the virtuoso, he demonstrates the satanic trait of playing with otherworldly brio. In allegro and adagio passages and vocalizations in soprano, contralto, and bass registers, he sings of Muhammad's love and rage. His emphatic and velvety delivery is compressed in flowing and lilting tones, expositions, developments, and recapitulations. His thematic transformations, which he describes in terms of key, time, and amplitudes, are worked out with elegance and bravura, eliciting emotions that range from pathos and sensuality to anger, passion, and melancholia. As Gambara performs, his muscles grow taut, his fingers tense, and his senses plumb unheard-of depths. He has become an archetypal figure—Muhammad himself—both psychologically and physically. In short, he conveys the very aura of the being who was God's mouthpiece.

Written in C minor and played in three beats, the overture to *Muhammad* tells, in steady andante tempo, of the young Prophet's ambitions. His despondency and complaints are revealed in transitional passages of E-flat in a rapid allegro sequence of four beats, while his cries of despair and furor and his need to fight, shine, and conquer are conveyed in rhythmic tonalities suited to his mood. Modulations into A-flat major, as Khadija sings of her love and awe, are followed by clashing visceral transitions as the powerful magistrates and priests, believing their authority to be threatened, force Muhammad out of Mecca.

At this point, cadences in E-flat major and G minor announce a new spiritual attitude. Muhammad has converted many people, and, as a result, the new, energetic power is conveyed in thunderous crescendos of brasses sounding their triumphal notes, paralleling in music the Hegira;

Muhammad's struggle against the pagans, Jews, and Christians; his pilgrimage to Mecca; and, finally, his establishment of a theocratic state. The musical accompaniments of the opera's love motifs are sounded in soprano tones: Muhammad's marriage to his favorite, the virgin Aisha; his relationships with his family; his proclamation of polygamy. According to Gambara, Muhammad is a volatile being whose moods are constantly shifting. This changeableness is expressed by majestic, lilting harmonies and also by harsh and violent cacophonies that expand the very limits of melody and acoustics. "Didn't I have to explain the marvels of this great movement of men that created their own music, architecture, poetry, costume and mores?" Gambara asks, justifying his composition (p. 601). He feels compelled to communicate every idea and emotion through music. The brass instruments have to blare out their powerful tones for the strident, triumphant moments; timpani have to create the feeling of conquest, mass movements, and crowds surrounding the holy man; the strings yield their laments and, along with woodwinds, convey throbbing, sensual desires.

What was highly effective in this demonstrative sequence was the manner in which Gambara built his sonorous dreamworld on musical volleys, succession of pitches, transpositions into various registers, resonances, and contrasts in tonal colorations—all of which were brought on by his visionary experiences.

Gambara seemed to *feel into* the cosmos and experience its dynamism and its variegated intensities. He took on the stature of the divinely inspired Muhammad—thus combining legend and reality. His spasmodic rendering of the lines and his emotional climaxes as he sang out the recitatives and arias reverberated with such intensity that they aroused Marianna and Andrea: "The madness of the husband had been eclipsed by that of the composer" (p. 602).

What accounts, psychologically, for the viscerality of Gambara's performance? As we suggested earlier, Gambara has been victimized by a complex—in his case, revolving around music. Complexes may be considered as having a type of electric current: they possess affective charges and feeling tones. The affects given off by a complex are sometimes so great as to be capable of acting physically upon the person experiencing it. Respiration and blood pressure and circulation may be altered, depending upon the power of the complex over the individual. When certain exceptionally deep-rooted complexes break through into consciousness, they can erupt with such extreme violence that they invade an entire personality. This kind of situation occurs in cases of psychosis, which may very well have been Gambara's mental condition.[6]

What happens to a person who comes to be dominated by a complex?

The complex inflates, distends, and grows like a cancer. As it invades the psyche, its energy, released in affective charges and feeling tones, bombards rational attitudes and thought processes. As the complex increases in dynamism, the entire psyche falls under its dominion; almost everything the individual does, thinks, or feels is centered on this complex. The complex, the autonomous psychic entity, keeps attracting to itself energy that properly belongs to, and that should nourish, the psyche as a whole. With what result? As the complex gains in strength and vigor, the rest of the psyche starves, atrophies, and finally disintegrates.[7]

At the finale Andrea reveals that he is shocked by the cacophonies in *Muhammad*—not surprising in view of Gambara's psychological condition. Andrea has been accustomed to harmonious tones and velvety sonorities. The discords grate on his sensibilities and lacerate his nerves. Yet, it is these very dissonances that give joy to Gambara in composing and that mark his work as revolutionary. Gambara believes that he has divested himself of the composition principles and harmony rules governing the opera world of his day. For him, a note or chord does not lead into the next in a conventional manner. The sequences of fifths, sevenths, octaves, major and minor thirds, fourths, and sixths create a conglomeration of jarring tonalities: "The strange discordances that howled under his fingers had evidently resounded in his ears as celestial harmonies" (p. 602). So moved is Gambara by the fresh cadences and pitches emanating from his vocal rendition that he reaches a state of *ekstasis*. His blue eyes are like repositories of celestial forces; his face reflects the agitation and visceral qualities of his music; and his head thrust back in exhaustion signals the close of an incredible musical adventure.

The stunning orchestrations and melodious tonalities of romantic opera were nonexistent in *Muhammad*. Gambara must have felt that, by not using the full resources of the chromatic scale, he could introduce greater variety and emotional appeal into his modulations through *pivotal points*, thereby underscoring inner harmonies and so paving the way for easier transitions. He did not abandon the tonic note in favor of primary relations in an atonal system, as Arnold Schoenberg, Anton Webern, and Alban Berg were to do. Gambara had extended the limits of musical harmony and introduced clashing sounds reminiscent of Stravinsky's harsh dissonances, irregular beats, and fresh rhythmic qualities and orchestral colorations. The jarring and grating tones and unexpected progressions issuing from Gambara's piano, the variety of tempi, the dynamics and duration of the notes, the vibratory quality of his melodies, conveyed by what he described as strings, woodwinds, brasses, and percussion, had disconcerted Andrea—but had also impressed him. "All the harmonies emanate from a common center and retain an intimate relationship between them; or rather, harmony, like light, is decomposed by our arts as rays are in a prism" (p. 602).

Gambara's mystico-scientific discussion of his opera includes an explanation of the instruments involved. Instruments in general, he believed, emanate from a unique prototype, which was differentiated in accordance with tone, timbre, pitch, and so forth, and regulated by mathematical relationships. Thus, the *one* was incorporated into the *many*. In accordance with the theories of Etienne Geoffroy Saint-Hilaire (1772–1844), the founder of embryology, who believed in the unity of composition of human and animal organisms, Balzac, via Gambara, suggested that all creation stems from a *mother-substance*—a single faculty from which all others emerge. When creating instruments, therefore, one works from a *prima materia*, known, yet unknown. Each new amalgam brings different tones into existence; each constituent creates its own principles, modifications, laws, disciplines, and emotional impact (p. 596). To understand chromatic fluctuations, dynamics, pitch, and acoustics is to extend not only the boundaries of music but of physics and mathematics as well.

Gambara proceeds to show Andrea his *Panharmonicon*. This *complete* and *unique* instrument that he has constructed will, he asserts, replace an entire orchestra. Interestingly, though Balzac was writing fiction, such an instrument had been invented by J. N. Maelzel, the creator of the metronome, early in the nineteenth century. In fact, Beethoven had written his *Battle Symphony* for it.

Andrea was so excited—and repelled—by Gambara's ideas that he insisted upon questioning him still further. This time, Giacomo Meyerbeer's (1791–1864) opera *Robert the Devil* (1831) came under scrutiny. As Gambara began explaining its sequences and musical interludes, he was again carried away by the music—its themes, evolution, development, progressions, and passionate outbursts. Excitement, perhaps even madness, radiated from his face as he imitated the raucous laughter of Robert, the son of Bertram (really the Devil).

> Roll on music, envelop us in your intensified folds; roll on and seduce. Infernal powers have seized their prey; they hold it, they dance. This handsome genius destined to conquer, to reign, is lost! The demons are jubilant. Misery will strangle genius, passion will destroy the knight. (p. 607)

Robert's viciousness increased despite his love for the beautiful and saintly Isabelle, and hers for him. Forever tempted by the evil Bertram, he gambles his fortune away and loses his honor in the process.

Vast canvases and universal principles are also at stake in *Robert the*

Devil, as they had been in *Muhammad*. Gambara's piano-playing, depicting evil fighting good, vocally and verbally, brings to mind Paganini and Liszt—virtuosi who had generated a sense of mystery and divine and demonic powers as they performed. Gambara's brilliance terrified and exhilarated Andrea; it moved and instilled fear into Marianna's soul. The two watched the gaunt figure before them contort, as if possessed by some otherworldly power!

Balzac concludes his tale of tragedy and woe with Marianna's desertion of her husband, her enjoyment of Andrea's love for a few years, and his subsequent abandonment of her. Left in need and reduced to skeleton form, she returned to Paris and to her husband six years later, in 1837. Gambara had not fared much better. Incapable of earning a livelihood by repairing instruments, he had been forced to sell his Panharmonicon; as for his musical scores, the merchants of the Halles who bought them used these "sublime" works to wrap their meats, fish, fruits, and vegetables.

Music lived in Gambara's unconscious as an anima—an autonomous entity, luring him into the ideal realm where he could tear off the mask, rend the barriers of the empirical world, and live as *vates*. It was through the intricate vibratory experience—the emanations exuded from the mind in waves, sheets, and particles—that Gambara glimpsed the *uncreated* and that he sensed the *void*. In these endlessly shifting spheres (the collective unconscious, in psychological terms), Gambara, the genius, heard his archetypal music, anticipating future innovations, sparking fresh principles, and developing potentials.

Gambara's gigantic orchestral arrangements and the way his vital, dynamic urges conveyed sound, idea, rhythm, and amplitude anticipated Richard Wagner and Richard Strauss. In relatively primitive terms, he was also the forerunner of the novel tonalities of Arnold Schoenberg, Anton Webern, Alban Berg, and other composers who, in emphasizing the twelve-tone resources of the chromatic scale, believed they were introducing more varied modulations from one key to another.

Freed from the many musical conventions of the time, Gambara could give rein to his instinct and mind. He did so on a visceral level to be sure, but also archetypally, since he experienced and conveyed transpersonal images in his musical compositions. Being victimized by his *musical complex* only served to stimulate his visionary experience and to endow his works with intense energy and rare momentum. Gambara, for whom sound was both a science and an art, was, indeed, the "unknown Orpheus of modern music" (p. 610). Fire was his sounding board, energy his wand, fluid and wavelike particles his inspirational forces, through which he participated endlessly and fully in cosmic spheres.

3 Baudelaire and Wagner's Archetypal Operas

Richard Wagner's archetypal operas actuated powerful concepts and images in Charles Baudelaire's imagination. No sooner did he hear the composer's leitmotifs, the poet tells us in his essay "Richard Wagner and 'Tannhäuser' " (1861), than his entire being was electrified, affording him "the most intense musical pleasure" he had ever known.[1] He felt himself floating out of the empirical world: "I experienced one of those happy impressions. . . . I felt myself liberated *from those weighty bonds,* able through souvenir, to rediscover the extraordinary *voluptuousness* that circulates in these high spheres" (p. 1213). Timelessness and spacelessness opened him to "a great reverie," to ever-renewing sensations of flame and whiteness which accelerated and slackened in pace, paralleling the rhythms and tonal sweep of Wagner's music.

> I see a vast expanse of somber red before my eyes. If this red represents passion, I view it as going through all the shades of red and rose, gradually taking on the incandescence of a furnace. Although it would seem difficult, if not impossible to experience anything more fiery, a last flare traces a furrow, whiter than the white used as a backdrop. This is, if you wish, the supreme gasp of a soul risen to its paroxystic heights. (p. 1206)

Archetypal images, endowed with their own energy charge, worked powerfully on Baudelaire's psyche. Emanating from both the personal unconscious (representing the private aspect of an individual's psychic life) and the collective unconscious (the profoundest suprapersonal layer within the psyche), archetypal images have existed in the collective psyche of humanity since earliest times. They are the basic content of religions, mythologies, legends, and great works of pictorial, literary, or musical arts. These archetypes (*arche*, meaning beginning, origin, primal source and principle; and *typos*, translated as imprint, form, prototype), C. G. Jung suggests, disclose psychic or life energy that eludes consciousness and rational thinking.[2] They are "mnemic deposits . . . patterns, unseen determinants of psychic nature."[3]

Because the archetype possesses its own *libido* (psychic energy), it attracts to it "contents of consciousness—conscious ideas that render it perceptible and hence capable of conscious realization."[4] When passing over into consciousness, the archetype, invested with its own dynamism, may catapult into the dream or vision, thus paving the way for a *numinous* or *ecstatic experience*. Such was the effect of Wagner's music upon Baudelaire; and upon Wagner himself when in the throes of composition.

Baudelaire's intense response to Wagner's music points to the psychological affinities between these two artists. Both descended to the source of their creativity—"to the wordless and imageless" amorphous realm of the collective unconscious. Each conveyed his feelings and sensations in his own way—in primordial images and archaic forms endowed with color and feeling, which give form and substance to what is generally considered nebulous and indeterminate.[5]

Wagner's innovative ideas concerning poetry, composition, drama, and stagecraft were expressed in his treatises *Art and Revolution* (1849), *The Art-work of the Future* (1849), and *Opera and Drama* (1850–51). The myth was vital to his credo, as it was to Baudelaire's. The very subject matter of his operas is drawn from the *myth:* the conveyor of the archaic communal life and beliefs of a people. As a result, the whole cultural and psychological dimension of Wagner's Germanic forebears—his *Vaterland*—became accessible to him, not merely through the intellect, but through *feeling*. "In the Drama," Wagner wrote, "we must become knowers through Feeling." The myth, an original experience emanating from the psyche of a people, speaks directly to the personal unconscious, representing the private aspects of the psychological life and the collective psyche of a people in all periods and lands. "The incomparable thing about myth," wrote Wagner, "is that it is true for all time, and its content, however compressed, is inexhaustible throughout the ages."[6] This reaching into the heart of mythical life enabled Wagner to integrate, at least momentarily, those factors that had been alienated within his personality, among which was the dichotomy between flesh and spirit.[7]

Baudelaire considered the myth as a restatement of an original and unique experience that had really happened in some indeterminate past, perhaps at the very outset of the creation of the world. Since myths, in general, narrate a cosmological event—the beginning of the Cosmos, of the Earth, of heroes, and so forth—they bathe *in illo tempore,* that is, in *archetypal history.* They reveal in universal terms the very structure of reality in all of its many modalities. Mythology, then, is *ontophany* as well as *theophany* and *hierophany.* The creators of the world were gods, partially divine beings, or heroes; it is they who narrate the history of what came into being *in illo tempore* and thereby reveal the emergence of the *sacred* into the world.[8]

Mythical in dimension, Wagner's operas bathed in unlimited time schemes, thereby touching upon the *sacred.* They recounted the intervention of the gods (or God), the birth of heroes and heroines, their trajectories through life, their death and redemption. No longer could opera consist of arias designed to show off the talents of singers; nor could music alone be the goal of drama. Wagner united in his music dramas those very forces that had been diffused onstage in the works of his contemporaries. He also accomplished, through projection, a unification of his own spirit and psyche.

To put his innovative ideas into practice, "Tone-speech" would replace "Word-speech." He wrote: "Tone-speech is the beginning and end of Word-Speech: as feeling is the beginning and end of Understanding, as Mythos is beginning and end of History, the Lyric beginning and end of Poetry." Language, Wagner believed, was born from emotion or the *feeling domain:* vowel sounds were first uttered by humans when reacting tonally and qualitatively to events and situations around them. Consonants, which developed later, framed and thereby limited the vowel sounds. At this point, intellectual and abstract notions participated in the transformative process. For Wagner, then, the basis of language and of music (tone) is associated with humanity's affective nature. In keeping with Wagner's emotional approach to language and sound in general, music is to be fluid, moving about in continuous, "infinite" melody. Wagner was convinced that "the orchestra indisputably possesses a *faculty of speech.* . . . We have plainly to denote this Speaking-faculty of the Orchestra as the faculty of uttering the *unspeakable.*"[9]

Wagner's operas and Baudelaire's writings are mythical and archetypal expressions of living intuitions and perceptions emanating from their collective unconscious. They are concentrations and distillations of energies which, when manifested in visions, dreams, fantasies, tones, and rhythms, altered their inner world, allowing their works to take shape from within—not merely from the exterior domain—and enabling them to float out of finitude and linearity into a space-time continuum.

The Intuitive Versus the Rational

That both Wagner and Baudelaire were hounded by excoriating conflicts in the workaday world stemmed in part from a fundamental opposition between the powers of reason, defined by Wagner as "consciously or rationally formed ideas," and "the exquisite unconscious of artistic creation."[10] "We can form no abstract idea of a thing," Wagner wrote, "unless we have already taken it in as a living intuition."[11]

For Baudelaire, the creative spirit learns through a *kind of recognition*, in the Platonic sense. He *"recognized"* Wagner's music when listening to it for the first time: it was as if it had emanated from some anterior existence. "I knew this music. . . . It seemed to me that this music was mine . . . and I recognized it as all men recognize things they are destined to love" (p. 1205). For Wagner and Baudelaire, music existed in the psyche—in the form of potentialities—as did archetypal images, awaiting their emergence into the conscious sphere at the appropriate moment. From nonbeing to being: only after its manifestation in the form (visual, oral, or otherwise) does the rational principle take hold, develop, order, and refine the contrapuntal and polyphonic combinations, the mental images, and the Tone-speech and Word-speech essential to composer and poet.

Wagner composed like a man possessed—as if in a *trance*, with "divine and demonic excitement," receiving idea, tone, and gesture from his unconscious without any conscious direction on his part.[12] His Dionysian side and his exalted spirituality took precedence over all else. The empirical world no longer existed during the tempestuous moments alluded to as Wagner's "period of creative withdrawal." Wagner lived in a state of "complete self-forgetfulness, forgetfulness of the world," as he fixed into form what had been fluid and transient in his unconscious.[13]

Some of the material existing within Wagner's collective unconscious was striving to be communicated to the world. It was "like a whirlwind that seized everything within reach" as it swirled upward into visible shape. Although he could perceive only glimpses of this matrix of unconscious contents (when in the process of transforming the amorphous into musical and dramatic form), feelings of *exaltation*—the *numinosum*—swept over him. He felt *redeemed* and filled with an inner harmony. Psychologically speaking, he knew *wholeness*. No longer was he fragmented; no longer was he tortured by conflict.[14]

For Baudelaire, who was more cerebral than Wagner, *ideas* were perceived intuitively amid the whirling sensations brought on by the composer's leitmotifs. He conceived of a soul "moving in luminous spheres, of ecstasy that comes from voluptuousness and knowledge, and gliding above and far from the natural world" (p. 1214). The intermingling of

idea/intuition and sense perception paved the way for "a spiritual operation . . . a revelation," inviting Baudelaire—as Wagner—to bathe in *mystery* and to hear, see, palpate, and inhale the new structures, orders, and
methods of the unknown.

The idea of wholeness—a monistic view—enabled Baudelaire, like Wagner, to experience feelings of cohesion and unity, which he called "spiritual
and physical beatitude" (p. 1214). He now felt linked to cosmic realms
through "a reciprocal analogy." He recognized the fact that timelessness
and spacelessness existed within as well as outside him, ever since "the day
God proffered to the world a complete and indivisible totality" (p. 1213).
For Baudelaire, tones reverberated in his psyche when triggered by Wagner's resonances and residues from a distant past and anterior worlds.
These he probed by penetrating their amplitudes, vibrations, and trajectories in a space-time continuum. His approach to music and to poetry was
analogical, consisting in experiencing connections between networks of
correspondences, thus enabling him to restore the primordial unity for
which he so longed. Sounds, colors, aromas, textures blended through
mutuality into a harmonious whole:

> The shadows displace themselves slowly, forcing before them or
> extinguishing the tones that light itself displaces, and seeks to have
> resonate anew. These return their reflections, and modify their quali-
> ties by icing them over with transparent and borrowed qualities,
> *multiplying infinitely their melodious marriages.* . . . This great day-
> time symphony which is the eternal variation of yesterday's *sym-
> phony*, this succession of melodies where variety always emerges
> from the infinite, this complicated hymn is called color.[15]

Wagner's approach, emanating from the *prima materia*, was intuitive,
and analogical as well. His operas were composed of coordinates of poems
(intellect through speech), music (heart, feeling in tone), and dance (pantomime, gesture). All issued from the collective unconscious. Equipoise
replaced what had been imbalanced, nutritive elements revived what had
grown arid, and depth filled the chasm beneath superficiality.

Wagner explained that, when composing, "strange melodies, never-felt
passions" imposed themselves upon his soul "like dreams full of presenti-
ment."[16] In Marienbad, for example, where he had gone for a medically
ordered cure in 1845, he brought with him Wolfram von Eschenbach's
poems and the anonymous epic *Lohengrin*, thinking that these books
would help him relax. Before taking the waters, he decided to take a walk
through the neighboring woods. Sitting down beside a brook to begin
reading, instead of experiencing greatly needed tranquility, he lost himself

"in Wolfram's strange, yet irresistibly charming poem. Soon, however, a longing seized me to give expression to the inspiration generated by this poem, so that I had the greatest difficulty in overcoming my desire to give up the rest I had prescribed. . . ." This "ever increasing state of excitement" mounted, encompassing his entire being, when

> *Lohengrin* . . . stood suddenly revealed before me, complete in every detail of its dramatic construction. The legend of the swan, which forms such an important feature of all the many versions of this series of myths that my studies had brought to my notice, exercised a singular fascination over my imagination. . . . I felt an over-powering desire to write out *Lohengrin*, and this longing so overcame me that I could not wait the prescribed hour for the bath. . . . I ran home to write out what I had in mind. I repeated this for several days until the complete sketch of *Lohengrin* was on paper.[17]

The doctor caring for Wagner at the spa realized the power of that irrepressible and incandescent force within him and suggested that the composer return home. The baths under such conditions would lose their healing effect. *Lohengrin*, however, had been born.

That music and poetry emerged full-blown from Wagner's unconscious is substantiated in his description of the changes which took place in him during the creation of the *Ring*. When conceiving it, Wagner had thought it out in a most rational manner. His intellect pointed the way: toward the depiction of a "Hellenic, optimistic world." His feelings, however, turned him in another direction:

> I had unconsciously followed an entirely different, much profounder view, and instead of a phase of world development, had perceived and recognized in its true character the essential nature of the world itself in all its conceivable phases . . . something came forth entirely different from what I had conceived.[18]

Wagner mentions his ability, when creating his operas, "to look down into those profoundest depths, which the human breast contains," and actually see "what stirs itself at the bottom of this unfathomable spring, now in divine and again in demonic excitement."[19]

Baudelaire, who projected onto Wagner's music perhaps more deeply than most of his contemporaries, could say with equanimity that when engulfed in the stream of Wagner's music he experienced that "tenebrous and profound unity"—that sphere where universals and primordial images live inchoate. The mysterious world of myth, legend, and mystery answered a need in both Baudelaire and Wagner: that of *redemption*.

The Redemption Motif in The Flying Dutchman, Tannhäuser, *and* Lohengrin

Wagner's obsession with the myth of *redemption* is particularly significant in the three operas which Baudelaire singled out for discussion in his essay on Wagner: *The Flying Dutchman, Tannhäuser*, and *Lohengrin*.
Wagner expressed his thoughts on redemption as follows:

> The period in which I have worked in response to my *intuitions* starts with *The Flying Dutchman*. Then came *Tannhäuser* and *Lohengrin*, and if in these works there is any underlying poetic theme, it must be looked for in the supreme tragedy of renunciation, the abnegation of the will, which is shown there as necessary and unavoidable and alone capable of achieving redemption.[20]

Wagner's redemption motifs invited Baudelaire to penetrate into both satanic and divine realms: descending into the blackest abyss—that giant maw where the Prince of Darkness reigned—and ascending to the most elevated of spheres, where souls roam in the light of the azure. As Baudelaire closed his eyes, bathing in the very essence of Wagner's archetypal tonalities, he felt himself "so to speak taken away from earth" (p. 1213):

> When the religious theme invades the precincts of evil unleashed, and begins reestablishing order little by little, and taking on the ascendancy; when it rises again in all of its solid beauty, above the chaos of agonizing sensuality, the entire soul experiences a kind of cooling down, a beatitude of redemption, ineffable feeling. . . . (p. 1224)

What is the notion of redemption that so attracted both poet and composer? The word (from the Latin verb *emere*) means barter, buy back, ransom. For the Christian, Christ came to earth to buy back Adam's sin, giving humanity the possibility of redemption. A rite of passage, redemption takes the acolyte from an earthbound and distressful state to a free and celestial condition, from the human to the divine sphere. Psychologically, redemption implies the awareness of the ego (center of consciousness) of the suprapersonal nature of the psyche. When such expansion and growth occur, a reconciliation of opposites may come into being, paving the way for the beginning of the process of *individuation* or *wholeness*.

Baudelaire and Wagner longed for redemption, which would heal, they felt, the split between the instinctual and the spiritual, the Christ and the anti-Christ, good and evil, flesh and spirit, the ideal and the real. The Christian prejudice against the world of instincts, earth force, and life equated with sinful and satanic powers, compelled them to long for its opposite: the *inhuman* or divine/ideal sphere. The example of martyrs and flagellants and their ascetic practices (fasting, isolation, self-torture, etc.) is implicit in Wagner's depiction of the Pilgrims as contrasted with the seekers of Venusberg. Baudelaire's feelings were equally ambivalent, tempted as he was by the orgiastic practices associated with the Prince of Darkness (lust, concupiscentia), but yearning also for the serenity of the divine domain.

Extreme asceticism elicits its opposite. Attempts on the part of Baudelaire and Wagner to repress the spontaneous impulses of an inner spirit by an overly conscious control of the ego only accentuated the imbalance within them, leading more urgently to a need for redemption.[21] To yearn for the ideal and for perfection in the domain of love, or any other domain, is to proscribe the imperfect human realm of life itself. To reject the principle of evil is to increase an already precarious *imbalance* within the psyche, which may become "*a causa instrumentalis* of redemption and individuation."[22] Individuation is defined as "the conscious realization and fulfillment of one's unique being."[23]

Baudelaire and Wagner were forever veering from excessive spirituality to the intense joy of basking in the delights of lust. Baudelaire was well aware of the polarities within him and remarked that "moderation never seemed to me to be the sign of a vigorous artistic nature. I like those healthful excesses, those overflowings of will inscribed in works . . ." (p. 1236).

Death, or the *sacrifice* of the ego, is represented by specific characters and leitmotifs in Wagner's *Flying Dutchman*, *Tannhäuser*, and *Lohengrin*. "His melodies," Baudelaire remarked, "are to a certain extent like personifications of ideas . . ." (p. 1231). The Dutchman/Senta, Tannhäuser/Elisabeth, Lohengrin/Elsa, and the specific musical phrases associated with each of them were organically connected to their deliberate and voluntary self-abnegating acts. In each case, they opted for death rather than life, for heaven instead of earth—disequilibrium from an empirical point of view.

The Flying Dutchman

The Flying Dutchman tells the story of a sea captain who had rashly vowed to round a cape of land though it might take him until Judgment Day. Satan hears his words, and the Dutchman is doomed to sail the seas without rest. Only once every seven years is he permitted to land, and then only to seek out a maiden who will be true to him unto death. When he meets Senta, the Dutchman feels strange sensations and a burning within him. "Is it love?" he questions. "Ah, no! It is salvation that I crave / Might such an angel come my soul to save." Despite warnings from the young man who loves her and from friends and neighbors, Senta cries out uncontrollably: "Tis I he seeks! To him must I go! His fate shall be mine!" As the Dutchman leaves in his Phantom Ship, Senta throws herself into the water and drowns. In the glow of a supernatural light, the Dutchman and Senta are seen in each other's arms ascending to Heaven. Her sacrificial love redeemed the Dutchman and led to his salvation.

The Dutchman, referred to frequently as "the Ahasuerus of the Seas," was punished for his hubris: his ego had identified with his Self when attempting to determine his destiny. Eternal wandering and the pain accompanying such a punishment seal his fate. Redemption alone will bring him the serenity for which he so desperately longs. Senta's love, Wagner believed, justified the sacrifice of her life. "The condition of lovelessness," the composer wrote to Liszt, "is the cause of suffering for the entire human race." Pity, he suggested elsewhere, if deeply felt, is the basis for true morality. For him, Senta, then, was a truly righteous being.[24]

Baudelaire considered Senta's unselfish love a paradigm of supernal love and the rejection of a vulgar earthly relationship. "To love the unfortunate man for his sorrow," he remarked, "is too great an idea to be placed in anyone's heart except that of an ingenuous person, and it is certainly a beautiful thought to have associated the idea of the redemption of a damned individual with the passionate imagination of a young girl" (p. 1234).

Tannhäuser

Wagner's adaptation of the thirteenth-century Tannhäuser myth focuses on redemption as a means of solving the conflict between flesh and spirit. Tannhäuser, a minnesinger, returns from Venusberg to the court of the Landgrave of Thuringia. Elisabeth, the Landgrave's niece, who had remained faithful in her love for the minnesinger, is deeply moved by his presence. Wolfram von Eschenbach, Tannhäuser's friend and a poet in his own right, convinces him to enter a singing contest. The winner is to marry Elisabeth. Tannhäuser agrees. When it is his turn to perform, he bursts into song praising Venus and her orgiastic love. Tannhäuser's wild paganism becomes so overt that the knights who had gathered to listen to him are scandalized and draw their swords. Elisabeth begs them to spare his life. Penitent, Tannhäuser leaves for Rome with a group of pilgrims to earn absolution. The Pope will grant him his wish only if a miracle comes to pass: his barren staff must flower. In despair, Tannhäuser decides to return to Thuringia and to Venus. Wolfram tries to dissuade him. As he mentions Elisabeth's name, her funeral cortege passes by. A group of pilgrims arrives and informs those present that the Pope's staff has burst into flower. Tannhäuser falls down beside Elisabeth's bier and dies, forgiven and redeemed.

Wagner stated that the *imprint* of *Tannhäuser* had been alive within him prior to the writing process. His hero's eternal restlessness, and his great conflict between sinful flesh and blissful spirit, were projections of his own inner torment. "All the sounds and characteristic motifs," including "the highest longing for love," not only existed in the composer's head prior to his setting them down on paper but "were transmutations and transliterations of his own psychological climate."[25] Redemption, for which Tannhäuser yearned so desperately, and which Wagner achieved momentarily while composing his work, is that single force capable of quelling *agony via agony*. Like the functioning of a vaccine, one poison cures another. About Tannhäuser Wagner wrote:

> From the excess of joy that he had known in the arms of Venus, he yearns for relief in—pain. This profoundly mortal yearning naturally leads him to Woman, that he might sorrow with her as he knew only pleasure with Venus. His longing is fulfilled, and thenceforth he cannot live without rapturous pain, just as his earlier joys had been rapturous. But the pains are not voluntary, not purposely assumed: with irresistible power they have filled his heart with compassion, and his whole life's energy is consumed to a point of self-denial. Here his love for Elisabeth expresses itself as completely unlike his love for Venus. . . .[26]

Elisabeth is the instrument of Tannhäuser's redemption: the *sacrificial agent*. She surrendered what was most precious to her—her life—to a higher principle, God; she redeemed Tannhäuser in an *imitatio Christi*. Such a deed cut her off from the profane world; it also indicated her need for deity. Both Wagner and Baudelaire considered her sacrifice—her sacredness—as a spiritual victory over humanity's animal instincts. Psychologically, ego/Elisabeth had given up its powerful position as the center of consciousness and martyred itself by yielding to more powerful values, affording renewal in another dimension.

For Baudelaire, *Tannhäuser* dramatizes "the struggle of two principles that chose the human heart as a battlefield, that is, spirit and flesh, hell and heaven, Satan and God" (p. 1223). *Tannhäuser*, then, revolves around two archetypes and two contrary principles, "psychic duality": the conflict between Venus and God, the religious and the voluptuous, sin and saintliness (p. 1226). "But as an intimate sense of God is soon to be consciously drowned out by the desire of the flesh, the aria representing saintliness, is slowly submerged by the sighs of voluptuousness," until such time as spirituality wins out (p. 1223). Commenting on Wagner's opera, Baudelaire wrote:

> Languishings, delights, blended with fevers cut through by anguish, incessant returnings to voluptuousness, always promising to quench one's thirst for it, but never does, raging palpitations of the heart and senses, imperious orders of the flesh, the entire dictionary of onomatopeias identified with love is heard here. Finally, the religious theme slowly takes back its empire, gradually absorbing the other in a peaceful and glorious victory, as does an irresistible being over a sickly and disorderly one, Saint Michael over Lucifer. (p. 1223)

Tannhäuser, "saturated with enervating delights, *aspires to pain*" (p. 1224). For Baudelaire, as for Wagner, pain alone brings healing and frees one from the world of the flesh, which so tormented both sensualists—the poet and the composer.

Lohengrin

The theme of redemption through love is also dominant in *Lohengrin*. Parsifal's son, Lohengrin, arrives at Antwerp in a skiff drawn by a swan. He will be the champion of Elsa, a princess of Brabant accused by the sorceress Ortrud and her husband, Telramund, of killing her brother. Lohengrin wins his combat against Telramund. He and Elsa express their mutual love and are to be married with one proviso: that she must not ask him his name or lineage. Under the influence of Ortrud, Elsa succumbs to her curiosity and questions Lohengrin on their wedding night. According to his vows to the Grail, Lohengrin must disclose his identity and then disappear. The swan returns to take him away. Before leaving, he prays, at which the swan is transformed into Elsa's brother, Gottfried, also a victim of the sorceress Ortrud. The Brabantians bow before Gottfried, who is to rule them henceforth. When Elsa sees Lohengrin sink into the distance, she falls lifeless into her brother's arms.

With the interpenetration of two worlds (the supernatural and the terrestrial), the protagonists earn redemption by sacrificing human for atemporal love. As Wagner wrote:

> Elsa is the unconscious, the unvolitional, into which Lohengrin's conscious, volitional being yearns to be redeemed; but that yearn-

ing is itself the unconscious, unvolitional in Lohengrin, through which he feels himself akin in being to Elsa.[27]

Baudelaire commented on Lohengrin's subordinating his will to the higher transpersonal principle of the Grail, thereby cutting himself off from the temporal sphere and earning redemption. Baudelaire also made mention of the similarity existing between the Lohengrin/Elsa and Cupid/ Psyche myths. In both cases, the hero's identity has to remain a secret; in both cases, the woman's curiosity unleashes evil forces. Such analogies, Baudelaire remarked, serve to confirm the single origin of myths, that is, the *single origin* of everything in the primordial realm.

> It is, if you will, the sign of a unique origin, the incontroversial proof of kinship, but only on the condition that one searches for its origins in the absolute principle and communal origin of all beings. One myth may be considered brother to another. . . . the myth is a tree that burgeons everywhere, in all climates, under all suns, spontaneously and without cuttings. . . . (p. 1229)

The same holds true for poetry—for all the arts—and for religion. "As sin is everywhere, redemption is everywhere, myth is everywhere" (p. 1229).

The French, who vilified Wagner's operas, fathomed neither the composer's innovative ideas nor his dual personality, which Baudelaire described as a composite of "the man of order and the man of passion" (p. 1221). Wagner's inner turmoil and instinctuality ("nervous intensity, violence in passion and will"), as manifested in his dramatic operas, were unacceptable to the French psyche, which prided itself on its *rational* and *structured* approach to life (p. 1235). Unable, therefore, to relate to Wagner's perturbations, the French could not understand his musical and dramatic world of the myth. Wagner's withdrawals into his collective unconscious allowed him to explore still further unknown realms—his own *illo tempore*—and revealed, Baudelaire wrote, "what is most hidden in the heart of man" (p. 1235). He spanned eternity in his primordial or archetypal depths and universal time from ancient to contemporary periods, making him "the truest representative of modern nature" (p. 1235).

Baudelaire admitted to being unable to articulate the depths of his emotional reactions to Wagner's music because *archetypes* consist of energies that cannot be fully defined by the intellect. That he recognized them in Wagner's operas, that he depicted these recurring patterns and images in his own terms, underscores his belief, though he did not use these words, in the collective unconscious, which is, according to Jung, the "focal or nodal point of psychic life."[28] Affinities between Baudelaire and Wagner existed, the French poet suggested, because within each being there lives the individual (ego consciousness) and the collective (unconscious, Self). Ontogeny recapitulates phylogeny.

> As each one is the diminutive of everyone, as the history of an individual brain, is the microcosm of a universal brain, it would be just and natural to suppose that the elaboration of Wagner's thought was analogous to the work of humanity as a whole. (p. 1222)

Baudelaire's confrontation with Wagner's archetypal motifs put him in contact with that transpersonal power within him, the Self, or, in religious terms, God. Such a trajectory took him beyond the ego or mortal sphere. Baudelaire experienced the sacrifice required to achieve such expanded consciousness in terms of loss (life, the empirical domain) and gain (redemption, Self, God): "Everywhere there is something rising and falling, something that aspires to even greater heights, something excessive and superlative" (p. 1206).

Wagner's archetypal music encouraged composer and poet to come into contact with a kind of "extra-musical" frame of reference: a brief, incisive composite of successive tones in the form of chords or harmonies. These leitmotifs, to be looked upon as remembrances of past emotions and forerunners of future ones, activated their passions, altering the very structure of their psyches and enabling Baudelaire and Wagner to express in their works the infinite in finite terms.

4 Tolstoy's *Kreutzer Sonata:* Archetypal Music as a Demonic Force

Leo Tolstoy drew the title of his short novel *The Kreutzer Sonata* (1891) from Beethoven's violin sonata (opus 47), an archetypal musical composition that was instrumental, according to the Russian novelist, in bringing out the animal in man. It affected Tolstoy's protagonist subliminally, *exciting* him to such an extent that he became victimized by a series of inner upheavals of volcanic force, which annihilated in him any semblance of rational behavior, balance, or logic. As Tolstoy's protagonist states:

> Music instantaneously transports me into that mental condition in which he who composed it found himself. I blend my soul with his, and together with him am transported from one mood to another; but why this is so I cannot tell. For instance, he who composed the Kreutzer sonata—Beethoven—he knew why he was in that mood. That mood impelled him to do certain things, and therefore that mood meant something for him, but it means nothing for me. And that is why music excites and does not bring to any conclusion.[1]

Archetypal music in Tolstoy's narrative creates havoc; it unleashes repressed instincts and opens the floodgates to the irrational. Music, therefore, is *demonic.*

To understand more fully Tolstoy's strange approach to music in *The Kreutzer Sonata* requires some background information concerning the writer's activities and psychological condition. After putting the final touches to *Anna Karenina* (1877), Tolstoy underwent a traumatic moral and spiritual experience which almost brought him to suicide. Although he seemingly led a happy, healthy, and successful life—he was adulated by his readers for *War and Peace* (1869) and admired for his autobiographical trilogy, *Childhood* (1852), *Boyhood* (1854), and *Youth* (1857), and for *The Cossacks* (1863) and many short stories—something was gnawing at him. His marriage in 1862 to Sophia Andreyevna Bers, a well-educated woman half his age who bore him thirteen children, was marred by his infidelities, his views on wifely obligations, and his own paradoxical obsessions with chastity.

Tolstoy rejected carnal love, basing his ideas on Saint Matthew's dicta, which he quoted in *The Kreutzer Sonata:* "But I say unto you, That whosoever looketh on a woman to lust after her hath committed adultery with her already in his heart" (5:8). In this view, the goal of marriage is to procreate, not to enjoy the fruits of sensual pleasures. Marriage is a sacred bond. The highest earthly state for a human being is chastity.

> His disciples say unto him, if the case of the man be so with his wife, it is not good to marry.
> But he said unto them, All men cannot receive this saying, save they to whom it is given. (19:10–11)

Existence for Tolstoy at this critical stage of his life seemed devoid of interest, goalless and senseless. What was his life in terms of the infinite? God? Eternity? Tolstoy eventually concluded that religion was the only answer to his search—but not organized religion, as practiced in the Russian Orthodox Church, which he considered dogmatic and hypocritical and not in keeping with the teachings of Christ, and from which he was excommunicated in 1901. Tolstoy contended that human beings were endowed with higher and lower natures and that it is the mind which enables one to choose between good and evil. To follow Christ's message, one must practice good and live out the dictates of the Gospels (especially the Sermon on the Mount). Only by a pragmatic application of Christ's counsel would our earthly condition be improved and joy experienced. Asceticism and the banishing of sensual pleasures were Tolstoy's *way*.[2]

Psychologically, one may say that Tolstoy was puritanical. It has been suggested that he suffered deep guilt feelings—the aftermath of a sexually active youth which continued after his marriage and included relationships with household servants and even fathering a child to one of them. These "excesses" preyed on his mind. He sought to be "clean" and "pure." His puritanical ideals were evidently at odds with his physical nature. In his writings—*Confession* (1879), *A Short Exposition of the Gospels* (1881),

What I Believe In (1882), *What Then Must We Do* (1886), *The Law of Love and the Law of Violence* (1908), and *The Kreutzer Sonata*—he attempted to probe his inner world through some of his protagonists. His intention was to discover and examine the motivations of certain acts and relationships. Questioning the power of evil, Tolstoy concluded that one must not resist it. One must obey Christ's commandments: not to grow angry, not to lust, not to bind oneself to oaths or to rebuff a person who is evil ("Resist not him that is evil"), Tolstoy rejected all government and religious institutions based on violence and force. Like Jean-Jacques Rousseau, whose works he had read, he admired the simple peasant, the tiller of the land, the woodcutter—those who understood the real meaning of life. Their exploitation by others caused the poor excoriating suffering; private property encouraged economic disparity. Such evils had to be eradicated. Tolstoy's decision to give his wealth to the needy aroused a bitter marital feud and a permanent break in relations with his wife. His children, save Alexandra, sided with their mother. She and her father, eighty-three years of age at the time, left home. While waiting at the railroad stationmaster's house, he caught a chill and died.

Tolstoy had always been deeply moved by music and seemed to enjoy it as much as he did his early hunting, gymnastics, and women. Throughout his student years at the University of Kazan, in the army when stationed in the Caucasus, during the Crimean War, at the siege of Sevastopol, and throughout his later years, music was one of his deep loves. In *Sevastopol in May*, a reportage in which he conveys his antimilitarism, Tolstoy structures various incidents, events, and scenes in sonata form with specific themes, variations, repetitions, restatements, and a coda at the finale.

In 1857, while in Europe, he composed a short story, *Albert*. Although didactic and moralistic, it focused on something dear to Tolstoy: the fate of a violinist. His protagonist, a sensitive and talented violinist, was given to drink and desperately needed help from others. No one offered it to him because no one understood him. Society was uninterested in the fate of the artist. The feelings and ideals Tolstoy expressed in *Albert* were unquestionably noble, but his characters lacked depth and, worse still, he neglected to underscore the violinist's greatness. He did not encourage his readers to *experience* the instrumentalist's music, thereby precluding their taking his virtuosity seriously.

In Tolstoy's tale *Lucerne* (1857), we are introduced to another musician—a Tyrolean singer—whose story is based on a real incident. Tolstoy, who happened to be at a Swiss tourist center, noted the following in his diary (July 7, 1857):

> Walked to *privathaus*. On the way back at night—cloudy, with the moon breaking through—heard several marvellous voices. Two

bell towers on a wide street. Little man with guitar singing
Tyrolean songs—superb. Gave him something and invited him to
sing opposite the Schweizerhof. He got nothing and walked away
ashamed, the crowd laughing as he went. . . . Caught him up and
invited him to the Schweizerhof for a drink. They put us in a
separate room. Singer vulgar but pathetic. We drank. The waiter
laughed and the doorkeeper sat down. This infuriated me—swore
at them and got terribly worked up.[3]

Another moral situation provoked Tolstoy to take pen in hand, but again
he neglected to explore the effects of song upon him. Interested more in
the tale's story line, he conveyed his annoyance with the wealthy English
guests at a Swiss mountain resort who listened to and enjoyed the songs of
a most charming Tyrolean singer. They admired his talent and spontane-
ity, but when, at the finale of the concert, he held out his cap for remunera-
tion, not one gave a farthing. As the singer leaves the hotel, the narrator
invites him to return and sip champagne with him. During the course of
their conversation, the narrator points out the economic and social injus-
tices to the singer but fails to arouse his anger; instead, he discovers the
essential goodness of this country person who accepts life as it is, maintaining his jolly, buoyant, and wholesome outlook.[4]

The Kreutzer Sonata

Tolstoy, who had based his plot on what an actor friend, Andreev-Burlak,
had told him about the infidelities of a friend's wife, entitled it at first
"Sexual Love." The following year, 1888, when Tolstoy saw Andreev-
Burlak and the painter I. E. Repin at a party where Beethoven's Kreutzer
Sonata was performed, the latter suggested that he write about the effects
music had upon him and include these in his tale. The Russian novelist
agreed, on the condition that Andreev-Burlak would read it in public and
that Repin would paint a canvas based on the story. Tolstoy alone completed his part of the agreement.

Beethoven's opus 47, written for piano and violin (in 1802; published in
1805), and the best-known of his ten sonatas, was dedicated to Rodolphe
Kreutzer (1766–1831), a French composer and violinist and professor at
the Paris Conservatory. His forty études for violin, unequalled in their
genre, must have impressed Beethoven, who wrote in a letter dated Octo-
ber 4, 1804, that he had heard the French violinist perform some of his
works.[5]

Tolstoy sought to convey Beethoven's infinite variety of moods, ranging
from deep sorrow to rapturous exaltation, in The Kreutzer Sonata. It may

be suggested that he used the composer's archetypal music to articulate his own emotions, dividing his tale into three parts as Beethoven had divided his violin sonata into three movements: *Adagio sostenuto Presto, Adante con variazoni, Finale* (*Presto*).

Adagio sostenuto Presto

Tolstoy's *Kreutzer Sonata* is told by a narrator in the first person, but his function is minimal. He is there only as a sounding board, so that the protagonist, Pozdnyshev, can air his feelings and relate the events that preoccupy him.

The action takes place on a train. Its constant rolling and the physical closeness of those seated in a compartment encourage communication between them. A lawyer, a married woman, and an older man discuss their ideas concerning marriage and love. In addition, another person makes his presence known every now and then by a tic: "strange noises like a cough or like a laugh begun and broken off" (p. 58). This involuntary spasmodic reaction, usually of neurotic origin, interests the reader because it so often hides inner conflicts. While the conversation of the others in the compartment is light and lively, the narrator focuses on the man with the tic, who looks "oppressed by his loneliness." There is something arresting about him and his "extraordinarily brilliant eyes which kept roving from object to object" (p. 58). At times they grow flamelike, as if he were attempting in some way to restrain himself.

Only with the beginning of chapter 3 does the *adagio sostenuto* take on rapidity, leading up to the *presto*—the highly emotional and suspenseful content of the interlude. As the travelers leave the compartment or go to sleep, Pozdnyshev, the man with the tic, comforted by the constant rolling of the train and the closed and protective universe in which he finds himself, begins to withdraw into a past—his inner world. Barriers are shed; Pozdnyshev's psychic energy is mobilized and increases in activity until it reaches *presto* force.

Pozdnyshev tells the narrator that until he got married he lived like a member of the landed aristocracy. A university graduate who enjoyed his dissipated and immoral life, he decided never to get really entangled. The sight of "woman in her nakedness" at the age of sixteen tormented him for days and weeks thereafter. He felt as if he had been *corrupted* and polluted; he also realized that until now he had never known the difference between right and wrong; he had never had to choose, nor had he ever been emotionally troubled. To pursue a life of debauchery could, so the "Priests of Science" had declared, bring on illness. More significant was that he felt like weeping for the loss of his *innocence*; like a drug addict or alcoholic, he knew that the *purity* he had once known would never return, and he was "overwhelmed with horror" (p. 74). Although "soiled with the rottenness of lewdness," he was very fortunate to find a *pure* girl, Lily, to whom he became engaged. When he showed her his diary so that she could learn more about him, her reaction was one of despair and disillusionment. They nevertheless married. He realized that this beautiful fantasy figure would have to change if she were to fulfill her function as wife and future mother. Marriage, he had to admit, is not based exclusively on poetry, love, or morality, but on "proximity," the body—that is, low-cut gowns, hair styles, perfumes, and a woman's wiles. The *anima* in Pozdnyshev was aroused at the sight of Lily's beautiful body.

Pozdnyshev sees the world and himself in terms of extremes: chastity is equated with good; sensuality, with evil. What he does not seem to take into consideration is that good and evil are opposite poles of a moral judgment. To attempt an *imitatio Christi* and try to become all good (all light, all spirit) is to reject the notion of evil and those factors of the human condition which are identified with it.

A split results and tyrannizes Pozdnyshev: the concretization of absolute good and light at odds with Satan or the Antichrist, standing for evil, dark, material, and carnal forces. He was neither alone in his torment nor was it merely symptomatic of a contemporary malaise. The divestiture of the Godhead's dark side in Christianity paved the way for a similar split in humankind's unconscious, since it projected onto Divinity. A dualistic formula is expressed in 2 Thessalonians: God's earthly or eschatological manifestation in Christ, and Satan's in the Antichrist. The conflict between these two opposing forces became inevitable. In Romans we read: "And the God of peace shall bruise Satan under your feet shortly" (16:20). To resist the Devil is proof of the strength of one's Christian faith (1 Peter 5:9), and of one's intelligence and understanding of Satan's ways: "Lest Satan should get an advantage of us: for we are not ignorant of his devices" (2 Corinthians 2:11). Saint Paul, a firm believer in ascetic practices, was convinced of the positive effects of discipline; it would help an individual evolve and, accordingly, rid him of his demonization: "To open their eyes, and to turn them from darkness to light, and from the power of Satan unto God, that they may receive forgiveness of sins, and inheritance among them which are sanctified by faith that is in me" (Acts 26:18).

To long to be like Christ, however—which is Pozdnyshev's goal—is not only to experience only half of one's nature and to relegate one's earthbound condition to infernal regions; it is also a paradigm of hubris. For the Greeks, hubris was one of the most serious of crimes, if not punishable by death, then by some form of chastisement. The imbalance in Pozdnyshev's attitude has created a dangerous split within his psyche.

Flesh is satanic; it is the "adversary" (the Hebrew meaning of *Satan*); it spreads chaos, doubt, and confusion. Satan's intrusion into Pozdnyshev's world has threatened his well-being—the rational order of things.

To label the *animal* in man as satanic or evil indicates psychologically, a *fear* of the irrational or instinctual domain—that whole unpredictable area within humankind and the universe. To attempt to cut away a person's sexuality is to eliminate his passionate nature, which is basic to him, and simply repress and imprison these instinctual forces in the unconscious. The natural response to imprisonment is rage. Blocked within the psyche, these negative powers become stronger and stronger. Every now and then they break out, uncontrollably and viciously.

Pozdnyshev suffers, he tells the narrator, because he feels women dominate the world in general, and his in particular. It is the woman who decides whether she wants her man or whether he must be kept at a distance. This is due, Pozdnyshev reasons, to the fact that women do not enjoy equal rights with men, and so they seek revenge; and they succeed because they know how to work on what is most vulnerable within man: his passions. They ensnare him in their nets. When a man falls under the influence of a woman's "deviltry," he "grows foolish" (p. 83). Here Pozdnyshev reminisces about his ancestor Adam and blames Eve for his weakness. Pozdnyshev, like countless others, was unable to assume responsibility for his acts. Rather than attempt to view Adam's acquiescence objectively, as an example of his own blindness and misguided ideas, Pozdnyshev looks for a scapegoat upon whom he can pile everything he finds objectionable. Nor does Pozdnyshev ever look upon woman as an individual, evolving being; rather he sees her in a self-serving manner—as an object to be repulsed because of her carnality and as a spreader of venality.

As Pozdnyshev describes the days and months following his marriage, his hostility toward his situation and his wife grows more and more overt. It accelerates, taking on *presto* force, as if he were overwhelmed by an unconscious rage. He regrets having married. His honeymoon was a disaster. Lily was totally unprepared for it all, and, he complains, when he put his arms around her, she burst into tears. Certainly, he must have forgotten the fact that a few days earlier he had given her his diary to read, shocking her to her very foundations. After soothing her, he realized that a "wall of cold venomous hostility" existed within, which was assuaged only when they made love. Thereafter their married life consisted, as do the introductory movements in Beethoven's sonata, in statements and restatements, in quarrels and reconciliations, which came about only after each had experienced complete sexual satisfaction. Nevertheless, beneath this veneer of passionate love, there was hatred between them. It was an "abomination" (p. 91).

Andante con variazoni

Chapters 13 to 19 restate similar situations in *andante* or *moderato* movement—a pace that flows along easily, steadily, with variations on the same theme.

Pozdnyshev gives examples from their conjugal life which rouse his repugnance for what people call love. "Love is something swinish," "shameful and disgusting," he remarks (p. 93). Nevertheless, he fathered five children, after which the doctors told his wife that another pregnancy would endanger her life. The worst of sins was committed at this point: these men of science taught her how to avoid conception. Women, then, and specifically his wife, would no longer be fulfilling their function. Pozdnyshev grew angry as well as jealous. For her not to be pregnant meant that she would have more time to herself and, worse, that she could devote her time to making herself more beautiful. The more his diatribes took on passion, the more irrational was his reasoning. "You see I am a kind of insane man" (p. 101).

Pozdnyshev's jealousy of his wife grew out of proportion. That she would be able to enjoy the sexual act without being burdened with pregnancies and have time to herself without the constant presence of the children "poisoned" their life together. They were transformed, he added, into "two convicts, fastened to one chain and hating each other, each poisoning the life of the other and striving not to recognize the fact" (p. 108). Only then did he realize, he says, that 99 percent of couples live as if in a vise.

Why had Pozdnyshev's psychosis so increased in dimension? His constant rejection and condemnation of his earthly side made him long for its opposite: an ethereal, spiritual relationship rather than a sexual attraction between himself and his wife. Ideals, however, are incompatible with life and are virtually made to crumble, bringing into play the opposite extreme, which plunges the idealist into the most turbid of mires. Since Pozdnyshev had cut himself off so drastically from his own nature and from life in general, every time he performed the sexual act he was revulsed by his own carnality and by the pleasure which he forever equated with evil.

If, psychologically speaking, instincts are properly understood and accepted as part of the life process, they may act in concert with other factors within a personality and become positive forces. When unattended—or rejected—they crave for what is rightly theirs and thereby may become virulent and destructive. That Pozdnyshev associates his wife with evil—as he does women in general—is an age-old attitude. Woman has from time immemorial been marked with infernal, dark, chthonic, devouring, hostile, and terrifying characteristics. Such beings and supernatural forces as Medea, Gorgon, Hecate, Cybele, and Eve, as *vagina dentata* types, are described throughout history and in religions as destroyers of man, castrators, "deadly mothers," impure creatures, and instigators of orgies. Symbolically, they have been associated with nature and the material world. Imagistically, their bodies are identified with earth, vessel, and cave, putting them in opposition to the spiritual values inherent in the male. Accordingly, they are considered inferior and damned, representatives of flesh and instinct. Eve is blamed for having seduced Adam and for the Fall. Is it any wonder that Pozdnyshev should share the universal contempt for women?

To vary the tempi and beats of their *andante* life together, with all of its variations on but a single theme—that of sexuality—Pozdnyshev decided that it might be best to move to the city. His wife's health would improve, he reasoned, and indeed it did. She not only grew more and more beautiful but also became increasingly conscious of her attractiveness. She took time out to care for herself, to see that she wore the right clothes and her hair in the right style. Her beauty became "fascinating and disturbing to men," Pozdnyshev remarked. At parties, he was convinced that all the men looked at her with longing. "She was like a well-fed and bridled horse which had not been driven for some time and from which the bridle was taken off. There was no longer any restraint . . ." (p. 110). A melodic and rhythmic interchange seemed to take place between the two: as his frenzy increased, so she seemed to *awaken* to the world outside of her home and outside of her role as childbearer and mother. She started to live "for the sake of love" (p. 112). Pozdnyshev's speech grew to tempi and diapason as his fantasy world became more and more dynamic, acting, as it were, of its own accord, creating image upon image, freely and actively replicating his own inner phobias.

Pozdnyshev was convinced at this point that his wife was bored with him because she wanted to improve herself. Before her marriage, she had been a fine pianist, and she was now determined to pursue this art form. "That was the beginning of the end," he stated categorically (p. 113). Just as sexuality undermined his spiritual longings, and so represented a threat to him, so music would also be experienced as a negative entity and as an evil force to be extirpated. Woman is a kind of *Hexe* who arouses him sexually; music is likewise demonic, penetrating as it does both his conscious and unconscious spheres. Like a seductress, it is tantalizing and therefore dangerous.

The more Pozdnyshev focuses on his wife's beauty, the more aroused he becomes. His hysterical symptoms, which are representations of unconscious events, cannot be discharged or expressed, because the contents of his fantasies are incompatible with his conscious outlook. Interiorized energy, diverted into the wrong channels, activates Pozdnyshev's fantasies, which then accrete in potency. Jung writes in this regard: "the patient constructs in his imagination little stories that are very coherent and very logical, but when he has to deal with reality, he is no longer capable of attention or comprehension."[6] Pozdnyshev's fantasies, ideas, notions, and sensations revolve around sexuality for the most part; he relates *everything* in the outer world to the fulfillment of an inner obsession or compulsion. There is no enlightenment or evolution in his monologue. It follows the same theme and variations: those of a man who projects his *shadow*. As defined by Jung, the shadow is an unconscious aspect of the psyche which contains what the ego may consider to be inferior or negative characteristics and which it will not recognize as its own. The consequences of Pozdnyshev's inability to come to terms with his shadow, and the hysteria which results, may be dangerous.

Soon Pozdnyshev mentions a musician friend of his wife—a violinist. Interestingly enough, he cannot recall this man's first name right away, blocking out the very memory of an *evil* force. In time we learn that the violinist, a society man of sorts, was a professional or semi-professional musician. Pozdnyshev's intense jealousy of the man he believes to have been his wife's lover peppers each of his statements. "He had almond-shaped humid eyes, handsome, smiling lips, little waxed mustaches, the latest and most fashionable method of dressing his hair, an insipidly handsome face, such as women call 'not bad,' a slender build, though not ill-shaped, and with a largely developed behind such as they say characterize Hottentot women. This it is said is musical" (p. 113). Although underscoring the violinist's fine points, he makes certain he belittles this rival as well, lumping together both the man and his art as a destructive and evil factor in society.

"Well, this man with his music was the cause of all the trouble," Pozdnyshev said, making him the scapegoat and heaping upon him all the evils of sex and marriage (p. 114). The violinist was to blame for Pozdnyshev's increasing misunderstandings with his wife. Psychologically speaking, Pozdnyshev was projecting his shadow—thereby casting out of himself onto others all those "despicable" characteristics which, in reality, existed within him. Everything Pozdnyshev associated with evil—the violinist and his art—was lumped together and condemned. Let us recall that in the olden days the collective shadow (the evils of the community) was heaped onto a goat by a priest; the animal was then sent out into the wilderness, and the clan, considered purged of its sins, did not have to face the pain of truth and the effort of resolving tensions and problems. By merely rejecting an unpleasant situation or person, one escapes a conflict that could have salutary effects.

By being projected, Pozdnyshev's shadow remains unconscious, so that he experiences it affectively and with virtually no discernment. Since the tension of opposites is nonexistent, he is now engulfed or *possessed* by his shadow. Having lost whatever capacity he had to differentiate, he can no longer be responsible for his actions. He lives in the darkened realm of his own manufacture, dominated by an ego alienated from reality.

The days, weeks, months pursue their course—as do the variations on the themes of sexuality, hostility, and jealousy. Every time he sees his wife at the piano accompanying the violinist, all blackens before him. He resents the pleasure she takes in her musical renditions and is convinced that the man with whom she makes this music is a lecher. Something is certainly going on between them, he muses, for when they play together it is "like an electrical shock, calling forth something like a uniformity in the expression of their eyes and their smiles" (p. 120).

When Pozdnyshev narrates what he believes to be the evolution of the relationship between the violinist and his wife, he does so in musical terms, viewing archetypal music as a go-between or bridge that encourages an illicit affair between the two.

> In the evening he came with his fiddle, and they played together. But for a long time the music did not go very well; we had not the pieces that he wanted, and those he had my wife could not play without preparation. I was very fond of music and sympathized with their playing, arranging the music-stand for him and turning over the leaves. They managed to play something—a few songs without words and a sonata by Mozart. He played excellently, and he had to the highest degree what is called "temperament"—moreover, a delicate, noble art, entirely out of keeping with his character. (p. 121)

Pozdnyshev tried to remain calm that evening, pretending to be interested in music, and even encouraging his wife to play on. Inside, however, he was "tortured by jealousy" (p. 121). His fantasies see only "the wild beast existing in them both" (p. 122).

The violinist and his wife continued their musicales, their talents for art linking them powerfully together. On one occasion, after an evening of music, a strange feeling took hold of Pozdnyshev: an urge to kill the violinist on the spot. Exercising control, he makes certain he has successfully buried his urge by inviting him to stay for dinner and treating him to the finest of wines.

Instruments, tones, melodies, and rhythms are all enemies for Pozdnyshev. The performers of music (Pozdnyshev's wife and the violinist) are

involved in rites and liturgies which arouse the wrath of a husband dominated by an obsession.

> Two people occupy themselves with the noblest of arts—music; in
> order to accomplish this a certain proximity is required, and this
> proximity has nothing reprehensible in it, and only a stupid, jealous
> husband could find anything undesirable in it. But meantime, all
> know that precisely by means of these very occupations, especially
> by music, the largest part of the adultery committed in the ranks of
> our society is committed. (p. 125)

They were days when their "proximity" caused Pozdnyshev such torment
that he could barely converse with his wife. One time, virtually beside
himself, he threatened to kill her and began hurling objects at her. She left
the room, fully aware that he was no longer "responsible for his madness"
(p. 128). Later that evening the usual "sexual" reconciliation took place,
and again Pozdnyshev concealed his anger.

Presto

No longer working with developing themes and the difficulties involved in
probing, combining, and knitting them together, Tolstoy launches into the
crisis, which now takes on *presto* force. Emotions break loose, relationships change, human nature emerges in all of its rawness. Beethovian
dynamism is released in this Tolstoyan drama—leading to its fulminating
conclusion.

Pozdnyshev agrees that a musicale be given at their home. Although he
feels ill at ease throughout the dinner, he watches every movement of his
wife and the violinist, "their motions and glances," in an attempt to ferret
out the least sign that will corroborate his obsessive jealousy. Pozdnyshev
recalls every detail of the evening: how the violinist "brought his fiddle,
opened the box, took off the covering which had been embroidered for
him by some lady, took out the instrument and began to tune it" (p. 130).
As for his wife, she acts relaxed and indifferent as she sits down at the
grand piano and strikes the "usual *a* which was followed by the pizzicato
of the fiddle and the getting into tune" (p. 130). After looking at each other
and glancing at the audience, they start to play: "His face grew grave,
stern, and sympathetic, and as he bent his head to listen to the sounds he
produced, he placed his fingers cautiously on the strings. The piano re-
plied" (p. 130).

An entente certainly exists between them, Pozdnyshev thinks, as he
looks at them both with hatred. The violinist, in his eyes, is the living
incarnation of the Devil and the instrument of perdition. He works in

opposition to God and to Light, Pozdnyshev maintains. He is the Great
Tempter, the Adversary, the one who prepares humankind for the Fall. He
may also be regarded as a projection of Pozdnyshev's disintegrating mental condition.

It is on this particular night that Pozdnyshev's wife and the violinist play
Beethoven's *Kreutzer Sonata*. "Do you know the first *presto*—You know it?"
he asks the narrator.

> U!U!U! . . . That sonata is a terrible thing. And especially that
> movement. And music in general is a terrible thing. I cannot
> comprehend it. What is music? What does it do? And why does it
> have the effect it has? They say music has the effect of elevating
> the soul—rubbish! falsehood! It has its effect, it has a terrible
> effect,—I am speaking about its effect on me,—but not at all by
> elevating the soul. Its effect is neither to elevate nor to degrade,
> but to excite. (p. 130)

The archetypal music he hears unleashes Pozdnyshev's emotions, working on his nerves, grating and grinding them so that the pain he feels
becomes unbearable. The inner tensions arouse the nuclear dynamism of
his psyche.[7] For a psychopath such as Pozdnyshev, Beethoven's *Kreutzer
Sonata* triggers an explosion of the ego complex, thus putting an end to
relatively smooth-running conscious personality. His acts, henceforth, will
be predictable.[8] As he is carried away by the flow of libido implicit in
Beethoven's music, it is as if he is being pulled by the undertow of an inner
ocean.

> Music makes me forget myself, my actual position; it transports me
> into another state not my natural one; under the influence of music
> it seems to me that I feel what I don't really really feel, that I
> understand what I do not really understand, that I can do what I
> can't do. I explain this by the fact that music acts like gaping or
> laughing; I am not sleepy but I gape, looking at anyone else who is
> gaping; I have nothing to laugh at but I laugh when I hear others
> laugh. (p. 130)

Music holds the power of a drug for Pozdnyshev; it is a spirit, as is
alcohol. Let us recall that when Noah began taking care of the vine he
became a "man of the ground" and was no longer the "pious one."[9] His
elixir caused a disorientation of the senses: "And he drank of the wine, and
was drunken; and he was uncovered within his tent" (Gen. 9:21). So, too,
was Pozdnyshev uncovered by music; the melody, pitch, timbre, and

rhythms encouraged him to disclose his fantasies, which emerged into life, taking on power in the empirical world. But just as wine is identified with drunkenness and ecstasy, and with the orgies and instincts of Dionysian rituals, so is it part of the Christian ceremony with its sacramental offerings (John 15:1–5).

The archetypal music emanating from the violin and piano transport Pozdnyshev into another domain, where, shedding all restraint and losing his identity, he claims that Beethoven had experienced a similar emotional condition when composing his *Kreutzer Sonata*. Pozdnyshev, then, is neither earthbound nor celestially oriented. He is in limbo. Confused and faceless, he is a pawn for any musical power that may entice him.

> Now they play a military march; the soldiers move forward under its strains, and the music accomplishes something; they play dance music and I dance, and the music accomplishes something; they perform a mass, I take the sacrament, again the music accomplishes its purpose. But in other cases there is only excitement, and it is impossible to tell what to do in this state of mind. And that is why music is so terrible, why it sometimes has such an awful effect. (p. 131)

Music "hypnotizes," he concedes. Like Mesmer's "animal fluid" that influences celestial bodies as well as earth beings, archetypal music is a force capable of communicating impressions and energizing the psyche. So powerful a force was Beethoven's *Kreutzer Sonata* that it took precedence over all else, and in the process it obliterated *logos*. Identifying archetypal music with the Devil, Pozdnyshev sees it as a metaphor for lovemaking, with its ultimate culmination in the orgasm.

How could anyone play the *Kreutzer Sonata*—this first *presto*—he questions, in a drawing room before ladies dressed in *décolletés?*

> To play that *presto* and then to applaud it, and then to eat ices and talk over the last bit of scandal? These things should be played only in certain grave, significant conditions, and only then when certain deeds corresponding to such music are to be accomplished: first play the music and perform that which this music was composed for. But to call forth an energy which is not consonant with the place or the time, and an impulse which does not manifest itself in anything, cannot fail to have a baneful effect. On me, at least, it had a horrible effect. It seemed to me that entirely new impulses, new possibilities, were revealed to me in myself, such as I had never dreamed of before. (p. 131)

Pozdnyshev was terrified by what he felt: something so unusual, so traumatic, that it seemed to "be whispered into my soul." He did not know what was happening to him. "This new state of mind" did feel delightful. Everything seemed to be altered now that music had penetrated his being. "After the *allegro* they played the beautiful but rather commonplace and far from original *andante*, with the cheap variations and the weak *finale*" (p. 132). A strange happiness flooded Pozdnyshev that evening—a feeling he attributed to the altered state of consciousness he had experienced listening to Beethoven's work.

Two days later, when Pozdnyshev had to go away on business, he was assured by his wife that she would not see the violinist during his absence. When she wrote to him and told him that the violinist had come to return some music, the "fatal step" had been taken. Pozdnyshev's fantasies about her love affair with the violinist gained full sway over his rationality. He returned to Moscow. During his long train ride home, visions of his wife kissing her lover and his own suffering were so intense that there were times when he wanted to throw himself on the tracks. "The one thing that prevented me from doing so was my self-pity which was the immediate source of my hatred for her" (p. 139). When Pozdnyshev arrived home in the morning, his anxiety had reached unparalleled proportions. The children were still asleep when he entered his house. He heard noises in the dining room, and when he pushed the door open, his wife and the violinist wore an expression of "despairing horror," which then turned into one of "annoyance," as if he were interrupting their pleasure (p. 145). Just as love has its sensual side, so rage has its inner pulsion toward violence.

> I threw myself on her, still concealing the dagger in order that he might prevent me from striking her in the side under the breast. I had chosen the spot at the very beginning. The instant I threw myself on her he saw my design, and with an action which I never expected from him, he seized me by the arm. (p. 146)

To touch her even in this manner was repulsive to Pozdnyshev; it "still further inflamed" his anger, and he "exulted in it" (p. 147). Withdrawing his arm, he strikes his wife in the face with his elbow as hard as he can. At the height of this paroxysmal moment, she confesses her innocence. Pozdnyshev, in his madness, concludes just the opposite, convinced more than ever that his worst fears has been realized. The *crescendo* has reached its climax. "Madness also has its laws," Pozdnyshev remarks (p. 148).

Rage overwhelms him. He seizes his wife by the throat and strangles her. The violinist turns white, and without uttering a word, "slipped under the piano and darted out the door" (p. 147). As Pozdnyshev's wife attempts to tear herself free, he "struck her with the dagger into the side under the ribs" (p. 148). That he recalled every detail of his act is not unusual for a psychotic.

Before his wife dies, Pozdnyshev begs her to forgive him. But she is by this time delirious, and her hatred seems to cascade forth. Pozdnyshev is taken to prison, where he spends eleven months awaiting trial. Only when he sees his wife's coffin does he realize the extent of his crime: "the terrible consciousness that I was killing and had killed a woman—a defenseless woman—my wife." He even remembers that right after plunging the dagger into her "I immediately withdrew it, with the desire to remedy what I had done and to put a stop to it" (p. 149).

That his protagonist reflected many of Tolstoy's thoughts and ideals is clearly evident in the "Afterword" of *The Kreutzer Sonata*, written a year later (1890). In it, he castigates doctors for spreading false rumors: that sexual relations are good for the health, that conjugal infidelity is common because relations between men and women are regarded as pleasurable ("something poetic and elevated, and a blessing to life"), that birth control allows women to enjoy sexual union without giving birth. Such aims are unworthy of mankind, although considered by some to be life's supreme goal. Chastity is the ideal: it was Christ's ideal. Tolstoy wrote: "the establishment of the kingdom of God on earth; an ideal already foretold by the prophets who spoke of a time when all men shall be taught of God, and shall beat their plowshares and their spears into pruning-hooks; when the lions shall lie down with the lambs, and all beings shall be united by love" (p. 160).

Morality for Tolstoy and his protagonist was looked upon as an end unto itself. As such it was a codification of life, an ossification of the human personality, and therefore it was easily turned into an evil, as in Pozdnyshev's case—perhaps even in Tolstoy's. The great Russian writer became the butt of ridicule. Concerning *The Kreutzer Sonata*, his wife noted in her diary (March 6, 1891):

> At tea we talked about . . . the vegetarianism which Lyova advocates. He said he saw a vegetarian menu in a German paper which was composed of bread and almonds. I expect the person who wrote the menu practises vegetarianism as much as the author of *The Kreutzer Sonata* practices chastity.[10]

In December 1890 she wrote in her diary of her fear of becoming pregnant, "for everybody will hear of the disgrace and jubilantly repeat the recent Moscow joke: 'Voilà le véritable postscriptum de la Sonate de Kreutzer.' "[11]

That Tolstoy was tyrannized or possessed by an idea or ideal indicates that he and his hero were under the spell of a powerful complex—"a splinter psyche"—or a split-off.[12] When the shadow remains unconscious and is not integrated into the total psyche, some of its unacceptable qualities may become autonomous and go their own way. Such was Pozdnyshev's situation and, to a lesser degree, Tolstoy's. The latter's once relatively harmonious psyche had become fragmented and split into various complexes. Each miniature complex developed a strange fantasy life of its own, assuming abnormal proportions. In Pozdnyshev's and Tolstoy's cases, fantasies may be regarded as *toxins*, because not only do they not fit into their conscious patternings but they resist all attempts on the part of the will to cope with them.

Tolstoy and Pozdnyshev were so deeply entrenched in their ideals and their ideologies that they lost contact with the world of reality and instead lived in the abyss of their own minds. There they abandoned themselves to torrents of thoughts, energized still further by Beethoven's archetypal *Kreutzer Sonata*. It was a one-way trajectory for both Tolstoy and his hero; like geologists, they burrowed deeply within their psyche, coming face to face with the raw matter that lay buried in their own rich substance. Neither was redeemed!

5 Kandinsky's *Sounds:* Archetypal Resonances in Word, Color, Line, and Rhythm

Wassily Kandinsky's *Sounds* (1912), comprising thirty-eight poems and fifty-six woodcuts, fuses various art forms: the written, the pictorial, and the aural. By drawing the differentiated together, he believed he was not only deepening and broadening the creative experience but reaching into that inner core, that *soul force,* alluded to by mystics as the *Creative Point:* a never-ending source from which life emanates.

Music, Kandinsky wrote, is "the best Teacher" and the most powerful means for an artist and mystic to realize himself. Unlike writing and painting, music is nonobjective: it does not reproduce natural phenomena, but rather it conveys a spiritual essence through vibratory dimensions in alternating rhythmic patterns.

> A painter, who finds no satisfaction in mere representation, how-ever artistic, in his longing to express his inner life, cannot but envy the ease with which music, the most non-material of the arts to-day, achieves this end. He naturally seeks to apply the methods of music to his own art. And from this results that modern desire for rhythm in painting, for mathematical, abstract construction, for repeated notes of colour, for setting colour in motion.[1]

The very title Kandinsky chose, *Sounds,* indicates the preeminence ac-corded to tone as it issues forth from the word, color, line, and rhythmic patterns in his verse. We call these resonances archetypal because Kandin-sky considered them primordial: "unfettered by nature," in need of no "definite form" for their expression; flowing forth from the heart of the word; entities unto themselves; a corpus, a living, breathing, spiritual power.[2] Just as Arnold Schoenberg's *panchromatic* musical scheme aimed for freedom of self-expression by rejecting conventional harmonic progression and traditional forms, so Kandinsky succeeded in expressing thought, feeling, and sonance in his poetry by divesting it of a logical frame of reference.

Kandinsky's exploration of sound in the word/verse is comparable to sequences of dream fantasies or free associations: the visualization accompanied by the clang resonances is perceived both in terms of the individual's personal experience and of factors emanating from the collaborative unconscious. As such, the abstractions or forms which leap into the poems in *Sounds* arrive raw: polymorphic and organic, real and identifiable, framed and unframed—always tonal—enticing the reader through endless mazes of vibratory experiences. The streams of audible sounds which flow forth from the verses are not always pleasant; frequently they are turbulent and jarring, as they thrash about in pain, angered by some seeming cruelty.

Colors, as to be expected, made a powerful impact on Kandinsky as a child. So, too, did music. Even at the age of three, "bright juicy green, white, carmine red, black, and yellow ochre" took on for Kandinsky their own natural shapes in line and tone.[3] Visual, aural, and tactile experiences formed a cohesive whole. In his recollections of dusk in Moscow, he wrote:

> The sun melts all Moscow into one spot which, like a mad tuba, sets one's whole inside, one's whole soul vibrating. No, this red unity is not the loveliest hour! It is only the final note of the symphony which brings every color to its greatest intensity, which lets, indeed forces, all Moscow to resound like the fff of a giant orchestra. Pink, lavender, yellow, white, blue, pistachio green, flame-red houses, churches—each an independent song—the raving green grass, the deep murmuring trees, or the snow, singing with a thousand voices, or the allegretto of the bare branches, the red, stiff, silent ring of the Kremlin walls, and above, towering over all like a cry of triumph, like a Hallelujah forgetful of itself, the long white, delicately earnest line of the Ivan Veliky Bell Tower.[4]

In time, Kandinsky sought to probe the creative process further, to penetrate that *other* dimension, where harmony and disharmony cohabit, sparks flame in incandescent and blue tones, upheavals alter configurations, and explosions occur in staccato beats. Drawn as he was to mysticism and theosophy, it is not surprising that the non-manifest aspect of the creative experience should attract him so powerfully. He was well versed in the works of Madame Helena P. Blavatsky and Rudolf Steiner, who rejected the then popular concepts of Positivism and Scientism, while lauding a metaphysical universe with all of its unfathomable mysteries. The very *mystery* of existence—spiritual and material—fascinated the artist. Even as a student at the University of Moscow, he had been tantalized by "the field of Non-Objective Thought."[5]

When Kandinsky first saw Monet's "Haystacks" in Moscow in 1889, he did not recognize them as such at first. Later he realized that objects were not the key factor in painting; they were, in fact, nonessential. *Color* was crucial, as was *music*.[6] Only when form was dematerialized and representationalism was eliminated could the transpersonal realm be glimpsed and color and tone be realized—stimulating and electrifying the painter's and the viewer's vibratory system, which reached directly into the soul.

Abstraction/Tone/Word

Munich, where Kandinsky moved in 1896, was to play a crucial role in his life. An enchanting city for the artist, it attracted at this period Naum Gabo, Rilke, Wedekind, Heinrich and Thomas Mann, Jawlensky, and others. Kandinsky first studied with Anton Azbé (1859–1905), drawing from a model, as did the other students in the class.[7] In time he outgrew what he must have felt to be Azbé's circumscribed views on art and enrolled in the class of one of Germany's great draftsmen, Franz von Stuck (1863–1928). Kandinsky's career burgeoned.

Kandinsky, along with others, founded a school and artists' club, the Phalanx, in 1901. A poster that he designed for the Phalanx's first exhibit, in the autumn of that same year, was innovative: by eliminating perspective, he brought space into focus, thereby intensifying it; by heightening black-and-white tonalities, he aroused jarring emotions.

Although influenced by the popular Jugendstil (Art Nouveau) group, which may account in part for his powerful stylizations, his decorative bent, and his use of thick pigments in his works in general, he was, nevertheless, moving steadily toward abstraction, satisfying his increasing thirst for the nonobjective. To "break the bonds" that shackled him to nature, Kandinsky combined "pure color and independent form." Such autonomous compositions moved and electrified him, setting off "vibrations of the spirit" that affected soul and senses, and laid the groundwork for a *numinous* experience. While forms in Kandinsky's early pictorial works, such as "Der Blaue Reiter" (1903), had been definable (horse, rider, and cloud), by 1909 similar objects depicted in "Improvisation No. 3" were not. Ambiguity in the shapes and rhythms of the picture predominated. In

"Improvisation No. 12—The Rider" (1910), featuring the same scene, the interplay of light and dark stirred such inner pulsations that a whole new geological fold leaped into being: the visible and the invisible, the silent and the sounded, each struggling for supremacy.

> Painting is a thundering collision of different worlds, destined to create a new world. Technically, every work comes into existence as the universe comes into existence, namely through catastrophes. Yet in the end the chaotic discord of the instruments makes for a symphony which we call music of the spheres.[8]

Why should Kandinsky have been so fascinated by the nonobjective, so deeply drawn to amorphous climes in which the spiritual was embedded? How could sonorous and visual elements help him experience the transpersonal domain for which he longed?

There may have been psychological reasons which compelled him to seek liberation from the tyranny of the object—the material world. As an introverted *thinking* type, to use Jung's category, Kandinsky could not relate with ease to the naked world of reality. He felt constricted— sometimes repulsed—when, for example, drawing or painting a body realistically. The *thinking* type finds the domain of the intellect safe and comfortable; he can direct his thoughts along rational spheres, arranging his ideas in keeping with conceptual lines. As Kandinsky developed, however, he must have found the cognitive realm, where the laws of logic predominated, unpalatable, dull, and dreary. He may have felt that living solely in his *head* allowed the rest of his being to atrophy. Unconsciously, he sought to balance this one-sided condition. To do so, however, would necessitate the development of his inferior *sensation* function. Such a type reacts to and perceives the world of reality through his senses.[9] When these powers exist on an archaic level in a personality, as they did in Kandinsky, the flooding of visual and aural sense impressions stirs and electrifies the individual.

Kandinsky describes one such incident, when, as a child, he related a scene in a German fairy tale: "The yellow mailboxes sang like canary birds on the corners. I welcomed the inscription 'Kunstmuhle' [art mill] and felt that I was in a city of art, which was the same to me as a city of fairies." On another occasion, while changing trains to go to Rothenburg ob der Tauber, a panoply of unreal impressions emerged in his mind's eye. "I felt as if a magic power, against all the laws of nature, had set me back century after century, even deeper into the past."[10] His inferior sensation function, like a psychopomp, carried the symbolic experience and led him directly to his unconscious.

Until Kandinsky's departure for Munich, his thinking function had operated continuously. His sensation side erupted every now and then, when the pull of instinctual forces could no longer be contained. In time his world had grown arid; his ego (the center of consciousness) was no longer excited by streams of facts, statistics, objects—all of which seemed to stifle the mystery embedded in the life process itself. Thinking types make interpretive associations: their sphere is *logos*, where logical or analogical conclusions are all-powerful and the principle of discrimination dominates. Relatedness takes over when *Eros* functions: a domain where relationships are encouraged, and dynamic associations between thinking and feeling are aroused.[11]

Kandinsky's departure for Munich could be labeled a *sacrificium intellectus*.[12] Had he remained in Azbé's drawing class, copying real-life models that he found uninteresting and even repulsive, he would have relived the same thinking experience on an artistic plane that he had known in Russia. Some part of him had to be probed and activated, so as to allow energy to surge forth, not independently in jarring and sometimes hurtful sequences, but assimilated by his overly developed thinking side.

Kandinsky's way of balancing the polarities within him could be called *introspecting sensation:* watching himself seeing. Such a process, which reveals the outer world or object to the individual in an inner dimension, may be said to have a *feeling* aspect to it, since it affects bodily changes. Such physical alterations were transmitted to his consciousness in bulk impulses, causing Kandinsky to experience disturbing visions relatively frequently. When traveling with his mother as a child, he viewed Italy as "black impressions."[13] Certain imprints and blocks of color coming into view troubled him intensely; others brought him joy. In either case, these *aesthetic perceptions* allowed him to glimpse another world, redolent with excitement. Such moments, which we might allude to as visitations, enabled Kandinsky to feel detached, cut off from both the object perceived and from the subjective world of the seer. Although he seemed outside of it all, he was embedded in the *prima materia*, knowing a high state of "purity" never attainable when viewing/sensing an object concretely or empirically.[14]

Abstract sensation, such as Kandinsky experienced in his reactions to Italy, separated one factor or attribute of an image—in this case, its blackness. His description of Moscow at dusk, quoted previously, likewise evoked both visual elements and a whole range of musical tonalities, thereby expanding still further the primordial experience.

To *abstract* involves an intellectual process: applying the thinking, rational principle to the work of art. When conveyed in musical terms, with its Apollonian side predominant, it does not necessarily evoke feeling. Rather, consciousness takes hold, drawing the composer or listener into an inhuman or nonobjective realm. Music is not to be sentimentalized. It is a mathematical science. Let us recall that Pythagoras laid down its ground rules: musical intervals are based on numerical ratios determined according to spatial distances; sound waves also depend upon spatial distances.[15] Music not only has mood; it has measure, symmetry, proportion, line, mathematical and physical constituents—as does painting.

Some critics have suggested that Kandinsky's fascination with nonobjective painting stemmed from his nearsightedness: he could make out only blurred shapes and colors when not wearing glasses, and, when wearing them, the differences were sharply underscored, thereby drastically altering his perception. Color and the search for new optical sensations—and not the object—were his goals. It has also been put forward that Kandinsky sought the nonobjective image because of his fear of impending disaster. Although such reasonings may in part be true, why then would the musical element in art and poetry be of such moment to Kandinsky? How is it that colors howled and were orchestrated into shrill or mellifluous pitches and timbres?

To dislocate the object in a painting, to dismember syntax in a poem, to reject the harmonious tonalities heard in a normal scale is to create a new language, a fresh vocabulary, and a tuning fork that enables the artist to impose an inner vision on external shapes, words, and tones. Communication is then experienced viscerally as well as spiritually—and without blockage. During Kandinsky's Munich years, he was still searching for the nonobjective: hurling pigments onto canvas and allowing form to flow freely, colors to ejaculate, and musical analogies to sing out their rhythms and pitches as they saw fit. Each form and line, he was convinced, had its own *true sound* which *vibrated* according to an *inner intensity*. Color dependent on the light wave, and sound on the sound wave, both revealed their secret natures to Kandinsky in the *word*—thereby enriching its power and mystery.

Kandinsky and Franz Marc, who had formed the New Artists' Association in 1909, decided, along with Gabriele Munter, to sever their connections with the group because, held by an earthbound vision, it did not foster a nonobjective and mystical reality. What the three sought to depict on canvas was not a world the artist conceived of, but a domain in which things appeared as if born from and perceived by themselves.

The goal of the "Blaue Reiter" group, founded by Marc and Kandinsky in 1911, was to free the artist still further from conventional tendencies. Their historical compendium of contemporary aesthetics, *Der Blaue Reiter Almanach* (1912), included Kandinsky's stage composition, *Der Gelbe Klang* (*The Yellow Noise*), an example of the play of the future, which was to synthesize color, movement, music, and abstract form. This plotless drama, with its fleshless and bloodless characters, its dialogue consisting of shrieks, groans, grunts, incredible phrasings, and strange actions, was made even more shocking by an interplay of lights, colors, and objects which moved along singly or in groups.

Kandinsky remarked that Schoenberg's music "leads us into a realm where musical experience is a matter not of the ear but of the soul alone—and from this point begins the music of the future"; likewise, *The Yellow Noise* draws artist and viewer into supernal and abstract domains.[16] In an article ("The Relationship to the Text," "Das Verhaltnis zum Text," published in *Der Blaue Reiter Almanach*, 1912), Schoenberg declared that he had composed his music to the poems of Stefan George, inspired not by a textual understanding of them, but by the resonance of the verses themselves.[17]

Kandinsky incorporated in *The Yellow Noise* and in his volume of poems and woodcuts, *Sounds*, what Schoenberg achieved in his music. The latter used the twelve tones of the tempered scale, which he considered a "practical" abstraction from the "*natural*" scale, to achieve his effect. He believed that each tone was interrelated only insofar as it occupies a position in a Tone Row, which he defines as follows:

> . . . the two-or-more dimensional space in which musical ideas are presented as a unit . . . [which] demands an absolute and unitary perception. In this space . . . there is no absolute own, no right or left, forward or backward. Every musical configuration, every movement of tones has to be comprehended primarily as a mutual relation of sounds, of oscillatory vibrations, appearing at different places and times. . . . Just as our mind always recognizes, for instance, a knife, a bottle or a watch, regardless of its position, and can reproduce it in the imagination in every possible position, even so a musical creator's mind can operate subconsciously with a row of tones, regardless of their duration, regardless of the way in which a mirror might show the mutual relations, which remain a given quantity.[18]

Prior to Schoenberg's innovations, tones were believed to be related and their functions determined in accordance with the ratio of their vibrations or the quality and function of the *leading tone*.

It is no wonder, then, that both Schoenberg and Kandinsky sought a synthesis of the arts. The latter expressed his views in a seminal work, *Concerning the Spiritual in Art* (begun in 1901 and completed in 1910), which is considered a breakthrough to abstraction and to a harmonics of music.

And so the arts are one upon another, and from a proper use of this encroachment will rise the art that is truly monumental. Every man who steeps himself in the spiritual possibilities of his art is a valuable helper in the building of the spiritual pyramid which will some day reach to heaven.[19]

Techniques in Sounds

Sounds may be considered a kind of bridge leading from Kandinsky's relatively objective to his nonobjective phase in painting and verse. Although some of the images in *Sounds* are representational, they are not weighed down with discursive meaning. His abstractions—even his figurations—are severed from the whole, thereby creating strange verbal hierarchies and associations and frightening visions, endowed with tonality, pitch, and rhythms, as well as with color.

Abstraction and Introverted Libido

Kandinsky's need to abstract corresponded to a subjective desire to draw out a content or image from its usual habitat and to sever it from worldly connections. In so doing, the usual comparisons could no longer be made. New spheres opened up, therefore, separating the object or segment from the whole, thereby disrupting an entire psycho-energic process. The concepts formerly associated with the object no longer applied, since they were not identifiable to the viewer.

To cut something away from the whole, as is required in abstraction, involves a rejection of those aspects considered irrelevant to it. Such a procedure invites a concentration of psychic energy (libido) onto the part abstracted, and a concomitant depletion of psychic energy onto the rest of the area. To *abstract* in this sense is to depreciate the whole in favor of its parts, increasing the favored segment in value and energy. Psychologically, we may say that Kandinsky was *introverting libido*, assimilating certain segments of an object or vision into the word, image, and tonality of his verses. The more he abstracted, the more detached his verses became from the empirical domain. The less representative they became, the greater was the libido distilled, centralized, and compressed.[20]

When an image is cut off from its empirical value and function, a reshuffling of libido takes place. Inner feelings once associated with the object as a whole may now dematerialize, allowing new textures, auralities, and meanings to come forth. An analogy may be drawn here between a hyphen or a period used as a punctuation mark, thereby fulfilling a function, and one placed on a canvas where it has no pragmatic use and so is freed from any connection with its original signification.

Kandinsky similarly envisaged his abstractions and even his representational forms in *Sounds:* they were released from all identification with their original functions. As autonomous entities, they became living, dynamic, and spiritually active forces in and of themselves.

Vibratory Tonal Processes

Mention must be made, in connection with Kandinsky's vibratory tonal technique in *Sounds,* of his admiration for Maurice Maeterlinck's "supernatural" stage plays, namely, *Princess Maleine, The Seven Princesses, The Blind,* and others. They heralded a whole new theatrical and artistic venture for Kandinsky. Souls lost in clouds and appearing in moonlight, windy marshes, and gloomy shadows stirred a panoply of audible, but unseen, objects in his *mind* which he sensed and *heard* only in terms of "an abstract impression," that is to say, as dematerialization of the object and its corresponding vibration which was "immediately set up in the *heart.*"[21]

The vibrations aroused in *Sounds* are compounded by repetitions of simple and prosaic words such as "no one, no one, no one . . . or wider, wider . . . or speaks, speaks . . . Ba-ackagain . . . Ba-ackagain . . ." Not only do these protracted tones intensify inner harmonies and discordant and jarring pitches, but (as Kandinsky remarked about Maeterlinck's works and as is also applicable to *Sounds*) they enlighten "unsuspected spiritual properties in the word itself."[22] Such a disclosure occurs, explains Kandinsky, because "the soul undergoes an emotion which has no relation to any definite object, an emotion more complicated, I might say more super-sensuous than the emotion caused by the sound of a bell or a stringed instrument."[23] Kandinsky's abstractions, then, sever relations with habitual concepts and feeling-tones, only to *construct* different ones after the dismemberment process has taken place.

Synesthesia

Synesthesia, as mentioned in a previous chapter, implies a unification of the senses; the visual may be heard, smelled, touched, and tasted, or the tasted may be heard, seen, smelled, and felt, and so on. Synesthesia may be looked upon as a giant awakening, a psychic happening, and a flaring up of forces within the unconscious. Such a process enables the artist to experience simultaneity of sense impressions, to see the work of art coming into being, and to come into contact with new languages, forgotten species, and preformal life. So that the synesthetic experience may bear its full fruit, the artist must be willing to undergo a momentary eclipse of his conscious personality and a dissociation of the ego, allowing him to be engulfed by the powers of the collective unconscious. Then the inner eye and ear *feel* cadences and aromas, as well as the material fullness and aerated atomizations of sublimated spheres.

Kandinsky writes of the psychological effects of "scented colours" and "the sound of colours," which entice him to experience those "spiritual vibrations" mentioned so frequently in his writings, and particularly in *Concerning the Spiritual in Art.*

> In highly sensitive people, the way to the soul is so direct and the soul itself so impressionable, that any impression of taste communicates itself immediately to the soul, and thence to the other organs of sense (in this case, the eyes). This would imply an echo or reverberation, such as occurs sometimes in musical instruments which, without being touched, sound in harmony with some other instruments struck at the moment.[24]

Kandinsky's forays into the synesthetic experience capture life in its flux, and action in its counteraction. According to Heraclitean doctrine, the only reality is change; the notion of permanence is an illusion—the product of sophistry, paradox, and of casuistic reasoning. Within each entity (organic or inorganic), opposites exist: being and nonbeing. The only true state is that of transition. If strife were to end, Heraclitus wrote, so would life.

In Kandinsky's "Bassoon," "Oboe," and "Hills," included in *Sounds*, the flow of archetypal resonances reverberates within the images, colorations, lines, and rhythms. All types of auralities play their visceral and spiritual roles. Strident and mellifluous sounds, grinding and velvety pitches, whisperings and silences pierce husks and shear off layers of matter which had formerly screened the source of creativity. By dissociating word from object and reassembling them in new contrapuntal melodic schemes and in variously paced beats, he heightens vibrations, creating double and triple sounds—a whole orchestration of *overtones* which "hang" over the verses as a whole. Each word possesses not only its own tonal value but also its texture, coloration, and feeling-tones as well—its coldness and its warmth. The poems feed upon themselves, arousing kaleidoscopic sensations and developing rich nutrients embedded in the autonomous verbal and sonant abstractions and/or concretions.

"Bassoon"

"Bassoon" opens with a stylized image: a group of collapsed houses, an orange-colored cloud hanging over the town, a tower radiating violet hues, a naked tree, and blackness. A yellow town is set against a backdrop which is utterly silent, save for hoofbeats that ring out, filling the space-time continuum.

Everything is hierarchized, geometrized. The images are placed in perspective and thereby intellectualized. Viscerality opens the reader and poet to a thinking and sensate world—exciting but intimidating.

> Though elongated, extended, somewhat expressionless, unsympathetic notes of a bassoon rolling far, far away deep in the distant emptiness, everything slowly turning green. First low and rather dirty. Then brighter and brighter, colder and colder, poisonous and more poisonous, even brighter, even colder, even more poisonous. (p. 26)

Though the bassoon is identified in the title and alluded to in the poem per se, the object itself is never drawn; its attributes are identified, but never explicitly. It appears, therefore, as a kind of nonobject, further increasing the detachment of the word from the perceptual appearance of the object in question. Still, the personality of the musical instrument is captured through its tones. Its dynamics and strident resonances are activated as they progress in their inflammatory radiance.

Why the title "Bassoon"? Why call into being this double-reed woodwind instrument, with its long U-shaped conical tube connected to the mouthpiece by a thin metal tube? Let us recall that Kandinsky is tyrannized neither by language nor by context. Like Schoenberg, he rejects functional harmonious progressions and conventional forms, permitting as much self-expression as possible. Just as Schoenberg's music is *panchromatic*, Kandinsky writes, leading us into a realm where musical experience takes on audible but also spiritual dimension, so, too, does the bassoon assume this role in his poem. Its range is two octaves lower than the oboe's and ushers readers into the shadowy realm of a secretive world. The sound of the word itself in German, *Fagott*, with its fricative and dentals, rings out its plaintive cries or earthy shrieks, affecting the reader, who listens to its message of distress and alienation. Cool sounds, which Kandinsky identifies with the violet colorations radiating from the tower, impose an ailing quality onto the scene, lending a sense of mourning.

As this large, unfriendly instrument infiltrates its way into the poem, expanding and dominating open spaces within the town, terror spreads over the airways, producing cataclysmic sensations. The hanging orange cloud flames and crackles, intensifying the aurality of the scene. Contrapuntal sequences intrude: green tones instill restfulness, but also weariness and passivity.[25]

The tones conveyed by the bassoon usher in "low" and "dirty" sensations, which merge with and emerge from one another, their blendings transformed into "brighter, colder and colder" tones, and even "poisonous" ones. Auditive and spatial indications and variations increase the haptic, visual, and aural sensations, conveying deepening feelings of uneasiness. Proportions grow out of control; pitch and rhythm introduce a whole new range of physical and psychological conditions. No longer compressed horizontally in bass/base visions, feelings radiate as they soar upward and take on amplitude and vitality. The eye follows the building line, reaching a point—a single dot to the right—that thrusts toward the rational domain. As the vision ascends, it yields to an inner urge to penetrate a non-material sphere, "striving toward morning," toward the new, toward the beginning. This is the time span which mystics allude to as the *renovatio*—that eternal rebirth of life.

As the eye movement grows increasingly active, moving from the sublimity of a dematerialized sky world to the hard-crusted earth below, the viewer focuses on people walking about in bright and cold colorations, dominated by a "poisonous green" vision. Each stares ahead in his or her loneliness: "And the sky, the houses, the pavement and the people who walked on the pavement became brighter, colder, more poisonously green. The people walked constantly, continually, slowly, always staring straight ahead. And always alone" (p. 26). Soundlessness emanates from form and color and from shape and texture, as the motility of the previous ascents and descents turns into stasis.

The images seen thus far are never merely retinal projections of an inner experience. Each aspect of the visual and oral segment has found its own form and structure, or its soul and spirit, to use Kandinsky's words. The "naked tree," mentioned at the outset of the poem, now grown in size and bearing its luxurious crown of branches and leaves, is compared, humorously enough, to a "sausage," thereby deflating what has always been poetized: "But the naked tree correspondingly grew a large, luxurious crown. This crown sat up high and had a compact, sausage-like shape that curved upward. The crown alone was so shrilly yellow that no soul would endure it" (p. 26). To juxtapose a crown, symbolizing the highest possible function of humankind, with a sausage not only elicits laughter; it also topples conventional values. The ugliness marring the crown presages disaster: it was so "shrilly yellow that no soul would endure it."

Kandinsky describes yellow as a "disturbing," "aggressive," and "sour" color tone. "The intensification of the yellow increases the painful shrillness of its note," he wrote in *Concerning the Spiritual in Art*. A parallel disquietude, created by the shrill sounds of the bassoon, increases the piercing, virtually deafening tones. Action accelerates as horizontality and verticality vie for predominance, reaching out to confront obstacles and tear down barriers. "Yellow is the typically earthly colour," Kandinsky continues. "It can never have profound meaning." With the addition of the "piercing blue" sky, mentioned previously in the poem, the situation grows increasingly harrowing. The blending of yellow and blue is equated "with madness, not with melancholy or hypochondriacal mania, but rather with violent raving lunacy."[26]

Madness takes over in this apocalyptic vision. Chaos spreads throughout the world. Only the poet senses the impending disaster; the others are oblivious to the erupting stridencies and merely peer straight ahead, as had those ignorant, bound, blind, and constricted inhabitants in Plato's "Allegory of the Cave." "Only the bassoon attempted to describe the color. It rose higher and higher, became shrill and nasal in its outstretched note. How good that the bassoon couldn't reach this note" (p. 26).

The poet/bassoon is the prophet of his time. It is he who sees deep into the future. Because he enjoys a very special talent as forerunner of what is to be, he must be taken seriously. A prototype of the prophet, he is comparable, psychologically, to a "retort in which [the] poisons and antidotes of the collective are distilled."[27]

"It's good that none of the people walking below saw this crown," the poem continues, since the ordinary person would not know how to cope with this rounded force. Like the *ouroborus* (the Gnostic image of the snake eating its own tail), humankind during its earthly sojourn is blind, embedded in matter, and completely devoid of imagination and inner flame. Even the bassoon, at this critical moment, fails to prevent the further collapse of the large houses dotting the scene. It is powerless to dispel the havoc wreaked by the large orange cloud permeating the environs. Violet and black colorations, related to "the silence of death," encroach on the scene "with least harmony" (p. 39). After the crushing crunch of the falling buildings disturbs and vibrates ("Ganz grosse Häuser stürzten plötzlich"), silence invades the atmosphere, bringing overwhelming sensations of death. The bassoon had done all it could to heal what had been lacerated and to cleanse the wound through its description of the yellow crown. "Shrill and nasal in its outstretched note," it failed, however, to "reach this note"—its destination.

Like the bassoon, the poet seeks to perform miracles and to intuit the unknown by transmuting the impalpable into the palpable, the evanescent into the eternal. Although his responses are powerful, the contents that spring forth from his collective unconscious are limited.

Malaise permeates the atmosphere. Feelings of hopelessness spread throughout the infinitely empty spaces. Such feelings may well have been Kandinsky's own as he faced a world of imponderables, peering as it were

into a giant maw and horrified by the vastness of its emptiness. Years later
he wrote: "In my mind the collapse of the atom was the collapse of the
whole world: Suddenly the stoutest walls fell. Everything turned unstable,
insecure, and soft. I would not have been surprised if a stone had melted
into thin air before my eyes. Science seemed to have been annihilated."[28]

Kandinsky's only certainty was his creative élan, which he called that
"inner necessity." Renewal was in order: the breaking up still further of
pat concepts and fixed, concrete images, thereby opening up unsuspected
climes beyond the world of appearances. The artist must not depict exter-
nals, Kandinsky suggested; he must dig deep into the "root of all roots."

"*Oboe*"

Kandinsky's "Oboe," a metaphor for the creative spirit that suffers dismemberment, pain, and laceration, is a crucifixion. It is antipodal to
Charles Baudelaire's vision in "Correspondances" of this same instrument,
whose smooth, soft sounds are comparable to tender perfumes and green
prairies.

"Oboe" opens on a stylized image: "a little round flat hill" where a
young man, Nepomuk, wearing a new and very beautiful dress coat, sits
looking down at a "little green lake."

> Nepomuk leaned his back against the trunk of the little white green
> birch tree, pulled out his big long black oboe and played many
> beautiful songs which everybody knows. He played for a long time
> with deep feeling. Maybe going on two hours. Just as he started up
> with "There came a bird a-flying" and had gotten to "a-fly,"
> Meinrad came running up the hill all hot and out of breath and
> with his crooked, pointed, sharp, curved, shining sword struck off a
> nice fat chunk of the oboe. (p. 47)

Feelings of serenity permeate the stilled vision of the opening phrases
and determine their tonalities. The green birch tree and the silent blue-
green lake at the foot of the hill blend celestial and earthly spheres into a
new unity, thereby encouraging horizontal and circular movements, going
from the periphery to the center. The oboist's heart beats as he plays,
interrupting and disrupting the static quality of the primary images. Musical overtones flood the scene. The musician sitting on the hill, above the
madding crowd, knows how to appeal to the multitude, by playing those
melodies which invoke their simple inner values. All is contentment as the
serene tone of the flowing waters accompanies his own soundings in
hypnotic patterns, which serve to prolong a kind of trance state. The tree,
steady and serene, with its roots digging deep into the ground, is both a

protective force, because the instrumentalist leans on it, and an inspiration, because he draws sustenance from it by his proximity, as roots do from the earth.

That the oboist wears a black coat may indicate a need on his part to mask the turmoil within him. Until now, his woodwind instrument has helped him descant his happy melodies in understandable tones. Now, however, different sonorities emerge: archetypal music, embedded in its own beat, rhythm, and disruptive and quiescent pitches, diffuses strange intonations. When these filled the air, "There came a bird a-flying." The intrusion of the bird image alters the course of things: a soul image, free to roam the heavens as it wishes, is not caught up in the miasmic, earthly world. It is, then, a metaphor for the instrumentalist, who struggles with his own dual nature, both thirsting for spirituality and needing the earth force. He suffers the lacerations imposed upon him along with ignominy.

Meinrad, the harbinger of change, runs up the hill, breathless. This crushing, relentless being upsets the beauty of the moment and breaks up the peaceful tonal undulations as he severs the oboe, cutting what was whole. The oboe's lively and appealing tones have now halted. Nature no longer rings out freely in ascending and descending sonances. The freshness of the life experience is no longer able to roam and breathe at will. Instinctual forces have intruded, refusing to allow facile harmonies to pursue their course. Discord has usurped the place where accord once reigned. An onslaught of jarring, nerve-wracking vibrations rends the heavens. The atmosphere is filled with the raucous sounds of the dismembered oboe, which corresponds to the spiritual and psychological laceration predominating at this point.

Alliterations (spitzen, scharfen; gebogenen, glänzenden) heighten the disruptive forces at work and increase the cutting nature of the crooked, pointed, sharp, and abrasive sword used to sever the oboe. The pounding of the glottals, nasals, and labials in the German forces out the frenzy of the situation. ("Meinrad den Hügel herauf und schlug mit seinem krummen, spitzen, scharfen, gebogenen, glänzenden Säbel ein gutes Stück von der Hoboe ab.") The sword, associated with bravery, power, and the military, may also be looked upon as a positive force and identified with justice, because it separates good from evil, as well as with inner spiritual conquest, because it cuts away the purulent from the healthy part of the human being (Matt. 10:34). Psychologically speaking, the sword cuts what is whole, not only dividing an object, but dismembering a thought, feeling, or sensation, thus permitting an examination of its various components. To cut, for Kandinsky, implies an abstraction, since it invites the creative individual to peer deep into his own inner world, where he can then explore—even dissect—what he experiences via the thinking/sensation functions.

Creation emerges from destruction: the new is buried within the old and must willfully and cruelly be liberated, torn out, and extracted in order to come into its own. In *Reminiscences*, Kandinsky describes this process:

> It sometimes seemed to me that the brush, which with unyielding will tore pieces from this living color creation, evoked a musical sound in this tearing process. Sometimes I heard a hissing of the colors as they were blending. It was like an experience that one could hear in the secret kitchen of the alchemist, cloaked in mystery.[29]

As depicted in "Oboe," there is nothing sweet or beautiful in the act of creation. As when a woman gives birth, flesh must be torn and pain experienced. Who better than Kandinsky understood that painting is doing "battle with the canvas," which always resists the artist's wishes (dream) and fights his brush strokes?

> At first it stands there like a pure chaste virgin with clear eye and heavenly joy—this pure canvas which itself is as *beautiful* as a painting. And then comes the willful brush which first here, then there, gradually conquers it with all the energy peculiar to it, like a European colonist, who pushes into the wild virgin nature, hitherto untouched, using axe, spade, hammer, and saw to shape it to his wishes.[30]

Artist and poet, Kandinsky had trained his inner eye and ear to see and to hear. Bergson has suggested that intuition is a direct and instantaneous way of knowing. Kandinsky's musician in "Oboe" played effortlessly but not intuitively. He needed to undergo the dismembering process in order to penetrate the unknown. As for the bassoon, it not only mirrored an inner climate; it foretold the disaster of the creative force of both the individual and the collective. In both cases, the poet/musician, abstracted from the phenomenal world, penetrated deep into geological spheres—out of reach of the normal being, but bathing in pleromatic spheres and prototypal existences.

"Hills"

In "Hills," we are again dealing with undifferentiated archaic content and stylized, hierarchized visualizations. Filtered out from the primal substance, each object and nonobject lives out its independent existence, musically and rhythmically, through form, color, and texture.

"Hills" opens with "a mass of hills of all colors" and all sizes, "but the shapes always alike, i.e. just one: Fat at the bottom, puffed out around the sides, flat round up above." A "narrow path simply white, i.e. neither bluish, nor yellowish," runs through the hills. A man is walking along, his long black coat reaching down to his heels; his face is pale, and two red spots are visible on his cheeks; his lips are equally red.

> He has a big drum hung around his neck and he is drumming . . .
> Sometimes he runs and beats his drum with feverish, irregular strokes.
> Sometimes he walks slowly, perhaps absorbed in his thoughts and drums almost mechanically in a long drawn-out tempo: one . . . one . . . one . . . one . . . sometimes he stands stock still and drums like the little soft white toy rabbit that we all love so well.
> This standing doesn't last long though.
> The man is running again, beating his drum with feverish, irregular strokes.
> As if utterly exhausted he lies there, the black man, all stretched out over the white path, among the hills of all colors. His drum lies beside him and the two drumsticks too.
> He's standing up already. Now he'll start running again.
> All this I have seen from above and beg you too to look on it from above. (p. 18)

As in the opening scene of "Oboe," the background is static, increasing in dynamism as the drumming begins its energetic activations. The instrumentalist chooses his direction, then proceeds down the narrow path through the hills, sounding his percussion instrument as he walks. The air fills with successions of vibrating tones, throbbings, and stirring rhythms, thereby activating a whole mysterious invisible and silent dimension.

In olden days, the beating of the drum, harbinger of aggression, was viewed principally as a call to war. The very act of hitting the drum, of expelling sound from its frame, brings to mind emerging unconscious contents. Tones burn and sear, like flashes of lightning, discharging their bulletlike sonances into a formerly quiescent landscape. This instrument/weapon, with its primordial sonances, is analogous to the metaphor of the sword in "Oboe." It pierces the silence, crushes resistance, and penetrates aerated spheres. Drums are also spiritual forces. When used in shamanistic rituals, they help the man of religion prepare for his moment of ecstasy. As he strikes his drum, its sounds shatter nature's stillness; its reverberations crackle as matter is energized, linking superior to inferior worlds. (Kandinsky was familiar with shamanism, having studied Russian folk customs in areas where such worship is still practiced.)

Kandinsky's choice of a clownlike figure, dressed in black, with a white face, two bright red spots on his cheeks, and a drum, to convey his ideations is a satirical way of conveying his bitterness. In the poem the clown, whose function it is to make people laugh, is the bearer of the drum: the aggressive and spiritual instrument. Embodying the spirit that ridicules sovereign values, strikes back when struck, mocks, derides, and parodies what is considered sacred, the clown and his drum are tolerated because they entertain and are loved by adults and children alike. When Kandinsky introduces the simile of the "soft white toy rabbit," also beating a drum, he underscores a need to regress into childhood. The clown functions freely at this archaic-authentic level, divested of the hypocrisies of "culture." He mocks all so-called civilizing accoutrements.

That the clown is the artist's double is evident in the dichotomy of colors used in the poem: the black cloak and the white face. Linking these colors to sound, Kandinsky writes:

> . . . white, although often considered as no colour . . . is a symbol of a world from which all colour as a definite attribute has disappeared. This world is too far above us for its harmony to touch our souls. A great silence, like an impenetrable wall, shrouds its life from our understanding. White, therefore, has this harmony of silence, which works upon us negatively, like many pauses in music that break temporarily the melody. It is not a dead silence, but one pregnant with possibilities. White has the appeal of the nothingness that is before birth, of the world in the ice age.
>
> A totally dead silence, on the other hand, a silence with no possibilities, has the inner harmony of black. In music it is represented by one of those profound and final pauses, after which any continuation of the melody seems the dawn of another world. Black is something burnt out, like the ashes of a funeral pyre, something motionless like a corpse. The silence of black is the silence of death. Outwardly black is the colour with the least harmony of all, a kind of neutral background against which the minutest shades of other colours stand clearly forward. It differs from white in this also, for with white nearly every colour is in discord, or even mute altogether.[31]

Regarding the color of the clown's lips and the two spots on his cheeks, red, Kandinsky writes, may arouse "a sensation analogous to that caused by flame." It is "exciting," triggering physical reactions on the part of the viewer, awakening feelings of "strength, vigour, determination." In music, Kandinsky further remarks, red is brought into being by the "sound of trumpets, strong, harsh, and ringing." Its reverberation "rings out a powerful inner harmony" which "thunders like a drum." Nevertheless, there are moments when red ushers in moods of sadness, discord, or a frenzy of unsolved disharmonies.[32]

That the clown is a composite of black, white, and red indicates the divisions in his personality. As a mirror image of the creative spirit, his pace alters constantly. Tone, pace, and pitch accelerate or slacken in keeping with the rhythms of an inner climate. The clown pursues the "narrow path" through the hills and valleys, ascending and descending, entering into the very heart of nature, confronting difficult hurdles and suffering the ignominies of worldly contacts—as the clown does when he entertains.

The drummer, who stops and starts, walks and runs, beating upon his instrument feverishly and irregularly, exhausting himself in the process, is also representative of the person who seeks to be heard. Repetitions of words increase the jarring tempo and heighten vibrations, becoming "a source of elementary rhythm which, in turn, is a means to the attainment of elementary harmony in every form of art."[33]

We are dealing here with proto-, or original, sound. Earth force, as lived out in "counterpoint," invites moments of repose and stillness, of barely audible whisperings, followed by disruptive nerve-piercing beats. Rhythms, tones, and moods alter, paralleling the clown's course up and down the hills. A metaphor for the path of life, they also replicate Kandinsky's meteoric and dismembering view of the creative principle. Diversity and discord are important psychological, physiological, spiritual, and aesthetic factors in the evolution of a painting, a poem, or a musical composition. Opposition and contradiction in the life process, though arousing violent antitheses, strengthen the artistic endeavor. They engender passion, activate growth, break up hardened and stereotyped attitudes, and thereby prepare the individual to create fresh yields. According to doxographic documents, Heraclitus wrote: "War is the father of all and the king of all, and some he has made gods and some men, some bound and some free. . . . the immortals are mortal, the mortals are immortal, each living in the other's death and dying in the other's life."[34]

Kandinsky was not the first to write "new" poetry, with its strange word associations, neologisms, harsh alliterations, and bizarre analogies; nor was he the initiator of nonobjective verse. Baudelaire, Rimbaud, Mallarmé, Jarry, Apollinaire, and others preceded him. He was, however, one of the first painters to do so, using verse to convey his disdain for the world of appearance and dislocating or dissociating what seemed rational in the character or object at hand.

A city is viewed in terms of a bassoon; it takes on its character, lives out its antinomies, and expands its tonal range, reaching shrill and piercing sonances. A landscape emerges in "Oboe" as joyous and pleasing melodies permeate the surroundings. A disruptive force suddenly enters the image and breaks up its order, cuts open its pat sequences, preparing it for a return to its own roots and the possibility of creating an authentic and eternal melody. In "Hills," the clown drums his way through life in harsh, jarring beats, experiencing the dichotomy within him via the conflict of forces, thereby reaching deep into the *prima materia*—that world from which he will extract his work of art.

Words, for Kandinsky, are wafted into existence and cut the air into— for the uninitiated—seemingly irrational patterns. For others, nouns, adjectives, and adverbs, along with all types of figures of speech, are piled up in blocks, multiple amplitudes, and rhythmic patterns, all of which create new orchestrations, fresh cacophonies, and unfamiliar harmonies, via Kandinsky's unique semantic order and syntactical structure.

Sounds, which answered a spiritual need, also introduced to the world a language in which word, image, color, line, and texture were intertwined in archetypal sonorities linking the dual forces of matter/spirit into a new unity—the *One* in the poem.

6 Joyce's "Eveline": An Archetypal Auditory Experience

Although "Eveline" is considered the most rudimentary, structurally and thematically, of the tales in *Dubliners* (1914), it nevertheless reveals James Joyce's early use of music as metaphor and as organizing agent. The auditory experience implicit in Joyce's tale is further accentuated by his complex system of figures of speech and by his use of stressed and unstressed phonemes of beguiling sonority. The tonal qualities inherent in his images, their psychological associations, and the variety of rhythms interwoven into these pictures help convey feeling, mood, and character. Joyce's application of background noises, which infiltrate into specific scenes, serves to heighten pace and moments of suspense or anguish.

To appreciate "Eveline" fully—and this is true of Joyce's works in general—one must read it aloud. Its tones, rhythms, screeching sounds, and modulations convey covert attitudes, trigger subliminal meanderings, and work on the reader's ear and nervous system. They are devices that set off the interior monologue and stream-of-consciousness sequences. Words pronounced inwardly, in cadences or staccato beats, echo and reecho unheard melodies.

"Eveline" is told in the third person, through the consciousness of the main character, Eveline, as she sits and ponders certain past and present events. It is dusk as the story opens; the daily activities have slackened in pace. Eveline speaks out her litany in hard but sensitive modes—the painfully pure song which is her life.

The very name Eveline, which comes from the Celtic and means "pleasant," indicates her nature: gentle, affable, acquiescing. In this regard, she resembles Joyce's mother as well as his dutiful sister Margaret, who, at twenty years of age, took charge of her sisters and brothers after her mother's demise. Eveline is nineteen. She is depicted as repressed—the product of a social and psychological incarceration.

Eveline's intuitive, circuitous, repetitive, and introspective existence is brought into view immediately via Joyce's main image, which features her sitting in front of a window. Her thoughts are controlled as they issue forth in her interior monologue, meandering along, spreading their tones of grief and distress in variously paced crescendos and diminuendos. Like other Dubliners, she suffers from that psychological infection which prevents her from moving out of her regressive, miasmic stagnation. "Eveline sat at the window watching the evening invade the avenue. Her head leaned against the window curtains and in her nostrils was the odour of dusty cretonne. She was tired."[1]

Joyce's opening image of Eveline, framed by the window, is a perfect iconographic replica of her spiritual and psychological condition. The repetition of the lip-rounded, tongue-back semivowel w (window, watching) contains an airy, breezy quality, indicative of a need to move about freely. The voiced fricative labio-dental v (evening, invade) has the opposite effect. As the lower lip is pressed against the upper teeth, activity is suddenly brought to a halt. A battle seems to be brewing somewhere in Eveline's unconscious, and understandably, since her culture and her religion dictate her destiny, imprisoning her in a hard home environment that brings to mind the ancient dolmens—those large monuments which once were used as burial chambers and consisted usually of several upright stones capped by a large stone slab. Like the heroes of old who were buried in dolmens in crouched positions awaiting rebirth, and like the Christian martyrs who imprisoned themselves in grottoes as they prayed for purity of soul in order to enter paradise, Eveline sits within the window frame, longing for life to yield its excitement. To break out of her burial chamber, so to speak, is her fervent desire. She knows it to be her only salvation, for in this cavelike edifice she hears the reverberations of a heart that longs for love; she listens to her thoughts, intoned in long and agonizing melopoeia, as they echo her pain and distress. If she could only step beyond this death passage into life, darkness would give way to brightness, and morosity to celebration.

With an economy of words, Joyce traces the salient characteristics of this pious and righteous young girl. An inner melody manifests itself in her monologue as she recollects her tedious, dreary past. Eveline observes, from a distance, a whole *outside* world—reality, but also a fantasy. In a personification, the "evening" is seen through the "window" as an "invading" force. Its conflicting sonorities (w and v, as mentioned above) indicate action versus stasis, freedom as opposed to imprisonment. Eveline senses the ruthless march of time: her youth speeding by; hours, days, months passing relentlessly, vanishing into nothingness. She leans her head "against the window curtains" and looks toward the open spaces and unconstricted areas *out there*. She stares ahead, as though spanning horizons, but also drifting into other dimensions—remote, timeless regions of her inner being. She inhales the "odour of dusty cretonne," those curtains which, like veils, serve to block her view, dull her vision, prevent her from leaping out of her staid, fixed condition. As she contemplates her silent words, her lungs fill with the dust from the cretonnes within the room/tomb. The *d* in *dust*, a voiced tongue apex stop, coupled with the dental *t*, occludes any passage from one state or stage to another. Dust represents particles of a past, diffused experiences, disparate, powdery, unchanneled matter that has left its residue everywhere. Identified with the earthly sphere which fixes and paralyzes Eveline, dust, paradoxically, cements her to her family, culture, and religion. Like dust, she is a mortal remnant, a relic and product of her inheritance, a humble being living in a disintegrating environment which breeds estrangement, decay, and secret grief. Dust is a constant reminder to her that she is shackled to what is, unable to discover herself and her potential. She is a servant in the true sense of the word, never having done anything but obey.

Joyce takes Eveline's thoughts and sensations from within the tomblike edifice and projects them outside, into the world beyond. Eveline's mood, her extreme sensitivity, and her ambiguity of purpose are depicted by Joyce, musically, in array of complex phonemes and figures of speech: "The man out of the last house passed on his way home; she heard his footsteps clacking along the concrete pavement and afterwards crunching on the cinder path before the new red house" (p. 36). The orality of these clauses is striking. The experience is lived through Eveline's ear in contrapuntal episodes. The tones she hears are sounded in the words themselves, which vary in pace, in harshness and softness, depending upon the need of the moment.

The sonances of the alliterations (clacking, concrete, crunching) foster a climate of harshness, aggressivity, and dissatisfaction. These tones not only expel Eveline's distress but also accentuate her spirit of frustration and her need to tear, cut, and untie what binds. Smothering feelings of rejection and alienation come to the fore as these consonants convey the cruelty of a life based on sacrifice. The tones evoked by the "crunching" and the "cinder path" jar and annihilate; they communicate an organic need to eviscerate something within her so that her days may be lived fully and her yearnings and desires realized. These cacophonies reverberate in Eveline's head, disclosing the schism existing within her psyche.

Joyce's use of dentals and fricatives, as in "footsteps," and guttural and nasal phonemes, as in "clacking" and "crunching," creates sensations of friction. The harsh tones produced by the throat in uttering gutturals, dentals, fricatives, and nasals lend a raspy, hoarse tonality to the picture. Phonetically speaking, they suggest that a bridge leads from the mouth and the nose to the stomach and lungs. The passageway that exists from the inner being (stomach, heart, lungs) to the outer person (mouth and nose) is blocked by specific impediments: glottal stops which prevent ready access from one world to the other. The "footsteps" indicate that someone is going someplace. But where? Only to the "last house," and no further.

The "concrete pavement" which stands immediately outside Eveline's home is merely an extension of the hard and material world within the room/tomb. Although the concrete pavement and the cinder path represent the collective world, each is confining and restrictive in its own way. The man crunches along, grinding out, pressing in, treading the same line, transcribing the age-old ways of his ancestors, replicating images of what has been. The man who is entering the last house on the street is walking on "concrete pavement": a solid ground of coalesced particles, compacted sand and gravel, cemented together with water. He knows his obligations and duties and follows traditional ways—just like the Dublin streets, which were laid out according to certain conventions centuries before.

The word "crunching," with its guttural and affricate consonants, may also be identified with the activity of pressing, grinding, biting, and masticating, indicating the taking in of an experience and the aggressive act of apprehending elements from the outer world to feed the inner domain. By chewing or grinding something within the mouth, one alters matter, content and form. As Eveline hears the image, synesthetically speaking, the cacophony of harsh, conflicting sounds and of intricate tonal and rhythmic effects reverberates in her mind's eye. Abrasive, triturating tonal and rhythmic structures serve to increase her disquietude.

The "crunching" sounds of the "footsteps" hitting the cinder path indicate, paradoxically, both proximity and distance. The man in question has come from the outer, concrete, or hard world to the softer, unpaved area (from the collective to the individual domain). Cinders, like the dusty cretonne of the first image, take the reader even further into Eveline's slaglike existence. The product of matter, cinders are made of burned-out wood which has been reduced to ashes. Alchemically speaking, cinders have been through the fire process and thus stand for triturated, purified, and transformed matter. The alliance of dust and cinders, and of roads and paths, symbolizes the difficulties involved in seeking to step out of traditional thoroughfares. To step out of the individual and personal existence marked by dust and cinders requires a cutting off—a brutal and cruel act which only heroes and heroines are courageous enough to perform. The glow of desire is insufficient; a fire that sears must burn.

That Joyce chose *c* for his alliterations in this same passage underscores the musicality of the entire clause, which revolves around the first note of the natural scale—that basic tone to which pianos and organs are tuned. So important is this pitch that Joyce wrote: "Literature is kept alive by tonics."[2] Eveline's passive, servantlike existence is relational to the *c:* it is basic to her nature and her heredity. As for the window metaphor and the sonant sentence, they indicate that Eveline is taking *note* of her situation; she is singing out that *basic tone* of the scale and conveying her needs. For the first time, she is able and willing to look at the world and at herself as part of it.

That the "red house" at the end of the path is "new" introduces another rhythmic scheme into the tonal image. Time, divided into years, months, and so forth, is linear; in that the past is compared to the present, the simultaneity of experience or the concept of cyclicality is likewise present, emphasizing duration and a sense of doomed eternality. Eveline and her stonelike house, her entombment and her puritanical conscience, are covered with the dust of past attitudes. The pace slackens in this clause; then stops. The "red house," a metaphor for the fire principle, ushers in new, activating, and energizing elements. Rhythms heighten and reach incandescent force. The juxtaposition of the old and the new, in terms of time as well as of color tones and tempo, is a musical device which replicates Eveline's inner attitude. Her home is brown; heavy and terrestrial, it stands for earth, matter, and conventional attitudes. Preoccupied with chores, helping her family survive a life of poverty, Eveline lives in an apathetic condition of immobility and non-growth. Joyce speaks of the "last house" in this passage as if it were the limit of Eveline's circumscribed existence. The new house, with its "shining roof," is polished, refined, smooth, and it gleams mirrorlike even though it is rooted in a similar climate and tradition.

Shifting thought patterns begin to fluidify Eveline's views. Rhythms and pace accelerate as Joyce starts to use the stream-of-consciousness technique. Mental images waft her back to her childhood days: to a past when no house existed in this area. She used to play with her brothers and sisters on what was then an open field. Their happiness, however, was of short duration. The rhythm slackens; then comes to a halt. Her thoughts resume. An intruder from Belfast bought the vacant lot on which to build the redbrick house. As for the friends with whom she used to play, they have grown up and moved away. She questions: Was her childhood really happy? When the children were at play, Eveline's father used to come with

his "blackthorn stick" to "hunt them out of the field." (Let us recall that
Joyce's father had no patience with his children; as the years went by and
his drunkenness increased, he became insulting and deriding. According
to Stanislaus, Joyce's brother, his will had been "dissipated" and his intellect "besotted"; he had become "spiteful like all drunkards who are
thwarted."[3] Eveline's father beat his children each time they seemed to be
enjoying themselves. The aggressive and rough tonalities associated with
the aspirate h in "hunt," the hissing, snakelike sound in the sibilant
"stick," were too harsh for Eveline to bear. She retreated into her traditional role: that of a submissive and dutiful daughter, who dared not think
evil of her father, for to do so would have led her into sin. Anyway, her
father "was not so bad then," she muses, "and besides," she remembers,
"her mother was alive." As if dissatisfied with her present passivity and
inertia, she adds, "That was a long time ago." Plaintive once again, she
lingers on the past, vowels (o) and nasal (on) echoing her immersion in a
beginning. Her childhood ushers in a climate of hope which blocks free
access to the metrical pattern of her formerly circular, circuitous, repetitive existence.

"That was a long time ago," she murmurs inwardly, not only interjecting new rhythmic effects (in the backward and forward space-time continuum of her thoughts and feelings), but also introducing nasal sounds
without stops. The tones are held for a relatively long period, underscoring
the duration of it all. These consonantal sequences, with their variations of
vowels, arouse a whole unspecified segment of a past existence—almost
mythical in that it seems to have no beginning or end. The nasal consonants and the vowels included in such words as "long" and "ago" encourage tonalities to linger on, preserving a culture that breeds sameness,
stagnation, and unchangeability. The aspirate h ("hunt") of the previous
passage, which induces breath to pass through the mouth, when coupled
with nasalized vowels, entices the olfactory senses into participation, reminiscent of the time when Eveline recalled the odor of the cretonne. Such
sonants create a *pedal effect:* when tones are prolonged, as these are, they
swell in dimension, recombining and encouraging fresh, imitative tonalities to be heard.

Eveline's mention of the death of her mother and some of her brothers
and sisters sustains the mood and time span. Antithetically, the d's in
"dead" are alveolar stops, onomatopoeias of sorts, which rout movement.
Death indicates a break, a schism, a cruel and shocking intrusion into the
relative serenity of Eveline's stream-of-consciousness imaginings. Nevertheless, her thought clusters and their tonal recombinants pursue their rhythmic meanderings. Eveline comes to accept life's vagaries: "Everything
changes," she states silently.

And, indeed, things do seem about to change. "Now she was going away like the others, to leave home" and marry a sailor. In so doing, she intends to cut herself off from tradition, from a past, a family, a way of life. "Home! She looked round the room, reviewing all its familiar objects which she had dusted once a week for so many years, wondering where on earth all the dust came from. Perhaps she would never see again those familiar objects from which she had never dreamed of being divided" (p. 37). The placing of the word "home" at the outset of the paragraph, followed by an exclamation mark, emphasizes the very special nature of the image/sound. The aspirate *h* and the long-drawn-out vowel *o* perpetuate that secure feeling—that past which dominates and virtually stifles her very being. "Home," for Eveline, is a *temenos:* a sacred area, associated room/tomb, the inner space where the feminine principle reigns. In this case, as we know, it constricts and encloses; but it is also a repository for nourishment and a secret inner sphere—a personal and collective unconscious. Her home is described in slow-motion narrative and in plaintive terms, as if Joyce intended to reveal his protagonist's paralytic outlook and her frustrations in confessional style, in uncritical mental images with all of their auditory ramifications.

Eveline peers into the inner sanctum now, and no longer gazes through the window into the outside world. Introspectively, she *looks* within the round *r*oom of her home (in the same paragraph), reviewing her past, as though she still lived in some Neolithic period, inhabiting her cairn or dolmen. Nonfrictional consonants (*r*) flow freely now, almost vowel-like in their smoothness and sonancy, revealing an unconscious need to break out of this tomblike enclosure which is smothering her every spark of life.

The flowing rhythms and sonant reverberations of the *round room* are underscored semiotically: circular contours prolong activity but usher in the notion of sameness as well. Circles, like the *ouroborus*, suggest the eternality of Eveline's life-style, its stagnant and repetitive movement without a goal and without any alteration of focus. Stuck in routine, embedded in habit, systems, and a certain order, Eveline is not yet strong enough to carve out a new course. She is and must remain the dutiful girl who cares for the motherless children left in her charge. Yet, and in this same paragraph (p. 12), Joyce builds up tension by interjecting the word "reviewing" (*revidere:* the prefix *re* reaffirming the idea of seeing again). Will her ability to look inward, to take stock of her life, to objectify her ways encourage her to divest herself of her servantlike mentality? Will a survey and retrospective study of her world, a reassessment and inspection of her feelings and her destiny, permeated as they are with grief and pain, generate the energy necessary to break her ties with a nonconstructive past? Similar to the plainchant of the medieval period, the vowel-like consonant *r* virtually plays the role of a constant, underscoring Eveline's almost hopeless psychological condition, which forever revolves around fear of the new and terror of sin, damnation, and burning in hell for all eternity.

What does Eveline see as she gazes about the room? Dust, the residue of centuries of tradition. Though she keeps removing these gray particles, she cannot rid the objects in the room of the detritus of past existences. Dust, as previously stated, stands for disintegration. Dental and sibilant sonorities reverberate again in a harsh, cold, jarring medley which echoes throughout the tomblike room. The *d*, as in "dust," an alveolar stop which entices the jaw into participation, helps create tooth-ridge sounds and is also reminiscent in sonancy to "dead," mentioned before. As such, it is antagonistic to the previous liquid tonalities and nasalized vowels, with their mellifluous sameness and their velvety melodies that spell duration, eternality, and security. Will Eveline's past alter in direction? Or are the objects covered with dust simply passive witnesses and remnants of a static and single-toned world?

The alliteration ("dreamed" and "divided") indicates, musically and semiotically, Eveline's need to cut herself off from her past activities. The word "dream," on the other hand, suggests a subliminal domain replete with phantasms of all sorts: an imaginative world which her ascetic upbringing sought to crush ("crunching," "dead") so that servile religious, political, and social conventions could be observed. Tension grows in Eveline's unconscious as friction between "dream" and "divide" increases. She will have to choose one or the other: separation, a cutting off from her past, as she follows her dream; or pursuit of her time-worn ways, as she sinks in the miasmic waters of a nonproductive past.

Eveline's gaze falls on the "yellowing photograph" of a priest that hangs on the wall. She knows almost nothing about him except that he had once been her father's friend, but had gone to Melbourne with other Irish emigrants. He embarked in a new direction, opting for the unknown—a world of perils and difficulties, but one which may also spell excitement and even joy.

Eveline focuses on the colored print of the blessed Margaret Mary Alacoque (1647–1690), a saint connected with popular devotion in Ireland. French by birth, she was ascetic to the extreme, eating human dejecta in the hospitals in which she worked and inflicting torture upon herself in an *imitatio Christi*. Her masochism led to paralysis; her faith, she maintained, miraculously cured her. For Eveline, and the Irish in general, Saint Alacoque stands for sacrificial Catholicism and the purging of sin-ridden humanity—a psychological experience which many inhabitants of the Emerald Isle have been living for centuries.

Interestingly enough, Joyce's sister Margaret (note that her first name is the same as the saint's) was also saintly in her own way. At the age of twenty, she sacrificed herself to her family. She had wanted to become a nun, but because she had promised her mother on her deathbed to care for the children until they were older, she could not fulfill her own wishes for six more years. She took her vows in 1909, became a Sister of Mercy, and then sailed to a convent in New Zealand.[4] Stanislaus describes Margaret as follows:

> Poppie [Margaret's nickname] is the most unselfish person I know. She is obstinate and inclined to answer back a great deal, but she is gentle and takes the affairs of the house very much to heart. She seems to wish, if anyone is to suffer, that she should be the victim. What an extraordinary sense of duty women have![5]

Eveline also had a choice: to remain at home and care for her family in a saintly manner, or to give up her symbolical priesthood and sail forth into life. That the photographs of Saint Alacoque and the priest who went to Melbourne should have been placed next to each other on the wall, above "the broken harmonium," seems to be but a trivial detail; yet, it is of the utmost importance. Music and feeling come into play at this point, enabling Joyce to pass from a photographic reality to aesthetic impressionism, integrating an inner conflict through sensory apparatus.

A harmonium is a small keyboard organ in which tones are produced by forcing air through metal reeds by means of bellows operated by pedals. The word *harmonia*, or "harmony," identified with this instrument, ushers in a mood of agreement, coordination, and structure—not static or fixed, necessarily, but modulated, arranged in progressions and multiple rhythmic patterns. That the harmonium was broken suggests that the principle which had been in working order when the mother was alive, during that happy period the children spent playing in green fields, broke down or went askew after her death. In this instance, music represents the mother/feeling principle; although acquiescing and always yielding to the father's dictates, the mother was, nevertheless, a nourishing and protective force and a dispenser of love. Now that this element has been shorn away (that the harmonium is broken), only a negative *senex* (old) figure remains: a drunken, abusive, unfeeling, and parsimonious father.

As Eveline keeps "reviewing" her life and analyzing her future, she questions her desire to escape, weighing each factor against the other, and in so doing, always retaining that *c* note, that basic tonal structure, that tonic first sound which serves to ground and balance all the others. If she were to embark, she thinks, "she would not cry many tears at leaving the Stores." Here the dental *t* (tears), blended with the sibilant *s* (she) and the guttural and liquid *cr* (cry), gives the impression of choking, of having reached an impasse—like closures or impediments in the psychological sphere. Whatever course Eveline chooses, tears will be shed.

As she meditates about her imminent departure, her "new home, in a distant unknown country," and her marriage to Frank, the sailor she loves, her attitude grows increasingly defiant; her prose hardens, fortissimos are sounded during the course of her interior monologue. She will be treated "with respect," she reflects, not deprecated and abused as her mother had been, and as she is now by her father. These veiled disclosures introduce a new tonal quality: increasing self-awareness. Sounds coalesce with anger and fear. No longer will she have to stand her "father's violence"—it gives her "palpitations." Labials (*f, v, p*) usher in a climate of fear and grief, underscoring the negativity of her existence and her rejection of the destructive patriarchal force. During her mother's lifetime, she felt protected; her father had not threatened her; her brothers were there. Her anger mounts, as does the stridency of her inner tones. She lists her grievances: she gives her father her earnings, which he squanders on drink; he is so stingy she can barely make ends meet. (Margaret had also found it difficult to extract money from her father to buy food for the children.) It's "hard work" feeding the young, Eveline thinks. Rhythms accelerate; energy is expended. Whenever her father finally does hand her some money, she rushes out as rapidly as possible and does her marketing, clutching her "black leather purse tightly in her hand as she elbow[s] her way through the crowds." Combative intonations are conveyed by "tightly," "elbow," "crowds," and in the dentals, labials, liquids, and back palatals of these words. Eveline alters her passivity in this sequence. When she goes marketing, she forces her way through the crowd, instinctively protecting the smaller members of her family, like a lioness with her cubs. From the passive daughter she is transformed into an aggressive mother figure. Eveline has the potential to change her life.

Eveline's courage, however, begins to slacken. Although she admits that she has to work hard and leads a "hard life," having now decided to leave with Frank, the sailor, she does not find her life "wholly undesirable." Her thoughts wander to Frank, "the very kind, manly, open-hearted" young man with whom she plans to go away on "the night-boat." She will be his wife, and together they will live in Buenos Ayres—that is, *good air*— leaving the stuffy, dusty ("cretonne") atmosphere behind. The image of the night-boat brings to mind the adventures of Ulysses, who sailed the seas for ten long years. Navigation myths—for example, that of the Flying Dutchman, who would know forgiveness for his sins only through the love of a young girl—are indicative of rites of passage. The ship represents victory over the perils of the water; psychologically, it is the symbol of the triumph of consciousness over the powerful subliminal forces roaming about the collective unconscious.

Eveline recalls the first time she saw Frank, "standing at the gate, his peaked cap, pushed back on his head and his hair tumbled forward over a face of bronze." The labials, gutturals, and glottal fricatives used in the alliterations are associated iconographically with the hat and head, signifying a fusion of feeling and thinking functions; they also represent force and energy, the ability to change direction and to leave one frame of existence for another. Frank is determined and courageous, Eveline believes, as well as sincere, kind, and loving. He is a positive masculine figure, in contrast to the negative *senex* father. He stands for that force in Eveline's life which can help her escape from her rigidly framed world into a fluid and airy domain, leading her from a violent and dangerous sphere to one of beauty and love.

Frank is candid and honest, as his name indicates. He already extricated her temporarily from her humdrum existence when he took her to see the operetta *The Bohemian Girl*—an exciting and romantic work that included a kidnapping, a Prince Charming, a royal court, foreign lands, and so many more dream visions. One of many operettas written by the Irish composer Michael William Balfe (1808–1870), it has lilting refrains that usher feelings of love into Eveline's world, once again triggering her auditory imagination. She hears her inner voice flow in cadences in an interior monologue dictated by the rhythms and melodies of the operetta, following the beat of her heart and not merely those of duty and obligation. Euphony reigns in her being. The silence and sorrow ushered in by the image of the broken harmonium in her home have been dispelled by Balfe's sun-filled, whimsical melodies.

Eveline knew that people were aware of the fact that she and Frank "were courting"; and when "he sang about the lass that loves a sailor, she always felt pleasantly confused." The lyrics of the song and the opera, with which she identifies, suit the mood and situation. Music takes her out of herself; it also sustains the emotional impact which the operetta and the song made on her.

Singing has yet another allurement for Eveline: it triggers further associations with her desire to escape. Mention must be made of the fact that when Frank took her to the operetta he had her sit in a more expensive seat than she usually sat in, thus already introducing her to a whole new frame of reference. When present at *The Bohemian Girl*, she did not hear those familiar religious chants sung in church or the popular Irish jigs; she is exposed to what a young girl likes best: love. Frank inspires these feelings; he stimulates her dreams and imagination, until she begins to sing out

Balfe's melody in her own inner chamber—her rational world lulled by its tonalities.

As Eveline thinks back to Frank and his lively ditties, she experiences a spiritual and emotional *upheaval*, as if she were participating in a collective inhalation/exhalation. The wavering sounds and tremulous tones of Frank's voice, to which she listens in retrospect, echo like vibrating chords which give access to a supernatural world, wafting her into a dream sphere where the unconscious reigns. The city of Buenos Ayres—that distant place Frank has told her about—leaps into her mind. The excitement of the music motivates her to reject her circumscribed world. (Joyce himself said: "No one who has any self-respect stays in Ireland, but flees afar as though from a country that has undergone the visitation of an angered Jove.")[6]

Reality suddenly intrudes as Eveline recalls the time when her father had discovered "the affair" with Frank and "had forbidden her to have anything to say to him." (Let us recall that Joyce also had kept his departure for the Continent with his sweetheart Nora a secret from his father. So, too, had Joyce's grandparents done everything in their power to prevent John Joyce from marrying their daughter, Mary Jane Murray.)[7] Now "the evening deepen[s] in the avenue"; time comes to a close, so to speak. Eveline must decide. Darkness has made the handwriting indistinct on the two farewell letters she has prepared for her father and brother. All seems blurred as she once again retreats into the blackness of her subliminal world. She dwells on her old father again, with a twinge of regret: "He would miss her," she feels. There are times when he can be so nice: when she was ill a while back, he read to her; when their mother was alive, the family went on a picnic, and her father put on her mother's bonnet in a spirit of merriment.

Eveline sits transfixed in the window frame, unable to move. Once again, as at the outset of the story, she leans "her head against the window curtain, inhaling the odour of dusty cretonne." The tones of a "street organ" playing down the avenue make their way to her. Like the broken harmonium and *The Bohemian Girl*, they are authentic lyrical elements which mirror Eveline's psychological torment. A synchronistic event or a meaningful coincidence occurs here. "Strange that it should come that very night to remind her of the promise to her mother"—the promise that she would maintain the family home as long as possible. It is the street organ that takes her out of herself and places her forthcoming decision in perspective. She recalls the "melancholy air of Italy" that the "organ player" had played outside her mother's window the night she died. Italy, identified with adventure and romance, sun and joyous climes, is antithetical to all her father represents. In fact, on that long-ago night, he gave the musician sixpence to leave the vicinity; and strutting back into the dying woman's room, he said: "Damned Italians! coming over here!"

Italy holds the key to lyrical sensuality and passion. The cadences Eveline hears brings to mind love, health, excitement, and adventure, not a world of sacrifice, sickness, and dementia. Her mother did become insane at the end, repeating nonsensical words: "Deveraun, Seraun! Deveraun Seraun!" These auditory impressions made inroads into Eveline's fiber, cloying, gripping, and nailing her to the cross of sorrow in life.

The combination of Balfe's operetta and the song Frank sang to her, as well as the street organ's melodies, which she associates both with romance and her mother's death, unleashes powerful forces within Eveline. Her auditory imagination overwhelms her: she feels dizzy and unbound, and she stands up "in a sudden impulse of terror." There are no glottal stops to bar her way toward life: liquid (l, r) sounds predominate; feelings of anger, as in the dental sibilants (s, t), propel her on. She rushes toward her savior, Frank, to escape from a life of interdiction to a world of love.

Eveline arrives at the station at the North Wall, where she is to meet Frank and then sail away with him. No inner monologue or stream-of-consciousness sequence is given here. Her libido (psychic energy) is so powerfully charged that it blocks out all thought patterns, values, associations, impressions, tonalities, and even feelings. Her instinct of self-preservation alone dictates her actions, forces her along, compels her to reach out into the world, to sing her song. Like Senta in *The Flying Dutchman*, she, too, yearns to follow her lover to the ends of the earth.

The sound effects reach crescendo force: polyphonic prose takes precedence as Eveline enters the station filled with soldiers and baggage. She hears hard, hammering noises of opening and shutting doors; she sees "the black mass of the boat, lying in beside the quay wall, with illumined portholes." The ship's portholes now play the role of the window in the opening passage: they dazzle as they offer Eveline a world beyond her wildest expectations. The sea beckons to her to immerse herself in its salubrious waters. She must choose. She hears the whistle; it signals a summoning of her inner energy. The ship will move out of the harbor in minutes, into the expanse of the sea, and she will be on it with Frank, her love—her only hope. Like a cosmic breath, the strident whistle is the sign of a change of orientation. It is *pneuma*—a spiritual force crying out to her to seek the new, to carve out a life for herself, and to awaken what has been dormant for years.

"A bell clanged upon her heart," adding to the already potent inner activity and calling her to freedom. Or does Eveline interpret the clanging sounds as those of a church bell, replicating those polyphonic modes and sonorities that prolong a culture gone awry?

Frank calls to her and seizes her hand. "Come!" he says. The *epiphany* now occurs. Joyce has labeled this literary technique, which he used with such felicity, as a "sudden spiritual manifestation" brought on by a remark or symbolic event that clarifies the meaning of the complex experience taking place. A gesture, word, or figure of speech can trigger such a memorable experience. Joyce defines the "eucharistic" feeling of an epiphany, which he borrowed from religious ritual, as follows:

> Don't you think there is a certain resemblance between the mystery of the Mass and what I am trying to do? I mean that I am trying . . . to give people some kind of intellectual pleasure or spiritual enjoyment by converting the bread of everyday life into something that has a permanent artistic life of its own . . . for their mental, moral, and spiritual uplift.[8]

The epiphany occurs as Frank reaches out for Eveline. The mysterious curtains which blocked her view of the outside and inside worlds have thickened. Her hopelessly embroiled situation takes a decisive turn, as it must. Her ego retreats into the deepest spheres of her being: her collective unconscious. When, therefore, Frank calls her again, some part of her—an autonomous, unrecognizable voice—answers, "No! No! No!" It is impossible; it can never be. She stands there paralyzed, frozen, catatonic. Her hands clutch the iron bars. "Amid the seas she sen[ds] a cry of anguish!" Gutturals, labials, fricatives, glottal stops ring out: "clutch," "cry," "call," "come," "grip."

Eveline resists the call to life; she repulses the call of the flesh and heart. She grips the gate, forcing her hands to grasp those iron bars as tightly as possible, to make certain she will not escape with Frank. Only by rejecting the outside world of clean air can she live with her shriveled, undeveloped, and unawakened self. A negative *senex* figure grips Eveline's psyche. Browbeaten and church-indoctrinated, she is shot through with terror. Her face turns white; she has become a passive, "helpless animal," divested of all individuality and all personality. Her eyes glare and stare; they are fixed and transfixed, emotionless and feelingless. Like her mother, she has become insane. The folly of sacrifice and martyrdom—like that of Margaret Mary Alacoque—is so deeply embedded in her spirit and psyche that life, sun, and clean air give way to rot, depression, and dust. Eveline recognizes nothing; she hears nothing. Her eyes give Frank "no sign of love or farewell or recognition." She is—as at the outset of the story—incarcerated behind, not a window this time, but a fence, a wall, and iron bars. She is framed in the quiescent retrograde traditions of her contemporaries. The "broken harmonium" is to reign in her world—not the melancholy Italian love ditties played by the organ grinder, nor the romantic refrains of Frank's song, nor those of *The Bohemian Girl.*

Stylistically, Joyce's musical devices (emphasis on background noises, prosodic techniques including complex uses of figures of speech, phonemes, and their psychologically significant imagistic equivalents), his staccato or sustained intonations, which trigger inner monologue and stream-of-consciousness sequences, are used to foster feelings and ideations. Joyce's pacing of sonants is interwoven into the fabric of the tale, functioning like fugal and polyphonic interludes in order to increase tension, particularly during the flashback sequences or projections onto future happenings. Such interludes also accentuate the static, ingrained, and hopelessly senescent quality of Eveline's world. The flavor of the experiences conveyed through the different voices—the father's harsh, brittle tones, the happy cries of children at play, the clanging of the bells, the crunching of footsteps—increases the pain of Eveline's choice. Music is that vital force which links character and theme, space and time, climate and ideation—diatonically and synchronistically—in the orchestrated masterpiece which is "Eveline."

7 Proust's *Remembrance of Things Past:* Archetypal Music, an Exercise in Transcendence

Archetypal music was used by Marcel Proust as a literary device throughout *Remembrance of Things Past;* it also became an enticement for some of his protagonists to experience conditions of transcendence. Archetypal music may be defined as clusters of sound waves interwoven into specific patterns, which are turned into electrical impulses and then transmitted through the auditory nerve to the brain. The impact of certain vibrations on two of Proust's protagonists (Charles Swann, an art connoisseur and dilettante, and the Narrator, a creative writer-to-be) was so powerful as to trigger contents in their collective unconscious—the deepest folds within the psyche, which are usually inaccessible to conscious awareness.

Proust transliterated musical interludes into verbal images and motifs that swept his two auditors into new dimensions, inviting them to experience deeper levels of reality and altered states of consciousness. During such moments, feelings floated unhampered and unassailable, the limitations imposed by the rational sphere having vanished. The tones, rhythms, amplitudes, breadth, and swell created by Proust's accompanying verbalized forms, shapes, and colorations fostered a climate of reverie. The ineffable joy, as well as the lacerating anguish experienced by Swann and the Narrator, no longer empirically, but in a four-dimensional universe, disclosed certain personality traits. When the affective reactions brought on by the melodious sequences slackened and consciousness returned, the two protagonists alighted from their celestial or infernal inner journeys emboldened by their perceptions and clarified in their attitudes.

Not only did a specific piece of music take on archetypal power for Swann, but it clothed itself in the contours of an *anima figure:* the personi-

fication of the feminine principle in man. Swann identified music/anima
with the woman he loved; it had the power to evoke past situations—both
blissful and painful. So obsessed with and dependent upon this archetypal
music did he become, that it acted on him as a narcotic, which he used to
dull or heighten his senses. The Narrator, on the other hand, also experienced certain musical sequences in terms of a past love, but their suggestive power led in his case to greater self-awareness. It encouraged him to
decode the mysteries and encode the secret networks of relationships hidden within the auditive interludes. He became, it could be said, a
cryptanalyst, studying the wizardry of sound, its gestural and literary
expressions, and its vibratory and incantatory powers.

That the magic of sound should have taken on archetypal magnitude in
Proust's novel is not surprising. He had always been captivated by music,
not only for the emotions it actuated in him, but also for philosophical,
aesthetic, and scientific reasons. Music was a way for him to penetrate the
hidden meanings of things, people, and events. It paralleled emotional
states; it enabled him to slip into mythical modes of consciousness. Like a
mantra, music allowed him to feel attuned to the universe.

How could music accomplish such feats? Notes, which are resonant
bodies having their own frequency ratios, are made up of vibrating particles of matter which collide and interact with each other. As they fly forth
into a spaceless and timeless sphere, they are continuously being transformed. When listening to instrumentalists, the ear and brain react to
overtones, harmonies, cacophonies, and rhythms which come within their
range; their multi-voiced messages make inroads on the psyche.

Since sound modulations emptying out into spatial spheres cannot, according to modern physics, be separated from time, we must include time
in our discussion (see p. 115). Time, as we know, obsessed Proust. *Remembrance of Things Past* (the literal translation of the first and last sections of
the novel being *In Search of Lost Time* and *Time Recaptured*) attests to this
preoccupation. Indeed, the entire novel may be regarded as Proust's investi-
gation into a space-time continuum. He could not accept the fact that
everything one experiences during one's life simply vanishes, that time just
flows away and nothing remains. Although existence may be regarded
realistically as a constant struggle against physical erosion (the alterations
the body undergoes as one grows old), changing relationships, and changing economic, political, and aesthetic conditions, something must nevertheless remain. To believe that people have their hour on earth and then
are heard no more is to consider life linearly or empirically and to remove
it from a larger scheme of things. For Proust, fourth-dimensional time was
to be experienced cyclically or mythically, memory being a key factor.

Proust described two types of memory: *voluntary recall* and *involuntary recall.* The former is relatively superficial: it brings facts, dates, and events to the surface. This type of recall is accompanied by a sharp realization of the gap between the present and the past. For example, if you try to relive a happy childhood experience by returning to an old house that you loved in your youth, you may be overwhelmed by emptiness and sadness instead of experiencing the expected elation. The house has changed and you have changed, and the perception is acutely painful. Instead of the warmth, conviviality, and joy that characterized the original experience you seek to recapture, you are faced with desolation, stemming from a linear time experience, which is divided into past, present, and future; birth, growth, and decay. As such, linear time becomes a depleter of earthly days and an inimical destroyer.

Involuntary recall, based on intuition, is quite different. It allows an individual to transcend the world of contingencies and enter into a fourth dimension, which we may call, in psychological terminology, the *collective unconscious.* Proust's Narrator tells us how he discovered involuntary recall—a condition which revolutionized his whole way of thinking and consequently his whole approach to life and art. One overcast winter afternoon in Paris, the Narrator returned to his apartment. Since there was a chill in the air, his mother offered him a cup of tea and some cakes called *petites madeleines.* Dejected by the prospect of a "sad tomorrow," he put his spoon into the tea, into which he had already put part of his madeleine. When he filled his spoon with the mixture and put it into his mouth, something *incredible* happened. "A delicious pleasure invaded me, isolated, without any notion of its cause."[1] No longer did he consider himself a mediocre victim of a vanishing world. This "precious essence" had filled him with an ineffable joy; some power had taken hold of him. He began musing about the experience, took another spoonful, then another. Finally he realized that an entire segment of his past had catapulted into his present reality. What was it? He felt he was back at his aunt's country house in Combray, where he used to spend his summer vacations as a child. Every Sunday morning she offered him madeleines, which he dipped into an herbal tea. Now, many years later, the warmth of these recollections dispelled his mournfulness and ushered in a sense of well-being.

Sometime after this wonderful experience, the Narrator realized that such "privileged moments" were triggered by his senses: taste, sight, smell, feeling, and hearing. The involuntary recall mechanism, unlike voluntary recall, was not linked to the rational domain of intelligence, but rather to the unconscious—the world of perception and intuition. The tea and madeleine had stimulated his taste buds, arousing contents that lived inchoate in his collective unconscious. An orchestration of memories came to the fore, affording him the luxury of regressing into another space-time period. On other occasions, the sight of an object, a whiff of perfume, the touch of a smooth or rough surface, or the sound of a melody would likewise provoke impressions stored in his collective unconscious. When these sensations and visualizations flowed into consciousness, they not only brought back sequences of his past but integrated these segments into his present reality, thereby enriching his existence by broadening and deepening it. A past had been conquered; it had become a living and present reality. "As there is a geometry in space," Proust wrote, "there is a psychology in time."

For Proust's Narrator, involuntary recall was a way of vanquishing change and of experiencing a modicum of serenity. Certain musical sequences worked on his auditory faculties (and those of Charles Swann as well). Specific melodies aroused involuntary recall, diverting these listeners from the world of contingencies, which they found painful and banal. Like the mystics of old, they felt inundated with feelings of transcendence.

Although Proust mentions many composers in *Remembrance of Things Past*—Beethoven, Wagner, Mozart, Schumann, Liszt, Debussy, Gluck, Faure, and others—we are concerned here with compositions written by M. Vinteuil, a creature of Proust's fantasy, though he is in part modeled on César Franck.[2] In the two musical interludes to be explored, Proust uses the technique of involuntary recall metaphorically and analogically. Tone, pitch, rhythm, and silence are all embedded in the very fabric of his words and phrases; syntax is altered to change the harmonies or cacophonies. By his positioning of adjectives, adverbs, conjunctions, and prepositions and by means of other grammatical devices and figures of speech, he transforms thoughts and emotions, creating a spectacularly exciting verbal musical experience.

Vinteuil's Sonata

The elegant dilettante and art connoisseur Charles Swann is invited to the home of the very bourgeois Verdurins by the beautiful Odette de Crécy, who is one of their frequent guests. That evening, Swann listens to a pianist playing a composition he heard the year before at someone else's gathering. He remembers having been entranced by it, and at the time he made inquiries as to the composer's name. His search, however, proved fruitless. What so impressed him was the catalytic power of the tones: as the violinist and pianist performed, strange images came to his mind's eye. He could literally see sound, the "delicate, unyielding, substantial and governing line of the violin"; he envisaged the piano harmonies as masses of liquid, wavelike and "mauve," displacing each other as their agitated rhythms were "charmed and minored [*bémolisé*] by the moonlight" (p. 208). Symbolically speaking, one could say that the piano, massive and fixed as compared to the portable violin, represented the more passionate instinctual realm and stood for human relationships in the workaday world; whereas the fragile, aerial tonalities of the violin were identified with more sublimated and spiritual spheres. In that the violin and piano represented a couple, they perhaps preluded the psychological experience that Swann and Odette were yet to live.

It is at the Verdurins' that Swann learns the names of the composer (Vinteuil) and the composition (Sonata for Piano and Violin in F-sharp). Thus, the musical composition is given empirical reality and identity. What impresses him most deeply on second hearing, however, are a few bars in the andante movement. He keeps listening to these measures in his mind, filtering out the rest of the music and hence endowing this section—"the little phrase," as he calls it—with special status. When he hears this same air on succeeding evenings at the Verdurins', it takes on not only quantitative but qualitative value. It seems to lift him out of his conventional and individual existence and plunge him into transpersonal spheres. Time is no longer a series of disparate instances; it is linked and contiguous, like sound waves distilled in patterned sequences, fusing psychological phenomena organized around a group of notes. He feels transformed by the tones he hears, as if something within him were tapped; he no longer feels isolated and solitary, but rather part of a group—related. That images are also triggered by the muscial interlude encourages him to bask in a world of unending phantasmagorias and expanding universes. He perceives himself awakening to new dimensions, opening up to fresh sensations, able to breathe freely and to absorb the inexpressible feelings of the moment. His emotions parallel those expressed in the music. Its pace and melody are at first hesitant, then circle about in all of their transparency. As they grow in amplitude, a singular power seems to take hold of him in an until now inexplicable way. He is undergoing a synesthetic experience, which catalyzes his nerve endings, sweeping him into an undifferentiated mythical sphere where audible vibrations take on concretion.

The sensations aroused by the organized sequences of notes Swann hears have in fact sent signals to his brain, which he experiences in terms of color, form, odor, opacity, and liquidity, giving him the impression that the musical interlude has taken on an existence and consistency of its own. Indeed, it has. "The little phrase" is for him *archetypal*; it has become a universal power, with its own timbre, pace, color, and personality. It invites Swann to penetrate its virtualities. It is no wonder, then, that he *sees* it approach "after a high note held on through two whole bars . . . stealing forth from underneath that resonance, which [is] prolonged and stretched out over it, like a curtain of sound, to veil the mystery of its birth." He recognizes, "secret, whispering, articulate, the airy and fragrant phrase" that he loves (p. 211). It is unique, yet it is universal and collective. As Swann muses on its rhythms and its high and low notes, his feeling-tones ascend and descend, dilate and diminish, in keeping with the intensity of the vibrations. He metaphorizes his feelings, comparing them to perfumed roses opening up to the "humid night air." The emotional confusion brought on by "the little phrase" has diminished his rational outlook, allowing him to begin his descent into transpersonal folds.

As Swann listens, he interiorizes, and *libido* (psychic energy) flows inward, nourishing his unconscious and catalyzing a whole subliminal sphere. His *ego*, that factor within the psyche that relates to both outer and inner worlds, is still sufficiently objective to ask certain questions. The music he has just heard has already disappeared; why and how can it still work its miracle upon him? Has it really vanished? We may suggest that these sound waves, after their initial impact, simply became inaudible to the human ear. Weren't they still present as uninterrupted progressions inhabiting an invisible, unexplored, and silent domain? According to Newtonian physics, musical notes existing in the empirical world do vanish, since change is considered in terms of a separate dimension called time, which proceeds unalterably from past to present toward the future. However, the concept of an unchangeable, universal flow of time, as posited by the Newtonian model, was disproved in 1905 by Einstein and his theory of relativity and twenty years later by the quantum theory.[3]

Einstein suggested that neither space nor time is separate. On the contrary, they are linked in a four-dimensional continuum. Hence, the flow of time is not to be looked upon as divided into a past, present, and future. Space-time factors are the outcome of individual observations and calculations and are not absolute, but relative. When this view of the world was first put forth, it was so revolutionary that the individual's approach to existence had to be reconsidered: mass had to be looked upon as a form of energy and not as something distinct and fixed. That all objects have energy stored in their mass was proved by Einstein in his equation $E = mc^2$ (c being the speed of light). By 1915 Einstein had included gravity ("the mutual attraction of all massive bodies") in his theory: time, which cannot be separated from space, is also affected by matter, which moves about at various rates in various parts of the universe.[4]

Such concepts, which may or may not have been known to Proust, were intuited by him aesthetically. They are fundamental to the literary and psychological structure of his novel. Sound, as we have already pointed out, is a composite of vibrating particles of matter which move about in a space-time continuum; a four-dimensional sphere which is comparable to the collective unconscious. The tremolos, high-pitched notes, and lower registers heard by Swann act like magical rituals for him, serving as preambles to passion, ecstasy, and tragedy. The perpetually altering frequencies of the sound waves in "the little phrase" work on his nerves, and understandably, since we know that sound can break glass, deafen, and even kill. Therefore, when Swann listens to the musical interlude, it is not surprising to find him describing himself as "submerged," "liquefied," and "enveloped" by the very essence of sonance.

He associates the musical interlude with his beloved idol, Odette de Crécy, who psychologically takes on the stature of an *anima figure*. In time, "the little phrase" becomes more important to him than the flesh-and-blood woman—understandably so, since an anima is an autonomous force and, as an archetype, is endowed with energetic power capable of triggering the involuntary recall system. Because of its very special virtue, Swann compares "the little phrase" to "a laborer who works at laying down a durable foundation in the midst of waves" (p. 209).

When experiencing an anima projection unconsciously, one may become its victim and fall subject to moods of all types. In Swann's case, his moods range from giddiness to pathos. On succeeding evenings at the Verdurins', Swann greets "the little phrase" as a voluptuous presence—a warm and tantalizing force which caresses and cajoles him. An autonomous power, as are all archetypes, this anima/music leads him to feel that he, too, is invested with special qualities, which enable him to grasp the very essence of the notes, beats, and measures and to draw their contours in arabesques, circles, and arches, computing them, as would an architect or mathematician, in terms of their height, depth, intensity, and timbre.

As his need for the anima/music intensifies, he grows increasingly dependent upon it. At times his ego even becomes overwhelmed by its resonance and reverberations. When he is at home, for example, or in the company of others, he may suddenly feel a need for "the little phrase" which parallels an addict's longing for narcotics. At such times, Swann's thinking function vanishes, limitations imposed upon him in the world of contingencies are dispelled, and he floats into transpersonal spheres: his ego weakens during these forays, as is to be expected, since it is living in a virtually static condition, fed constantly by the music/anima, never having to fend for itself. Swann confesses that these musical interludes deliver him from any kind of biological attachment; he feels himself drifting and weightless in some pleromatic sphere, experiencing the unlived and the unlivable, in a fantasy world where no distinctions exist between subject and object, mind and flesh. As Swann plunges ever deeper into his collective unconscious, virtually mesmerized by the music/anima, subliminal contents are re-forming, reconstituting, and recomposing themselves in keeping with their own laws and rituals. There are times when Swann feels himself ennobled, heightened by the lulling and pitching cadences of the music, the rapid and slackening visualizations which follow, and the sonorous and energetic patterns which come into existence; at other moments, he undergoes feelings of tenderness and melancholia, euphoria and wistfulness—introducing new perspectives and fresh vistas.

As his dependency upon "this unalterable essence" increases, so do his feelings of possessiveness toward it. He can no longer do without his music/anima. He looks upon it, Proust suggests metaphorically, as a companion and as a lover: he is "like a man into whose life a woman, whom he has seen for a moment passing by, has brought a new form of beauty, which strengthens and enlarges his own power of perception, without his knowing even whether he is ever to see her again whom he loves already, although he knows nothing of her, not even her name" (*SW*, p. 300).

The archetypal musical phrase has still other magical virtues: it can, Swann feels, rejuvenate him. In its presence, he feels able to regress into a space-time continuum and bathe in his own past—cleansed, joyful, ready and able to start life anew. The phrase can transform something which has grown arid into a richly giving force. Swann wonders at first whether these feelings of renewal might be due to some "elective influence." How else, he questions, could these tonalities inundate him with such a sense of youthful vigor? What power do they hold? When he visualizes the pianist in his mind's eye and hears "the little phrase," he "recognizes" the long sustained notes which last for two bars, and as he watches them "approach," then escape from beneath long, flowing sounds, it is as if they are reaching out to grasp a "sonorous curtain," turning up its edges ever so slightly so that they can penetrate the very heart of mystery (p. 211). So captivated is he by the phrase's "airy and fragrant" nature that he decides to learn its language and the secrets embedded in its vibrations—that axis which generates so many of his emotions. Like a hierophant preparing for an initiation ceremony, Swann approaches the musical construct once again, with the glow, warmth, and anticipation of sheer rapture. He feels himself gliding into the grouped sounds, experiencing a *participation mystique*. Gone are his identity and individuality. His purified and revivified ego, encapsulated in primordial spheres, is lulled still further into endlessly profound, dim or brilliantly aerated corridors. "Unknown perspectives" and unfathomable worlds of mobile, tactile, and tremulously exciting sensations open up to him.

It is characteristic of the *puer aeternus* personality type to long for aerated and diffused spheres, midway between heaven and earth, where formlessness and open spaces provide a sense of liberation from all commitment. Swann is indeed a *puer aeternus*, yielding to inner needs and impulses without ever really considering the consequences of his acts or objectifying his situations. An eternal adolescent, perpetually wandering in and out of relationships, moody, and frequently subject to a sense of overwhelming despair, Swann is incapable of assessing himself, evolving, or maturing. Rather than deal directly with problems at hand and his difficulties with Odette, he seeks refuge in the archetypal music—that anima figure which acts as a pacifier or escape mechanism, encouraging him to seek answers in flights of fantasy and dream, always elsewhere and at some future date.

As Swann's relationship with Odette grows increasingly intense, "the little phrase" acts as a support for him; it represents "the national anthem of their love" (p. 218). The sustained tones, the tremolos, and the slackening or accelerating harmonies order and concretize his feelings, sealing them off from the ordinary world. A canvas by a seventeenth-century Dutch painter of interiors, Pieter de Hooch, comes to Swann's mind: a narrow door, slightly ajar, framed by varying luminosities, among which Swann visualizes "the little phrase" dancing about in a kind of pastoral, discontinuous, "episodic" ambiance, as if it belonged "to another world," so different and so utterly enchanting. Feelings of "disenchantment" and "regret" follow this inner representation (p. 218).

Swann's vision of Pieter de Hooch's canvas may be considered a premonitory image: the door, the long hall, and the play of light reveal his waning love for Odette. Although he is consciously unaware of the painting's message, it implies a man deprived of sustenance, divested of that rich black earth with all its nutrients that comes with deepening affection and increased understanding of one partner for another. He, the *puer aeternus*, hovers about like a gadfly, and she tries to suck out what she can from every man who falls under her sway, thereby assuring her own economic well-being.

"This is *our* piece," Swann tells Odette, as he looks at the pianist's fingers flying over the keyboard. Indeed, like the Great Mother of old, the music/anima seems to want to embrace him and endow him with feelings of serenity and warmth; but at other moments, it takes on the contours of a "fantastic unicorn, a chimerical creature" (p. 237). As Swann follows "the little phrase" down the dismal and obscure halls of his psyche, depriving himself still further of his logical faculties, he can see the musical interlude filtering and distilling its images in seemingly endless vortices, in sound waves, sheets, and particles. He, responding to their implosions, feels the music's skin tones, its rhythmic breathing, its ebullience, and its threnodies. This complex of mass, contour, and tone, dilating his impressions and arousing them to a hyperactive state, allows him to peer into archaic dimensions where the temporal cohabits with the atemporal, where his faltering ego looks back, longingly, to those early days of his love for Odette, when kisses were so natural and life so authentic (p. 238).

Sometime later, at the home of the class-conscious Mme de Sainte-Euverte, Swann undergoes another transcendental experience. Odette's type—the kept woman—is never invited here. Swann knows this, and yet, as he enters Mme de Sainte-Euverte's home, he experiences feelings of disquietude. Later, when listening to Vinteuil's sonata, he grows sad. A vision of Odette floats into his mind's eye—warm, beautiful, and glowing. As he looks around at the other guests—"stupid," banal, their monstrous "monocles" masking their real intent—he suddenly feels something warm and ingratiating come toward him. It is "the little phrase"—anima/ Odette—approaching him. This apparition is so traumatic and causes him such feelings of uneasiness that he puts "his hand toward his heart," as if to ward off further pain.

> What had happened was that the violin had risen to a series of high notes, on which it rested as though expecting something, an expectancy which it prolonged without ceasing to hold onto the notes, in the exaltation with which it already saw the expected object approaching, and with a desperate effort to continue until its arrival, to welcome it before itself expired, to keep the way open for a moment longer, with all its remaining strength, that the stranger might enter in, as one holds a door open that would otherwise automatically close. And before Swann had had time to understand what was happening, to think: "It is the little phrase from Vinteuil's sonata. I mustn't listen!" all his memories of the days when Odette had been in love with him, which he had succeeded, up till that evening, in keeping invisible in the depths of his being, deceived by this sudden reflection of a season of love, whose sun, they supposed, had dawned again, had awakened from their slumber, had taken wing and risen to sing maddeningly in his ears, without pity for his present desolation, the forgotten strains of happiness. (*SW*, p. 496)

The dichotomy between Swann's feelings and the empirical situation— as depicted by metaphors, metonymies, altering tenses, and sonorous and rhythmic meanderings—parallels Swann's own quixotic relational patterns. Embedded in a world of imponderables, probabilities, and interconnected processes where events rather than individuals are emphasized, he is no longer merely a participant in a love affair, but is imbricated in a whole network of tonal, visual, vibrational, philosophical, and psychological factors, each insinuating its way into the black and white piano keys fingered by the musician.

The violin is frequently singled out for scrutiny: it may be looked upon as a transforming agent and a bridge between the heard and the unheard, the inner and outer worlds, feelings and thoughts, illusion and reality. It also takes on, perhaps more than other instruments, the amplitude of a voice or the murmur of a cry. It includes a human quality in its oscillating glissandos, its tonal nuances, and the velvety touch of its modulations. The violin has been looked upon as a paradigm of the androgyne; its feminine curves and the phalluslike handle represent the coupling of Swann and Odette. For Swann, it reveals "pure unfolding"; it is the mysterious container of an "invisible message" (p. 347). This boxlike instrument takes on numinosity, not only because of its androgynous qualities but because the sounds emanating from it resemble incantations and threnodies, filling the heart and lungs with plenitude and wonderment. It belongs to "an ultra-violet world," or a transpersonal sphere. As for "the little phrase" which emerges, it is comparable to a "protective deity" in whose love one has confidence because it singles out one among many to whom to speak, ever so caressingly. Proust writes of Swann's encounter with this deity/phrase:

> And as she passed him, light, soothing, as softly murmured as the perfume of a flower, telling him what she had to say, every word of which he closely scanned, sorry to see them fly away so fast, he made involuntarily with his lips the motion of kissing, as it went by him, the harmonious fleeting form. (*SW*, p. 500)

The sounds emanating from the violin, and those more liquid sonorities intoned by the piano, speak their own hermetic language, which agitates, petrifies, distends, materializes, and dematerializes Swann's sensations. He now realizes that music has become for him a "Synthesis of the Infinite"—a mythology, a religion with its own laws and rituals to be adhered to by one who seeks to be admitted to transcendental spheres (*SW*, p. 535). Archetypal music is a bridge to a buried world which exists inchoate in his collective unconscious: the "great impenetrable and discouraging night of our soul which we look upon as void and as nothingness," but which in reality is filled with infinite and incommensurable waves of energy packets and endless seas of imponderables (p. 345).

Vinteuil's Septet

Listening to Vinteuil's unpublished septet, the Narrator identifies the archetypal music with a love episode (in his case, with Albertine), but, perhaps more important for an incipient writer, the music is linked with *Idea*. He experiences music more conceptually than Swann does; its reverberations and essences are approached intellectually, to fulfill both psychological and literary needs.

The septet does convey "the intermittencies of the heart," particularly after the Narrator learns that Albertine has had a friendship with another woman. As was true for Swann, archetypal music parallels the Narrator's feelings of love, jealousy, suspicion, and rage. A transformation, or perhaps an intellectualization of his approach to music, occurs one afternoon as he is waiting for Albertine. He begins meditating on music in general and discovers that such a process helps him "descend into himself." His conclusion—that music is a tool for self-discovery—affords him the excitement of penetrating a fourth dimension and experiencing what mystics have termed the "unity of being" that relates them to the vastness of infinity.

For the Narrator music, which has been connected to the "richness" of Swann's soul, is linked in Platonic terms to the *Idea:* a transcendent universal substance (p. 349). Archetypal music, then, reflects another world and a different order of being, which can never be understood by an adherent of Cartesian logic. As the Narrator experiences sound-producing particles of various intensities and dimensions, distinct and unequal in their values, and feels them caressing him and enveloping him in their perfumed being, he becomes aware of the fact that the five notes included in "the little phrase" and the repetition of two of them, each separated by silence, enclose him in "refracted and chilly" tenderness. He understands that his reasoning faculties cannot be called into play and are incapable of explaining the mystery which he has experienced. The seven-note scale, as it exists in the empirical domain, simply cannot replicate the "incommensurable," unknown, invisible sphere that separates the known from the unknown—those "thick" and "unexplored shadows," those "air-pockets with their several million tender, passionate notes." For Swann, each modulation had brought about feeling-tones and intuitive forays. For the Narrator, though he is perceptive and sensual as well, the thinking function is more highly developed. Mind apprehends the Idea and singles out the concepts involved in the creation of the work of art. To experience the transcendental, therefore, is not sufficient for the Narrator; it must be transmuted into *praxis* (action) in order to nourish him as a writer.

At the Verdurins' one evening, the Narrator, who does not recognizes any of the themes in Vinteuil's septet, feels alienated, alone, and exiled from the madding crowd. Soon, however, he encounters *it;* "like a magical apparition," he feels it enveloping him, harnessing him in its silverness, "glittering with brilliant effects of sound, as light and soft as silken scarves" (III:249). It comes toward him, and he recognizes it in its new garb. The Narrator feels happy, as if he were meeting an old and trusted friend. But even this foray into a world where he feels so much more at ease does not satisfy him. He apprehends "the little phrase" as one does a sign or a symbol which points the way. His goal is to ferret out the direction he must take and be guided by this musical sequence. Like Swann, the Narrator is engulfed in a panoply of tonalities, but, unlike the former, he dwells in an orchestration of sounds, pitches, and intensities, and each of the instruments (cello, two violins, piano, harp, flute, oboe) is endowed with a personality of its own—as if he has penetrated a kind of no-man's-land. For example, he observes:

> The violinist dominated the instrument which he clutched between his knees, bowing his head to which its coarse features gave, in moments of mannerism, an involuntary expression of disgust; he leaned over it, fingered it with the same domestic patience with which he might have plucked a cabbage, while by his side the harpist (a mere girl) in a short skirt, bounded on either side by the lines of her golden quadrilateral like those which, in the magic chamber of a Sibyl, would arbitrarily denote the other, according to the consecrated rules, seemed to be going in quest, here and there, at the point required, of an exquisite sound, just as though, a little allegorical deity, placed in front of the golden trellis of the heavenly vault, she were gathering, one by one, its stars. (*SW*, p. 555)

One might say that the Narrator, who listens to the septet most intently, looks upon it as a kind of cauldron or urn which contains all of Vinteuil's previous themes, airs, refrains, but in refined and sublimated form. The septet, then, is his quintessential work, the Narrator concludes. Prior to its composition, Vinteuil had spent his time exploring themes and melodies, working them out as the writer does when putting his first book together. Timidly, then with greater vigor and confidence, Vinteuil singled out what he felt to be vital to his work, leaving aside those parts which were not fit for a magnum opus. Note upon note seemed to have been extracted from the as yet "unknown universe," torn "from the silence of the night," imbued in some magical way with a hierarchy of colorations and nuanced forms (p. 250).

That the Narrator labels Vinteuil's masterpiece "the *reddening* Septet," and his earlier work "the *white* Sonata," is of utmost significance (p. 255). Red may be identified with the creative process, since it is a paradigm of the life force: blood. It may also be likened to fire, which, for the alchemists, was the catalyzing element that burned off impurities from an underlying element, the diamond, allowing it to shine and glow in all of its unsullied splendor.

Perhaps the alchemists, those early scientists, knew best how to express the "reddening" process, or *rubedo*, in their operations. *Rubedo*, or flame, was the last phase prior to the creation of the philosophers' stone, considered the earthly counterpart of the sun, or perfection. The fire burned intensely in the *athanor*, the alchemist's oven, and during that time matter was transformed from its "leaden" to its "golden" condition; the black carbon became the resplendently brilliant diamond. The same may be said of the secrets buried within the mind and psyche of the composer and the writer. Those factors that exist in potential must be put through the "ordeal by fire" so that the essence of the work—the masterpiece— remains, and all other variations, themes, asides, and peripheral meanderings fall by the wayside.

That the Narrator associates Vinteuil's sonata with white, or the *albedo* operation, is also noteworthy. It was during the "whitening" phase that the alchemist washed, purified, and triturated his amalgams, thereby ridding matter of everything that was not essential to it. White represents absence rather than consummation; it also denotes the beginning or dawn of a work or experience. In Vinteuil's case, his early compositions held promise; they were "timid" interrogations, impressions, and "supplications," which haunted and mesmerized Swann.

For the Narrator, music—and art forms in general—encourages him to develop his potential as a writer by capturing as many experiences in life as his senses can apprehend and then distilling and purifying them. The metaphor of the sun's rays beating down on a windowpane, which, like a prism, decomposes and recomposes them in spectacular multicolored tonalities, illustrates most perfectly the dialectic existing between the created and the uncreated: the work to be written and the one already composed.

Music, as we have seen, is a catalyst for the Narrator. It permits him to project his inner riches onto the world of contingencies and integrate what his involuntary recall system has aroused within him. As he consciously assesses what he has gleaned from the past and from even anterior existences, he conceptualizes, objectifies, and analyzes. It must be noted also that he continuously questions every nuance of his ideations and sensations—everything that might expand his consciousness and deepen his understanding of the creative process. "If art were only a prolongation of life, would it be worth sacrificing anything for it?" he asks. And his answer is: "Wasn't it as unreal as itself?" (p. 57). The uniqueness of a work of art—the music given to society by great composers, or an author's novel, poem, or play—"is a proof of the irreducibly individual existence of the soul" (*SW*, p. 558).

Nor is it strange that the Narrator should refer to himself as a kind of Fallen Angel, who, after experiencing the sublime heights to which

Vinteuil's quintessential music has propelled him, returns to the banality of everyday existence. Indeed, he is a Fallen Angel—a Lucifer ("Light Bringer"), a Satan ("Adversary")—offering to humanity in the form of the written word the forbidden fruits he has discovered during his forays into the heart of mystery. As a Fallen Angel, he has to struggle in the world of matter, banality, and dross. To transliterate the visions produced by Vinteuil's music requires discipline, confrontation, and excoriating pain.

Once ejected from the transcendent sphere to which Vinteuil's music had swept him, the Narrator can no longer enjoy the condition referred to by the Epicureans as *ataraxia:* serenity. His reintegration into what he looks upon as the ugly and sordid world leads him to reflect still further on the "Meaning of Music" for the writer. Certainly, music could "have made for a communication of souls—had language not been invented or words formed or ideas analyzed" (p. 258). The narrator looks upon archetypal music as an "indivisible creature" that spoke a language "he did not know," yet "understood so well," and which brought him into contact with the Unknown—the very Mystery of Creation (p. 260).

How can one explain music's capacity to move both Swann and the Narrator to moments of joy and sorrow and to thought? C. G. Jung suggests that we look upon the human brain as a kind of computer or transforming agent, capable of toning down the particles or waves which exceed the speed of light, so that it may hear and understand what it might otherwise not have been able to catch. Jung wrote:

> It might be that psyche should be understood as *unextended intensity* and not as a body moving with time. One might assume the psyche gradually rising from minute extensity to infinite intensity, transcending for instance the velocity of light and thus irrealizing the body. . . . In the light of this view the brain might be a transformer station, in which the relative infinite tension or intensity of the psyche proper is transformed into perceptible frequencies or "extensions." Conversely, the fading of introspective perception of the body explains itself as due to a gradual "psychification," i.e., intensification at the expense of extension. Psyche = highest intensity in the smallest space.[5]

Psychological projection onto music, waves, and particles may be observable by the human eye only when frequencies diminish to the speed of light or less. At this point the brain "tunes down the intensity of the psyche until it becomes bound to lower frequencies," which are then interpreted according to one's empirical understanding.[6]

In the light of Jung's statement, we may be able to look upon Swann's and the Narrator's minds as mediating forces: "computers" with the power to transform high-frequency energy intensity into lower levels, and to then translate these lower levels into a comprehensible language. For Swann, music inhabited the domain of feeling; as a *puer aeternus*, he was a passive recipient of an unconscious anima projection. It was an escape mechanism for him, allowing him to bask in an *eternal present*. The Narrator, on the other hand, although he also descended into a fourth dimension, responded to the musical interludes more cerebrally. They opened up new vistas for him, fostered fresh ideas, and fecundated his creative instinct. Although both Swann and the Narrator underwent parapsychological experiences, only the latter transmuted the vibrational patterns, the altering intensities, the sound waves, and the electrical impulses, which he gathered unto himself, *into the word*. Like the ancient alchemist and like Vinteuil, he went through the operations from *albedo* to *rubedo* by means of music: "the only Stranger it has been my good fortune to meet" (p. 561).

8 Sartre's *Nausea:* Archetypal Jazz

Why did Antoine Roquentin, the protagonist of Jean-Paul Sartre's novel *Nausea* (1938), react so powerfully to "Some of These Days" and write the following about this jazz song?

> . . . a little melody began to sing and dance: "You must be like me; you must suffer in rhythm."
>   The voice sings:
> > *Some of these days*
> > *You'll miss me, honey*
>
> Someone must have scratched the record at that spot because it makes an odd noise. . . . the disc is scratched and is wearing out, perhaps the singer is dead. . . . But behind the existence which falls from one present to the other, without a past, without a future, behind these sounds which decompose from day to day, peel off and slip towards death, the melody stays the same, young and firm, like a pitiless witness.[1]

For Roquentin, "Some of These Days" had taken on archetypal dimension. It emerged from primordial *stuff* or from what C. G. Jung terms the "matrix of life experience," living preconsciously and representing a dominant within Roquentin's psyche.[2] It was an archaic biological pattern of behavior, recognizable only by its effect upon the person experiencing it.[3] The psychic energy inherent in archetypal music in general, and in "Some of These Days" in particular, was instrumental in effecting Roquentin's awakening into *existence* (the contingent) and in discovering the source of his creative élan.

To understand the significance of the role music plays in Sartre's novel, we must first learn something about Roquentin's background, his ideas, and his view of the world. Written in the form of a journal, so as to give credibility to Roquentin's thoughts and to the events narrated, *Nausea* tells the story of a thirty-five-year-old man going through a mid-life crisis. Depressed because he has not yet reached his anticipated (but undefined) goal, Roquentin has traveled widely through Central Europe, North Africa, and the Far East. After a strange and inexplicable incident, he decided to return to France. While in a friend's office, he happened to glance in the direction of the telephone and saw "a little Khmer statuette on a green carpet." Staring at this stone object, he suddenly felt "paralysed" and was stricken with aphasia. A sickening feeling took hold of him, and his zest for life vanished. Deadness, emptiness, and confusion filled his being. Back in France, Roquentin moved to Mudville (Bouville).[4] There would be no more adventures and no more traveling. His life became ordered, regulated, and measured. His days would be spent writing a historical study on an eighteenth-century libertine, the Marquis de Rollebon. Dividing his time among the library (where he conducted his research from 9:00 until 1:00), the bistro, the museum, the park, and the street, Roquentin pursued a bracketed existence. He was satisfied because his life, he thought, had taken on purpose and direction, giving him the security he needed.

Since the *traumatic* episode involving the Khmer statuette, something within him had changed. He felt detached and cut off from the world around him to such an extent that, when he looked at his hands and the way they picked up a fork, he saw them not as part of his body, but as objects. Feelings of insecurity, vulnerability, and terror overwhelmed him. So powerful were these onslaughts of sensations that they gave rise to episodes of nausea. "It came as an illness does . . . cunningly, little by little; I felt a little strange, a little put out, that's all" (p. 4).

Nausea was the physical expression of an emotional condition. Roquentin, the intellectual, with his reasoned and logical view of life, was living peripherally or, rather, *negatively* and *unconsciously*. He had become alienated because he was neither aware of himself as an individual nor conscious of his thoughts, neither understanding of his activities nor of his role in the world. Let us recall that, for Sartre, consciousness is *nonsubstantial*, or *nothingness*, as long as it is not conscious of an object, suggesting that Descartes's famous statement "I think therefore I am" be changed to "I think of something, therefore I am." *Nausea* relates the process by which Roquentin (*being*) became aware of himself (*existence*, contingency).[5] "The essential is contingency. I mean that, by definition, existence cannot be identified with necessity. To exist is to happen without reason. . . . Everything is purposeless, this garden, this town and myself" (p. 238).

The incident of the Khmer statuette and Roquentin's recurring bouts with nausea are factors involved in his growing realization of consciousness becoming aware of itself as nothingness and his heretofore unfulfilled, uncommitted, and inert life as negative *being*.[6] The *shock* of facing his own nothingness—that unlived part of himself—occurs in swift and successive incidents of disorientation and imbalance, which in turn provoke bouts of nausea. Roquentin feels *de trop*. The pat systems, with their ordered categories and their rational deductive thinking processes erected to comfort and cradle generations of people, no longer satisfy him. To assuage the chaos which has taken hold of him, Roquentin further orders his life and develops his *thinking function* still more powerfully, believing erroneously that his life would thereby take on greater meaning and fulfillment.

Mudville

That Roquentin chose Mudville as the locus for the development of his thinking function is significant. *Mud*, looked upon as something dirty, polluted, and repulsive to so-called civilized societies, also has its positive side. As a combination of earth and water, this archaic *stuff* may be associated with the Feminine Principle viewed as *Eros:* that capacity to relate to people and to things. Mud is malleable, rather than fixed and stable, and therefore can be molded into suitable shapes, making it a dynamic force within which the potential for life may take root. Mudville, then, is that place where Roquentin, severed from the Earth principle, will rediscover it. In Mudville Roquentin will find the necessary nutrients to effect a *deconstruction* of his inert, unlived, passive, and senseless life and a *reconstruction* or *rebirth*, lucidly accepting existence as contingent and absurd, but also as offering the opportunity of choosing his way in life freely and responsibly.

Saint Augustine wrote, "Between faeces and urine we are born."[7] The same may be said of Mudville, where Roquentin came into *existence* and where he depotentiated his overly developed *thinking function*, formerly held in such high esteem. Mudville, too, will fill a vacuum in his psyche, developing his inferior sensation function, which, when working in conjunction with *archetypal music*, will enable him to tap the source of his creative urge.

Thinking Versus Sensation

Until the incident of the Khmer statuette, Roquentin had trod along well-worn rational paths and functioned according to logical ideas and disembodied abstractions. He had philosophized, thought out systems, and idealized values, but all of his efforts had served further to enclose him in a dehumanized world of concepts. Because he felt secure and comfortable in this realm, he neither saw, felt, nor experienced the gratuitous nature of the *existential* world. Living inwardly, he not only could not confront the sensate world; he was unaware of its reality.

Why was the episode of the Khmer statuette so significant? That it was made of stone may shed some light on the matter. Stone (a metaphor used to convey durability), not subject to the laws of birth and decay to the same degree that people are, exists outside the human sphere and beyond the temporal realm. Stone serves also to differentiate Sartre's definitions of *being* and *existence:* the former is illustrated by brute or unrefined stone, which may be encountered any place in nature; the latter, although subject to contingencies, has been polished and refined and fashioned by the imagination of the artist who creates the work.

Roquentin's encounter with the Khmer statuette triggered his sensations, wrenched him from his state of *being*, and forced him to face the manifest world and his own mortality. Such a violent outward thrust upset his systematic and compartmentalized life-style and bracketed daily routine. Like a horse wearing blinders, Roquentin never looked out upon life's proliferating objects; he could not, therefore, respond to its vagaries. Roquentin preferred the secure rational sphere to the discomforts and anguish elicited when peering into the maw of the world's imponderables.

A whole side of Roquentin—his senses—had been unused and unfed and had virtually atrophied. Since his senses were so undeveloped, he could not express them conventionally, either with regard to objects (the *thinginess of life*) or in meaningful relationships. Such an attitude was evident in his affairs with women. When making love, for example, with the hostess of the café, neither he nor she ever talked. What would they talk about? And what would be the sense of talking? As for Anny, his former mistress, he thought he loved her. But here, too, he failed to realize his feelings. Soon he found her attitude toward life and love fallacious: she sought to eternalize the "privileged moments" which she experienced every now and then, justifying her existence in that way (p. 6). She was deluding herself, he reasoned, substituting one set of preconceived notions for another; she was *acting* out events, shaping them, living life through these episodes, through the world of appearances and never authentically, never grasping *existence* itself.

Nor did Roquentin enjoy the relationship with the Self-Made Man he met daily in the municipal library where he did his research. A clownlike figure with a passion—spending his time reading all the books in the library alphabetically, from A to Z—he is repulsive, disgusting, and insectlike, in Roquentin's view. The Self-Made Man believes that, if he succeeds in reading all the books, his life will take on meaning and focus. What makes matters even worse is that he believes everything he reads, never questioning an idea or developing any kind of critical sense. Like Anny, the Self-Made Man looks at the world through a mask of pseudo-learning and artificial goals. He represents the hypocrisy and vacuity of a life lived exclusively in an inert and unquestioning mind.

When Roquentin arrived in Bouville, he resembled the Self-Made Man in that he, too, had viewed the world as a comfortable place, and fulfillment as a distinct possibility. Like the Self-Made Man, Roquentin was an introverted *thinking type*, identifying with the patriarchal sphere and not with Mother Earth or the world of the senses. Unlike the Self-Made Man, who pursued the same course day in and day out, Roquentin reached an impasse in his life. He underwent a crisis, and his body rebelled. It fought against its banishment from the earth force and from the sensate, mineral, and vegetal world. It conveyed its distress and its needs through nausea.

Just as the presence of oxygen in a hermetically sealed jar causes an explosive condition, so Roquentin's chance encounter with the Khmer statuette suddenly released his repressed sensations. The energy brought forth by this outward thrust destroyed his *comfortable* but stultifying course. His repressed sensations bursting out drastically not only brought about episodes of malaise but also prolonged them.

It is not surprising that depression followed Roquentin's upsurge of sensations, which provoked his bouts with nausea. Let us recall that Sartre's original title for his novel was *Melancholia*, after Albrecht Dürer's celebrated engraving. Gallimard, his publisher, insisted he call his work *Nausea*, considering this title more appropriate. Melancholia implies, on the one hand, passivity and depression; on the other, a deep life-drive. Within Roquentin's psyche, there existed a force that sought and quested passionately for something.

To transform what is inert and passive into an active, lucid, and authentic force requires a dismemberment of illusory panaceas. The world could no longer be approached *a priori*. It had to be opened up to the unknown, the irrational—the disordered, the dizzy—a whole domain of imponderables. Trauma had to supersede torpor. Only then would Roquentin be free to question himself.

The body was the power that had to take over in order to topple a one-sided, ivory-tower existence. One day, for example, as Roquentin was walking along the seashore, he happened to pick up a pebble or two. "A sort of sweetish sickness" came over him. "How unpleasant it was! It came from the stone, I'm sure of it, it passed from the stone to my hand. Yes, that's it, that's just it—a sort of nausea in the hands" (p. 11). On another occasion, when looking into a mirror, he was horrified by what he considered to be his inhuman, fishlike face. As for the beer glass in the café, the piece of paper in the library, or the old rags at home—they all spelled revulsion. The entire world of things was experienced as a threat.

Why did the world of objects terrify him so? Objects stood for contingency, mortality, the gratuitousness of life. Objects did not exist for Roquentin in and of themselves; they served either as background material or functionally—to be used. "Objects should not *touch* because they are not alive. You use them, put them back in place, you live among them: they are useful, nothing more. But they touch me, it is unbearable. I am afraid of being in contact with them as though they were living beasts" (p. 10).

Until now Roquentin, the bachelor, had succeeded in coping with the dull, lonely, and boring city of Bouville and its inhabitants because he labored under the illusion that his life served some purpose. Once he began questioning the reasons behind his increasingly frequent bouts of nausea, *anguish* took over. That he never knew when nausea would strike him—in the library, the bistro, the street—forced the world of chance upon him. No longer could he escape into the domain of *a priori* reasoning. His only salvation lay in self-interrogation: to know himself truthfully and fully. He began by questioning the validity of his research work. Until now, his book on the Marquis de Rollebon was his *raison d'être*. He had to admit to himself that his entire point of view had changed, that his project bored him.

During Roquentin's period of self-interrogation, his body and psyche were on the alert. They never left him alone. That his episodes of nausea grew more acute, occurring in the café, which until now had been a refuge and a safety zone, is understandable. He had to face both inner and outer world, divested of subterfuge and illusions. He panicked.

> Things are bad! Things are very bad: I have it, the filth, the Nausea. . . . Nausea seized me, I dropped to a seat, I no longer knew where I was; I saw the colours spin slowly around me. I wanted to vomit. And since that time, the Nausea has not left me, it holds me. . . . The Nausea is not inside me: I feel it *out there* in the wall, in the suspenders, everywhere around me. It makes itself one with the cafe, I am the one who is within *it*. (p. 18)

Nausea, in Roquentin's case, is to be considered a positive sign, since it forces him to question his reactions to the outer world and their meaning with regard to the sensations and emotions it arouses. From the Latin *emoveo*, to move out or away from something, his emotions compel him to *move* outward rather than inward and to accept the world of contingencies, the fortuitous, and the concrete. Rational arguments or mental gymnastics could not possibly have affected him so drastically. Only by attacking the body and thereby affecting the *emotions and sensations* could the needed upheaval have occurred. Let us recall Sartre's well-known statement: "Emotional consciousness is, at first, consciousness *of* the world."[8]

As he moves out of conventional views and intellectually secure concepts, Roquentin becomes more and more subject to moods of *anguish*. Such a reaction is natural. He no longer feels in control of his life; his thinking function can order neither the world outside nor within himself. His deterministic approach, which had until now satisfied him in all ways, cannot explain the infinite mysteries existing in a world of imponderables. Nor does he feel detached, as he once had, from the domain of things. On the contrary, he realizes that he is very much involved and affected by all sorts of objects, such as pebbles or the purple suspenders worn by the barman.

His episodes of nausea and anguish should not be looked upon as a morbid condition, but rather as an indication of a growing awareness of the gratuitous nature of life. His body—the world of senses—cannot permit him the luxury of basking in lethargy, in a methodical, reasoned, logical, unquestioning, and automatic existence. Roquentin is growing and probing, and suffering as a result.

The world of cause and effect is no longer a reality for him, any more than objects are viewed as classifiable and reassuring presences which serve a purpose. Once Roquentin had thought that doorknobs opened doors, that glasses contained beer, and pipes, tobacco. Everything had its function, its explanation, its reason, its logical formula. Now that he has begun to question *being* and *existence*, nothing is definite, fixed, and comprehensible. What is reality? What is a face? a park gate? a bench? a lawn? a sea? the paw of an animal? a landscape? a dead donkey? The mask has been cast off. Self-interrogation has enabled him to perceive new domains, perhaps without meaning, coherence, and purpose—even absurd—but authentically. *Being* is now apprehended in its contingency and gratuity.[9]

Time Expands

One afternoon, Roquentin, the intellectual and world traveler, is standing at his window looking down at a woman walking in the street below. He makes his mental calculations as is his habit: she is a hundred yards away, and he figures out that it will take her ten minutes to reach a certain point. Suddenly, he experiences a kind of illumination, as if something new had been perceived: "I *see* the future. It is there, poised over the street, hardly more dim than the present" (p. 31).

What did this new insight indicate? Once viewing them as separate entities, Roquentin now sees time and space as indissolubly linked in a continuum. The classical Newtonian physical world, measured in terms of separate dimensions (time and space), had yielded to a new apprehension of the world: its connectedness. Since absolute space no longer existed for Roquentin, he could not continue to consider it as something unchangeable and forever at rest.

According to Newtonian physics, material particles, described as small, solid, indestructible, and passive, moved in accordance with fixed laws: cause and effect. Such a mechanistic view of nature, by implication, transformed the cosmos into a giant machine with everything within it predictable: the future determined via the past. Since Roquentin's body forced him to react to the sensate domain and concomitantly to experience nausea, he began tasting the flavor of existence, and in so doing, the *safe* and *secure* mechanistic view of the world of certainties vanished. What did he now face? A world of imponderables. Einstein's theory of relativity proved time and space to be connected in a four-dimensional continuum; it rejected the notion of a "universal flow of time," as Newton had once posited. Time was dependent upon the velocity of the movement relative to the event observed. Mass was a form of energy: $E = mc^2$ (c standing for the speed of light).[10]

Not only had Roquentin's philosophical and psychological safety zones been shattered by his expanded vision, but the physical world had also changed in contour. No sooner did Roquentin accept the fact that thinking and feeling people faced a world of uncertainties than his body again spoke to him. Dizziness set in.

> I don't know where I am any more: do I *see* her [the woman walking down the street] motions, or do I *foresee* them? I can no longer distinguish present from future and yet it lasts, it happens little by little. This is time, time laid bare, coming slowly into existence, keeping us waiting, and when it does come making us sick because we realise it's been there for a long time. . . . Calm. Calm. I can no longer feel the slipping, the rustling of time. (p. 31)

Abandoning his former linear view of time, and accepting its cyclicality or mythicality, he remarked, "There are no beginnings. Days are tacked on

to days without rhyme or reason, an interminable monotonous addition"
(p. 39). Time was no longer measurable, comprehensible, or determin-
able. "I wanted the moments of my life to follow and order themselves like
those of a life remembered," but "you might as well try and catch time by
the tail" (p. 40).

Roquentin was undergoing a drastic reorientation that enabled him to
experience *existence* lucidly, authentically, and without palliatives. Alienation had now given way to *sensations* of belonging. The world around
him did not pose a threat. Singular *feelings* of happiness poured into him
from objects: the "fleshy white plant at the bottom of the water" and the
"heavy air" (p. 57).

The Bouville Museum

When Roquentin visits the Bouville museum, he observes the self-satisfied
bourgeois engulfed by their own mediocrity. As they enter the museum's
"sacred" portals, they pause in front of the canvases of their ancestors,
those pilasters of society and leaders of commerce. These citizens, he
realizes, are enveloped in feelings of self-importance, respectability, and
morality. Not one understands the meaning of the *nothingness of the
human condition*. Nor do the humanitarians escape Roquentin's sharp
assessment: despite their good intentions, they, too, are people of *bad
faith*. They give to the poor so as to enhance their dignity and their prestige
and to assuage their guilt. The church is a *tricherie:* a conglomerate of false
certainties to circumvent the tragic nature of human existence.

The portrait painter whose works hang in the Bouville museum is also
given his due. Like the court jester or entertainer, he serves a social function. By accepting money from the ruling bourgeois, he is upholding their
institutions and prolonging domination by people who hide behind a
network of false values and meretricious concepts. Nor are his paintings
creative in the real sense of the word: they do not exist beyond or outside
linear time; they merely fulfill formalized, inauthentic concepts. Because
artists play a precise role in the social life of the city, they do not deal
directly with earth, with matter—the *stone*, which is the *hardness* that
lends life a kind of eternity. They limit themselves to characteristics and
qualities, thereby propitiating artifice. They are people of *bad faith*, as
guilty and as blind to their own foibles and deficiencies as are the bourgeois of Bouville. Roquentin turns his back on all of these *salauds*, as he
calls them, and on everything the museum contains: "Farewell beautiful
lilies, elegant in your painted little sanctuaries, good-bye, lovely lilies, our
pride and reason for existing, good-bye you bastards!" (p. 94).

The Past Rejected

Roquentin's condemnation of the *salauds* may be considered a psychological divestiture of his own formerly dishonest approach to life. Now he is prepared to shed yet another mask. He decides that to continue writing his book on the Marquis de Rollebon is to prolong a sham existence, as reprehensible as that led by the self-satisfied bourgeois of Bouville and their lackeys. The present alone exists, he claims; the world he was attempting to resurrect in his historical study is no longer *a reality* for him.

> The true nature of the present revealed itself: it was what exists, and all that was not present did not exist. The past did not exist. Not at all. Not in things, not even in my thoughts . . . until then I believed that it had simply gone out of my range. . . . Now I knew: things are entirely what they appear to be—and behind them . . . there is nothing. (p. 96)

Roquentin also realized that to re-create a life, as he was doing in his biography, is to live *through* a character and not directly, and therefore to deprive oneself of *existence*. His work, then, is fiction, drawing him away from his own raw and brute existence—the mud of life.

> I furnished the raw material, the material I had to re-sell, which I didn't know what to do with: existence, *my* existence. . . . He stood in front of me, took up my life to *lay bare* his own to me. I did not notice that I existed any more, I no longer existed in myself, but in him; I ate for him, breathed for him, each of my movements had its sense outside, there, just in front of me, in him; I no longer saw my hand writing letters on the paper, not even the sentence I had written—but behind, beyond the paper . . . I was only a means of making him live, he was my reason for living, he had delivered me from myself. What shall I do now? (p. 98)

Neither Proust's method of resurrecting a past via involuntary memory and then eternalizing it in the work of art, nor Joyce's technique of endowing an event with mythical dimension, nor Woolf's attempts to give permanence to the instant were valid any longer for Roquentin.

To abandon his writing and all that it implied, however, was no simple matter. Until now it had *filled* his time and his thoughts. It had been a justification for a life and a way of ordering the world and giving it meaning. To pursue this course, he now felt, was a falsification of life. "What am I going to do with my life?" he questioned anxiously (p. 94).

Forced once again to look out into the world, instead of within himself, objects again took precedence: his fingers, his limbs, his body, his whole animal side began tingling, as if each part of his body were bursting with renewed life.

Roquentin was *in existence*, no longer avoiding it or even standing outside it. He wanted to live life fully, actively, excitedly—gratuitously—no longer through identification with another, as when writing his historical study, or as a follower of classical philosophy and physics, or introvertedly, avoiding the world of objects. A fresh world was coming into being and bringing new ventures and adventures, lived freely, openly, and lucidly— free of false values and ideologies. Roquentin sees himself as an *individual*, living in contingency, and aware of the many ways "to *make* myself exist, to thrust myself into existence" (p. 100). To make certain of the reality of his newly realized identity, he calls upon his body as he jabs his hand with a knife.

> My body of living flesh which murmurs and turns gently, liquors which turn to cream, the flesh which turns, turns, the sweet sugary water of my flesh, the blood on my hand. I suffer in my wounded flesh which turns, walks, I walk, I flee, I am a criminal with bleeding flesh, bleeding with existence to these walls. (p. 101)

His hand hurts; his heart beats faster. Rollebon had died so that Roquentin could live.

The Chestnut Root

Roquentin goes to the municipal park, where chance again intervenes, followed by another malaise. He happens to glance at the root of a chestnut tree. Its "beastly," "black, knotty mass," growing up from beneath the earth, frightens him.

> . . . existence had suddenly unveiled itself. It had lost the harmless look of an abstract category; it was the very past of things, this root was kneaded into existence. Or rather the root, the park gates, the bench, the sparse grass, all that had vanished: the diversity of things, their individuality, were only an appearance, a veneer. This veneer had melted, leaving soft, monstrous masses, all in disorder— naked, in a frightful, obscene nakedness. I kept myself from making the slightest movement. . . . The chestnut tree pressed itself against my eyes. Green rust covered it half-way up; the bark, black and swollen, looked like boiled leather. (p. 127)

Like the Khmer statuette, the pebbles, the woman crossing the street, and the Bouville museum, the root is one of the inexplicable paradoxes of life: the brute, visceral world, which is at once obscene and beautiful, horrific and beatific, intriguing and repulsive, linear and cyclical. His apprehension of existence in all of its reality was a *jouissance*. Whatever remained of his previous worldview—signs, methods, reference points, signification of things—all vanished as he stared at the root. Only the acceptance of incoherence, of the absurdity of it all, could give coherence to the incoherent, stability to the unstable, immortality to mortality.[11] Without warning, the world outside of him flowed into existence. What had been dammed up within him or simply non-functioning, all those fortifications and fetishes he had erected around himself for protective reasons, suddenly withdrew. Roquentin understood finally that his acceptance of *existence* in all of its gratuitousness was in itself a justification of his life on earth. His newborn lucidity would allow him to choose his own course and thereby create his *essence:* to make something of himself, to commit himself (*engagé*), to participate in the world and not flee from it.

What do roots represent that such a vision should have been apocalyptic in dimension? In ancient times, roots and the tree itself were frequently endowed with spirit and sacredness. That Roquentin personifies the roots, and animates them in an embrace of understanding, discloses his relationship to them. This life force ministers to him, nourishes him, and feeds him the milk of life. Roots dig deep into Mother Earth and deal *directly* with matter— not through a sheath or covering. In like manner, Roquentin is prepared to face his own *prima materia*. No abstract theories affect him any more. Like the root upon which he projects so strongly, he is a striving power involved in a continuous and assiduous effort to force up the body (human potential) from inanimate matter: the *mana* power that lives outside of time and space and contains the essential sap and the inner moisture which sees to the continuance of the energetic life process.

The vision of the chestnut root as the body and flesh of existence helped Roquentin relate to what had formerly been his disembodied thoughts and abstract notions. Prepared to bring them into *existence*, he endowed them with form, shape, texture, and sustenance. Exhilarated, he said, "I had found the key to Existence." Everything was one and yet differentiated, absurd and yet relative and dependent on another absurdity. "Absurd: in relation to the stones, the tufts of yellow grass, the dry mud, the tree, the sky, the green benches. Absurd, irreducible; nothing—not even a profound, secret upheaval of nature—could explain it" (p. 129). Nothing was isolated, nothing was conclusive, nothing was definable.

The essential thing is contingency. I mean that one cannot define
existence as necessity. To exist is simply *to be* there; those who exist
let themselves be encountered, but you can never deduce anything
from them. I believe there are people who have understood this.
Only they tried to overcome this contingency by inventing a necessary, causal being. (p. 131)

Moving from passivity to action, from a contemplative, peripheral life-
style to a forceful, stirring, authentic existence, Roquentin was no longer
morose. Awakening to life, he felt blessed.

Every existing thing is born without reason, prolongs itself out of
weakness and dies by chance. I leaned back and closed my eyes. But
the images, forewarned, immediately leaped up and filled my
closed eyes with existence: existence is a fullness which man can
never abandon. (p. 133)

Archetypal Musical Experience

The divestiture of preconceived, rigid ideas and an overvalued thinking
function left Roquentin open to the emotions and sensations aroused by
the outside world. The archetypal music emanating from "Some of These
Days," which Roquentin listens to several times during the course of the
novel, struck a responsive chord in him, sweeping everything that had
been divided or repressed into a cohesive whole.

That Roquentin should feel a particular affinity toward jazz is understandable. An integral part of the life experience of the blacks of Louisiana
at the outset of the twentieth century, jazz conveyed a new musical language associated with the workaday world in all of its banality and spirituality: its weddings, funerals, christenings, picnics, birthdays, and so forth.
Since performances were given for the most part out of doors, its loudness
was as important as the ideas and techniques conveyed by the instrumentalists. It struck, invaded, and mesmerized the listener. Jazz was so instinctual and emotional an expressive form that it quickly spread to Tennessee,
Missouri, and Illinois. King Oliver, one of the greatest of New Orleans
artists, became the most sought-after entertainer of Chicago's nightlife.
When he sent for Louis Armstrong from New Orleans, jazz international
came into being. The powerfully rhythmic and melodious jazz song "Some
of These Days" was catchy and visceral, both rhythmically and aurally;
Roquentin—and millions of others throughout the world—could not help
but empathize with it.

Roquentin had first heard the old and banal ragtime "Some of These

Days" whistled by American soldiers in 1917 in the streets of La Rochelle. When he heard it again at the café in Bouville, it triggered some force within him which brought on acute nausea. The ordered notes making up the melody were no longer abstractions, or disembodied powers. Roquentin began personifying them and transforming them into living, moving, concrete, and *feelable* forces.

> The vocal chorus will be along shortly: I like that part especially and the abrupt manner in which it throws itself forward, like a cliff against the sea. For the moment, the jazz is playing; there is no melody, only notes, a myriad of tiny jolts. They know no rest, an inflexible order gives birth to them and destroys them without even giving them time to recuperate and exist for themselves. They race, they press forward, they strike me a sharp blow in passing and are obliterated. I would like to hold them back, but I know if I succeeded in stopping one it would remain between my fingers only as a raffish languishing sound. I must accept their death; I must even *will it*. I know few impressions stronger or more harsh. (p. 21)

Roquentin's personification of the notes humanized them, enabling him to respond and relate to their sonorities, rhythms, and diapasons: they are "young and firm," "hard" and "thin"; the music "transpierces"; the melody has its "metallic transparency," which "passes through time . . . crushing our miserable time against the walls . . . tearing at it with its dry little points. . . . there is another time" (pp. 21–22). His feelings of being superfluous and *de trop* have vanished. *Existence* is notes, he contends; it stands in opposition to melody, which follows another order in duration. Blended with sensation and feeling, the realization of "Some of These Days" causes Roquentin to experience a certain warmth and an unaccustomed happiness. "There is another happiness: outside there is this band of steel, the narrow duration of the music which traverses our time through and through, rejecting it, tearing at it with its dry little points; there is another time" (p. 21).

As the notes continue their ordered soundings, linear time vanishes and with it the perceptions it aroused: the "viscous puddle" made of "wide, soft instants, spreading at the edge, like an oil stain" (p. 21). The archetypal music he heard offered Roquentin another reality and a different form of life: youth and vigor of *existence*, not the lassitude and inertness of *being*. Notes are born to die, to decompose, and recompose, he realizes, whereas the *melody remains*, taking on reality in the here and now. Reasonless, timeless, and dimensionless, the present suddenly bursts in on Roquentin, traumatically: "I am *in* the music," he blurts out (p. 22).

Music is sensation and feeling; it is texture and resistance; it has become *thingified*. An object with which to empathize, it no longer represents danger, as had the softness on the beach. Humanized tonal sequences speak to him, sing to him, stimulate his sense perception and his entire *feeling realm*, thereby affecting his internal organs and his psyche.

No longer merely an aesthetic, objective, and detached admixture of thought alone, "Some of These Days" was *primordial* and therefore *archaic* and *reactive*. As concretion, this archetypal music transmitted not only the perception of the feelings and sensations associated with the individual notes and the melody as a whole, but also their analogues in the world of objects.

Like the primitive and the child, Roquentin reacts to archetypal music viscerally; senses and feelings predominate over the thinking function. The head no longer leads the way; no longer does it bask in objectivity; rather, it relates to material phenomena connected with feelings and sensations. Like the *fetish* in primitive societies, Roquentin's soma and psyche are transformed into a magical force. (Let us recall the *root* incident in this regard.)[12]

As an object of sensation and feeling, archetypal music becomes a dynamic capable of uniting feeling, sensations, and thought. It empowers Roquentin to experience a kind of *sensuous relatedness* with the outer world. His reactions to phenomena are experienced at first only on the body level, infiltrating ever so slowly his conscious thoughts. Aware of the change going on within him, and concomitantly his relationship with the outer world, he becomes transformed by the music as object. Notes are perceived not only as living and dying entities to be seen, touched, smelled, felt, and heard, but also as active forces that *press* and *"strike me a sharp blow in passing"* (p. 21). The impact of the archetypal music, which as we know is abnormally strong in Roquentin, corresponds to the intensity of the physical stimulus it arouses in him. Since the sonorities in "Some of These Days" touch him deeply, they enable him for the first time to empathize with his own *inner* song.

Just as "Some of These Days" exists both as ordered melody and as individual notes, so, too, does Roquentin now view himself as a composite of structured and single entities, alive inside and outside time, within and beyond the object of consciousness. His gestures take on a different consistency; his movements seem to have developed their own themes and their own gliding motions. A lightness and airiness invade his limbs. He feels as if he were dancing. Music has expanded his consciousness and liberated a whole repressed dimension within him, putting him in touch with his *essence*.

Roquentin's newly found unvarnished reality, experienced in listening to

"Some of These Days," is expressed in hard, metallic, stonelike metaphors, and no longer in viscous, flabby, passive, or inert images.

> Suddenly: it was almost unbearable to become so hard, so brilliant. At the same time the music was drawn out, dilated, swelled like a waterspout. It filled the room with its metallic transparency, crushing our miserable time against the walls. I am *in* the music. Globes of fire turn in the mirrors; encircled by rings of smoke, veiling and unveiling the hard smile of light. (p. 22)

Even if he were never to hear "Some of These Days" again, even if the record were to be smashed or a spring in the playing machine broken, Roquentin knew that *it was there.* So, too, had his view of the world altered in consistency: it was no longer something reasonable and rational, but rather it encompassed groupings of proliferating, purposeless, detached objects and actions. The world is not governed by ultimate laws, and people are not law-abiding. Regularities do exist, but they are subject to change. Roquentin's error was to have looked upon altering factors as laws and as absolutes, erecting pseudo-structures to allay his fear of the unknown and the unregulated. "Everything is purposeless, this garden, this town and myself." Neither comfortable nor friendly, Roquentin *exists* in a space-time continuum that has no beginning or end, no past or future. It *simply is;* and things simply occur, inexplicably.

> I exist. I think that I exist. Oh, the long coil, this sensation of existence—and I unwind it, gently. . . . If I could stop myself thinking! I try, I succeed; it seems as if my head is filled with smoke . . . and then it all begins again . . . I don't want to think. I must not think that I don't want to think because that is another thought. Will it never end.

The catalysis in Roquentin's system of reactions and aptitudes, brought about by archetypal music, is expressed not only in hard and metallic metaphors, as mentioned above, but also by a gamut of feelings and sensations revolving around music as love and beauty.

> It seems inevitable, so strong is the necessity of this music: nothing can interrupt it, nothing which comes from this time in which the world has fallen; it will stop of itself, as if by order. If I love this beautiful voice it is especially because of that: it is neither for its fulness nor its sadness, rather because it is the event for which so

many notes have been preparing, from so far away, dying that it
might be born. (p. 22)

Music may be alluded to as *anaplerotic*, that is, as an agent that pro-
motes the healing of a wound.[13] A *thinking* type, such as Roquentin prior
to his first bout with nausea, would never feel disoriented by intellectual
concepts, believing himself always capable of arguing against them, logi-
cally and rationally. Roquentin's inferior functions, *sensation* and *feeling*,
however, had remained undeveloped and vulnerable. Since he had never
really acknowledged their existence, he found himself unable to relate to
them in terms of the outside world—the domain of things and reality. The
incident of the Khmer statuette and the pebbles, among others, struck a
chord within him, arousing the latent realm of sense and feeling perception and dislodging what had managed to crush and repress a whole
unused portion of his psyche.

Because no one can talk *sensation* or *feeling* to a thinking type, the body
of necessity had to take over. It alone could create the excoriating havoc
necessary to effect a psychological transformation. A thinker believes fully
in the logic of his thought processes: should he be illogical, he would be
committing a transgression. Roquentin had always thought of thinking as
instinctively right. Nothing could topple this rigid and narrow view except
the *trauma* caused by the impact of powerful sensations and feelings.
Once the body toppled the denatured edifice that Roquentin had constructed for himself, the protective wall that he had erected around him
(the intellect which sheltered him from pain) crumbled.[14]

Archetypal music had helped him cross that fine line between passivity
and inertia, embedded in a world of abstract ideations, and an active,
realistic *existence* functioning in a sphere of multiplicity and conflict. "I
am touched, I feel my body at rest like a precision machine. I have had real
adventures. I can recapture no detail but I perceive the rigorous succession
of circumstances" (p. 23).

Roquentin not only accepts his finitude but discovers something else
about himself—still undetermined, still only a sensation, but that which
leads him to decide that nothing more holds him to Bouville. He will leave
for Paris. Before taking the train, he says his good-byes to the *patronne* of
the café where he first heard that crucial song "Some of These Days." As he
listens to it again, for the last time, he reacts freely to a new awareness,
that this archetypal music is

beyond—always beyond something, a voice, a violin note. Through
layers and layers of existence, it veils itself, thin and firm, and when
you want to seize it, you find only existants, you butt against ex-

istants devoid of sense. It is behind them. It is behind them: I don't even hear it, I hear sounds, vibrations in the air which unveil it. It does not exist because it has nothing superfluous: it is all the rest which in relation to it is superfluous. It is. (p. 175)

Roquentin listens to the notes as they slip into death, continuously decomposing, and to the melody that exists paradoxically in the present. He thinks of the Jewish composer who wrote the jazz tune in the heat of summer and in slum conditions, and of the Negress who sang it. Their pain and anguish have become his, not maudlin, weak, and flaccid, but hard and stonelike, possessing their own sacredness. That the composer and singer are dead is of little import to Roquentin. They are heroes of sorts, for they have, as much as is humanly possible, "washed themselves of the sin of existing." Suddenly Roquentin experienced something inexplicable. "I felt something brush against me lightly and I dare not move because I am afraid it will go away. Something I didn't know any more: a sort of joy" (p. 177).

Roquentin's senses and feelings have fluidified, warmed, and grown excited and joyous. Now positive in his outlook, he wonders whether he could *in good faith* justify his existence by writing a book. Not history. He would not resurrect a past, since "existence is without memory; of the vanished it retains nothing—not even memory" (p. 133). Rather, like "Some of These Days," his work would be "above existence," beyond the world of appearances and the rational domain. As such, it would be as "hard as steel" and "make people ashamed of their existence."

Roquentin's plans were purposely vague; he knew only that something *precious* had burgeoned within him and was struggling to be born— something which existed *outside* the vagaries and accidents of chance and contingency; *behind* the individual notes, but within the *melody*.

The book Roquentin has in mind would be nurtured and fed directly, authentically, from the dark, moist, muddy soil of his existential experience. For here lies the *source* of his creative principle—within the world of *sensation* and *feeling*, made accessible to him through archetypal music.

9 Yizhar's "Habakuk": Archetypal Violin Music and the Prophetic Experience

The violin in Yizhar Smilansky's short story "Habakuk" (1960) is the medium used to create the archetypal music that produces spacelessness and timelessness, by means of primordial sounds which are experienced subjectively by the protagonists. Affecting soma and psyche so powerfully that consciousness expands, the music opens up musician and listener to the prophetic experience.

Sober and classical in style, "Habakuk" is the literary expression of an emotionally charged event. It transcends the specificity of its locale: Jerusalem, not far from Rohovot, where the author was born (1916), schooled, and where he taught. Although landscapes are accurately described and the facts alluded to (the War of Independence, 1948, in which the author fought) are historically correct, the situations in the tale take on a suprapersonal cast.[1] Yizhar speaks in universals; he reaches deep into primordial spheres.

Habakuk, the story's namesake, is a violinist about whose personal life virtually nothing is known. He is mysterious and fascinating—a psychopomp of sorts. He yearns for beauty and spirituality, for he knows that they alone will release him from the tragic dilemma of the world struggle between victor and vanquished. Yizhar's expert use of internal monologue and dialogue, his lean vocabulary, his technically accurate musical references, and his metered rhythms endow his tale with a livingness and power which places it on a par with works by Gogol and Flaubert.

Structured with care and caution, "Habakuk" also follows the concerto patterning. It begins slowly at first, with asides interwoven into its very fabric; then tension mounts, subtly, via nuances of color tones and flashbacks. Finally a spectacular crescendo, reaching into the very heart of musical arcana, is unleashed, compelling the violinist and his listeners to flow forward, but also to repeat certain thematic interludes while also breaking with conventional ties and empirical reality, and in so doing, to reach out toward that impalpable, unnameable, immanence which is Divinity.

The original Habakkuk, after whom Yizhar named his protagonist, was a biblical prophet. Although nothing is really known about him, scholars speculate that he was a contemporary of Isaiah, or perhaps of Jeremiah. Nobility and poetry mark his visionary experience: he foretold the rise of the Chaldeans, their conquest of Nineveh, and Nebuchadnezzar's defeat of the Egyptians and invasion of Judah two years later. It was Habakkuk who, speaking out against the savageries perpetrated by these invaders, posed the eternal question: How and why does a merciful God permit *evil* to grow rampant?

Habakkuk, who attempted to understand the mysteries behind God's acts, cried out his anguish in tones that reverberated throughout the cosmos, reaching up into the endless clarity of the heavens.

> O Lord, how long shall I cry, and thou wilt not hear! even cry out unto thee of violence, and thou wilt not save! (Habakkuk 1:2)

> I will stand upon my watch, and set me upon the tower, and will watch to see what he will say unto me, and what I shall answer when I am reproved. (2:1)

Standing, as it were, on a symbolic tower, Habakkuk prayed and beseeched God to allow him to experience the inner light and to make His will known to him. Seeing apocalyptic visions, Habakkuk, quivering, spoke out his awe:

> O Lord, I have heard thy speech, and was afraid: O Lord, revive thy work in the midst of the years, in the midst of the years make known; in wrath remember mercy. (3:2)

The faithful and upright, he was told, would live; turmoil would be resolved.

The biblical Habakkuk—peering into the vaulted heavens and bathing in God's glory, listening as He spoke out His message in pure tones—inspired Yizhar to write his poignant tale.

Yizhar's "Habakuk," the narrator warns his readers, is a tale replete
with sadness. The protagonist's real name is not Habakuk, but Jedidiah.
"Why then do I call him Habakuk?" he questions with humor and point.
The answer is simply that everyone calls him by this name, an "empty
shell of a name" given a child at birth. The change in name, however, is
deeply significant: he does not identify with Jedidiah, which means "friend
of God," but rather with the biblical prophet. Thus Yizhar provides his
readers, as we shall see, with a new, secular, and psychological interpreta-
tion of the prophetic phenomenon. Interestingly, although Yizhar is a
secular Zionist who rejected many of the religious tenets of the orthodox,
his need to look beyond the temporal sphere is evident by the name that he
gives to his protagonist.

Habakuk has no real mark of distinction. He is thin and slightly bald;
his eyes are rather unusual in that they wear the expression of an Alsatian
dog.[2] Spiritually, however, he probes another dimension: a world that is
sensed and intuited, a world that may seem absurd to some at first glance,
but that to others may yield a transpersonal—perhaps divine—experience.

The narrator, who comes from a small town, has just arrived in Jerusalem, where he intends to pursue his studies. His mother, who has accompanied him, wishes to make certain that proper living arrangements have
been made for him. As the two wait at a bus stop, a "big-nosed man"
walks toward them. The narrator's mother greets him and introduces her
son as "the young resident scholar to be" (p. 79). The narrator thinks
nothing of the incident until the following morning; waiting alone in the
bus stop, he meets the same man, who is carrying a violin case. "I didn't
know you played," the narrator says to him with admiration. "Didn't
know you cared," the old man responds.

They chat for a while. The narrator mentions his love for music but
confesses he knows practically nothing about this art—not even what
most instruments look like. Such a void is not surprising in view of the fact
that the narrator had come from a small agricultural community. He has
lived embedded, so to speak, in orange groves, acacias, and water pumps.
The only sounds he has heard before coming to Jerusalem were the rustle
of eucalyptus leaves, the screeching of crows in the autumn air, donkeys
braying, Arabs selling their wares, and, of course, the marvelous musical
tonalities of the Yiddish language: his father's "occasional melancholy yah-
bim-bam-boom rendition of a Hassidic tune." He had Romain Rolland's
Jean Christophe, a novelized biography of Beethoven, but his greatest joy in
life had been listening to his Uncle Moshe's "wonder-box": a gramophone.

Uncle Moshe's "wonder-box" captivated the young lad's imagination. Its
polished surface gave it an "outlandish air"; its aroma was mesmerizing,
like that of a rare wine. *Mystery* was its name. That it occupied its own

stand, and was set apart from everything else in the home, likened it to a *hierophany*. The narrator listened day in and day out to the records he placed with great care on the machine; in time, he realized that, if he put his ear close to the latticed lid, the notes would grow louder, resound and echo more powerfully, cutting him off from the world about him and opening the door to a whole new level of being—that electrifying and soul-stirring world of the unknown. The swell and power of the notes which emanated from the "wonder-box" bathed him in feelings of elation. He found it increasingly difficult to tear himself away from this *magical* force which seemed to exercise some strangely hypnotic power over him. Like a narcotic, it dulled his lucidity, encouraging him to step into a land of enchantment.

> I could listen to the same record over and over again, till every-thing, every last detail had sunk down deep and been embedded in the core of my being, fused there with the swaying of eucalyptus branches beyond the window, merged with the flickering dots of light, tied up inextricably with the smell of the smooth box and rippling with the stillness in the large room. (p. 81)

Like a mantra, music repelled extraneous thoughts, purifying and clari-fying the mind in preparation for a spiritual ascension/descension and enlightenment. Psychologically speaking, the constant repetition of the recorded sounds put him in a trancelike state, inducing his libido (psychic energy) to flow inward, thus encouraging contemplation and meditation, and moving him out of the concrete or corporeal world into an abstract or spiritual dimension. As archetypal sound built up within him, subliminal contents were activated, creating new patterns of thought and feeling and formulating the inchoate. Music was the catalyst; it would enable the narrator to experience what Kabbalists call the creative *Center*, and what psychologists refer to as *identity*. Music was fluidifying those rigid or dormant factors within the psyche. Feeling could now become manifest, unrepressed, and the thinking factor could take second place, bringing harmony where there had been imbalance, and serenity and understand-ing where chaos had dominated. The groundwork was being set for nonspatiality and nontemporality, through the medium of music, which had always been part of the narrator's Hebrew tradition. David, let us recall, played on his harp and sang to Saul when he needed soothing. It was he, too, who organized Jewish musical life and trained groups of Levites in this art, being responsible also for the melodies and hymns which accompanied the Psalms. "I will sing unto the Lord as long as I live: I will sing praise to my God while I have my being" (Psalms 104:33). Music was part of the ancient temple service, harps, lyres, flutes, trumpets, the shofar, and other instruments serving liturgical purposes. Prayers and scriptures were intoned in keeping with traditional melodies frequently based on accented and unaccented syllables. Responsive or antiphonal singing was used to declaim sacred texts. Choruses intoned them, as did the head singer and the congregation.

Sacred music alone, however, did not captivate the narrator's psyche. He listened to profane works on the "wonder-box": Tchaikovsky, Caruso, Chaliapin, Galli-Curci, and Sarasate's *Andalusian Romance*, which he listened to so many times that he could even whistle the high and shrill notes, frightening "the ravens in the topmost branches" of the trees as he wandered by them (p. 82).

Beethoven's violin concerto was the narrator's favorite work. Although he had never seen an orchestra or a conductor, nor knew how to read music, he thrilled at the sounds he heard. Frequently, he stood in the middle of the room and began beating time with his hands and fingers, tossing his head and body about, reacting fervently to "the great Beethoven and his magical musicians." They transported him "from glory to glory up to the exultant moment of triumph" (p. 82). During these moments, the narrator was *in* the archetypal music; he felt, savored, and caressed its notes, rhythms, and modulations, thereby experiencing that transpersonal domain beyond time or place.

Having lived his earliest days in a climate of war, siege, and terror, Beethoven became the narrator's favorite composer: both loved freedom. Beethoven's music echoed an appreciation of nature, to which the young man responded. Rocks, trees, forests, and lush countrysides, as well as arid lands, spoke to him with love. The loftiness of the composer's inspiration, the dynamism of his shadings, the inexhaustible energy of his harmonic progressions, as well as their frequently explosive, boisterous, and sometimes unbridled themes, all made inroads on the narrator's psyche. Beethoven was his idol. Unconsciously, he must have sensed that Beethoven's archetypal music would lead him to a breakthrough into the realm of pure essence—that spiritual sphere known to the prophets of old.

While the narrator converses with Habakuk at the bus stop, he asks him whether he can play Beethoven's violin concerto. Yes, of course, though he admits to being no Heifetz. The two walk to the old man's house, altering their plans for the day. Psychologically speaking, the narrator is ready for reorientation, which will enable him to find a way out of the impasse he has evidently reached.

After walking through dismally poor streets, the old man and the young lad go down a flight of stairs into a cellar. Habakuk identifies this closed subterranean space, "whose small windows floated just above ground level," as "the vast depths," his home (p. 85). A metaphor for the unconscious, this underground room symbolizes that secret area where private thoughts and feelings cohabit and the locus for the transformation ritual which will be lived out. Within this vaulted sphere and this symbolically sealed world, the initiate will undergo his tests and disciplines, leading to the liberation of his *feeling* principle in the experience of archetypal music.

Music, then, in Yizhar's story, is the prime mover and its motivating force, all else being subject to its dictates. Habakuk, the psychopomp, will open the door for the lad to a world *in potentia*, enabling him to know a fusion among music, feeling, and spirit. The fifteenth-century Platonist Marsilio Ficino described the process most sensitively in *The Book of Life:*

> Musical spirit touches and works on the spirit as a medium between the body and the soul, affecting either one with its outpouring of affection. You will agree that this force is marvelous, exciting and spirit-brightening, if you agree with the Pythagoreans and Platonists that this is a heavenly spirit, arranging everything with its movements and tones.[3]

Habakuk's secluded cellar room, isolated and virtually bare, is reminiscent of the inner room of the soul. Not weighted down by anything, he has hardly any possessions: a table, chair, bed, and a few packing cases all pushed against the walls, leaving the center of the room empty. It is, as we shall see, a *temenos*, a sacred space consecrated to music.

As the old man takes out his violin most carefully from its case, he announces "Beethoven: Violin Concerto in D major." Then he begins to play.

> His fingers quivered on the strings, his hand flourished the bow, his eyebrows worked their way up, way up the height of his forehead, and his forehead contracted, and his brown eyes looked straight in front of him and his chin bulged atop the wedged violin. (p. 86)

Although there is no orchestra and every now and then Habakuk strikes a wrong note, plays out of tune, or simply squeaks a bit, startling the narrator *out* of the music, these imperfections do not detract from the composition's powerful impact.

> For I was absorbed, lost in this man and his playing, fascinated by the very reality of notes being produced before my eyes—a man standing here and making his violin sing; not some hidden mechanical device, but the product of these hands belonging to this

man here, these hands bringing the wonder to pass; and despite the
fact that the man was big-nosed and balding and brown-eyed like a
dog, here he was singing fervently in this basement of his that
contained nothing, nothing but him. (p. 78)

Habakuk, the prototype of the archetypal old man, the guide, or the
psychopomp, featured in so many myths, is a positive father figure for the
narrator, whose family life had been dominated by the struggle for sur-
vival and by daily exposure to danger, war, and terrorism. Music offers to
the narrator a world in which fantasy and dream—so important to children and youth—can roam at will. Habakuk, the patriarchal figure—a
kind of guru—will lead his protégé to *inwardness*, not through words
alone, but through music. Like Goethe, who guided Faust to the "World of
the Mothers" and healed his divided soul, so Habakuk will draw the
narrator into his arcane domain, where he will experience the secrets of
life and tradition—and the meaning of divine understanding.

In these deepest of spheres, alluded to as the collective unconscious, the
narrator will bathe in the latent energetic forces he carries within him—
arcane powers until now inaccessible to consciousness. The release of
potential contents will provide him with a continuous connection between
himself and past generations—the new and the traditional. The patriarchal image that figures so frequently in Judaism as a giver of laws and
symbol of authority is understandably transformed in Yizhar's tale into a
violinist with a *mana personality*, fructifying what has grown parched and
rejuvenating what has been withered.

As the narrator details Habakuk's performance of Beethoven's violin concerto, he is visibly moved. "His left hand flying and flickering on the strings"
pulsates in rhythm with his body movements, sideward gestures, and facial
expressions. Technical notations are also included in the narrator's verbal
metaphors. Themes, melodies, transitional passages, crescendos and diminuendos, major and minor modes, sharps and flats, rondo-allegro and
larghetto sequences are described iconographically. The narrator seems,
paradoxically, to *feel into the very body of melody*. His senses dilate to its
pitch and sway, enticing him ever deeper into a "wondrous valley" where he
can actually "feel the spirit expand and grow richer and everything around
him get clearer and brighter." A universe unfolds within and outside him.

Once the performance ends, fresh harmonies, oases of serene thoughts
and feelings, seem to have entered the narrator's being and calmed the
tumult within him, at least temporarily. For the Kabbalist, the sublime
nature of music can bring the human being closer to divine spheres and so
pave the way for the numinous experience to occur. In biblical times,
music was known to lead to altered states of consciousness, as, for exam-

ple, when David and his seers asked the sons of Asaph, Heman, and Jeduthun to prophesy and to bring their harps, psalteries, and cymbals to create the proper atmosphere.[4]

As the days pass, the narrator is exposed to more and more archetypal music, bringing his admiration for Habakuk to virtually unlimited proportions. Absorbed in the notes, melodies, and thematic patterns of Beethoven's works—the *Eroica* and *Pastoral* symphonies, the *Apassionata* Sonata, and the *Emperor* Concerto—he responds physically to his inner pulsations and to those latent *feelings* which had been repressed during all these years.

Time passes too quickly, laments the young man. "Time is always passing," Habakuk explains. "Space is fixed but time passes." Nevertheless, he reassures the narrator, who is only a lad, that time is on his side. Then, as if from nowhere, Habakuk asks him a very strange question, which triggers a whole new wave of sensations. Habakuk wants to know his age, as well as the day and hour of his birth. The narrator complies, and Habakuk, growing increasingly excited, takes out pen and paper. Like "a man crouching over a fire," he draws a circle and some figures; consults a graph with dots, triangles, houses, curves, squares, and blank spaces; and then mumbles some incomprehensible words (p. 91). The narrator does catch such names as Venus, Jupiter, Saturn. So deeply immersed is Habakuk in "some secret language" and in the computation of strange groupings of cyphers that he is oblivious to all else (p. 92).

What is the meaning of these glyphs? the narrator questions. "It's you and these are your stars. Everything's written here!" Habakuk speaks out solemnly. "Your horoscope! Written in the stars. . . . It's all written in the book of heaven. A man is born under his stars, inescapably. Man is, and the world is" (pp. 93–94).

Is this old man an astrologer? a soothsayer? or a prophet? the narrator wonders, growing uneasy, and even a bit frightened. Will Habakuk trespass into forbidden spheres? To provide human answers to questions about God's realm is dangerous and a sign of hubris!

Habakuk's astrological beliefs were in keeping with the system of Jewish theosophy (Kabbala), in which stars and planets played a significant role. One of the most important images for some Kabbalists was the vision of the Sefirotic Tree: a metaphor for God's Ten Divine Emanations or His Unmanifest Existence, it contained, it was believed, the very mystery of being. Only the initiate who progressively descended, by means of prayer and other disciplines, to the deepest levels of being could pass through the layers of matter which barred him from peering into God's domain and gleaning some of its arcana. Certain Kabbalists identified the Sefirotic Tree with planets: for example, Hokhmah was Uranus, and Kether was Neptune. Each sign of the zodiac, for others, represented one of the twelve

spiritual types determining an individual's fate. Kabbalists also had recourse to linguistics to prove their point: the Hebrew words *mazzel* ("fortune"), which implies that the soul has the ability to perfect itself, and
mazel tov ("to wish someone good luck") have the same root, *mazelot*,
which means "zodiac," indicating the relationship between human and
celestial spheres.[5] Mention must also be made, in this connection, of the
Sefer Yetsirah (*The Book of Creation*), composed sometime between the
third and sixth centuries. It offers a theoretical approach to the cosmological and cosmogonic world, numbers and letters for the Kabbalist being
metaphors for the mysteries of convergence of earthly and celestial
spheres. If properly computed, they, too, were supposed to lead to the
decantation of some of God's mysteries.[6] Kabbalists also cite Genesis to
strengthen their astrological argument: "And God said, let there be lights
in the firmament of the heavens to divide the day from the night; and let
them be for signs, and for seasons, and for days, and years" (1:14). Accordingly, two great luminaries came into being: the sun, the stronger one; and
the moon, the lesser light. Kabbalists and Talmudists were divided, however, on the subject of astrology: some (e.g., Rabbi Rava) suggested that
planets could determine a person's fate; others (e.g., Maimonides) were
convinced that Israel was not ruled by any celestial star.[7]

The zodiac, psychologically speaking, is a projection of unconscious
contents that lie embedded within subliminal spheres. It reflects humankind's empirical and spiritual knowledge and instinctual and emotional
reactions. Astrological notations and concepts have little or nothing to do
with the stars, psychologists maintain. The knowledge obtained from human computations and the future events detected from these *lumen
naturae* are based on unconscious experiences.[8] In this regard, they reveal
significant data concerning Habakuk's and the narrator's psychological
make-up.

The narrator, mesmerized by the arcane symbols and complicated calculations which Habakuk explains to him, returns regularly to the cellar
room—this "kingdom of music and the stars" (p. 95). He invites some
friends to share his new-found experience. They, too, "leave all the outside
and beyond-this-room beyond and outside," divesting themselves of all
empirical vestments so that they can be receptive to the forces they will
encounter in Habakuk's domain: the "great Beethoven on our right and
God's stars on our left." Like the narrator, they conduct either gesturally or
within their own minds the sonatas, symphonies, and concertos as
Habakuk performs them. Never once do they fear, falter, or question their
rhythmic patterns, as they ascend "to great heights of enthusiasm and
inspiration, rising to God and all his angels and higher yet" (p. 96).

During the astrological interludes, the young people in the cellar room watch entranced as Habakuk traces the positions of the stars to their houses. They listen with expectation to his explanations of the ciphers scattered about the pieces of paper. A world of "alien magic" has come alive; and he, the prophet, reveals their futures to them—always positive, glowing, and beautiful. The stars protect them, he tells them. Yet each time Habakuk delves into the mysteries of the stars and planets, they shudder a little at the "confrontation of its veiled secrets which no human eye may behold and whose misty distances only the sharp glance of this man could pierce" (p. 97).

This old man is a seer, the narrator and his friends conclude. He intuits the signs embedded in the cryptograms just as he interprets the esoteric markings in the realm of music, each releasing a rush of sonorous tones which cascade in audible and inaudible waves into the world of manifestation. Silences sound, and inarticulate tonalities are absorbed by the ear. The inanimate speaks to Habakuk. Nature as a whole is vocalized: orange groves, eucalyptus trees, acacia flowers, pinecones, rain, grass, and clouds all vibrate with life.

That Habakuk should associate astrology and music also stems from Kabbalistic readings of the Sefirotic Tree, which is frequently alluded to both as a musical Major Scale and as the Great Octave. Each of the Ten Divine Emanations was identified with an "active" or "passive" melodic interval, such as a semitone, triad, or subtriad, which crossed and crisscrossed around the central balancing column of the Sefirotic Tree. The greater the flow of activity between them, the more forceful were the accompanying tonal qualities. Such an approach to the Sefirotic Tree empowered the Kabbalist to bring about an interaction between the empirical and atemporal world. Music was one of the connecting principles which permitted the practitioner to descend/ascend into heretofore unknown levels in his subliminal sphere, depending upon the depth of his faith and the understanding and sensitivity of his psyche.[9]

Unlike Beethoven, Mozart, and Bach, Habakuk is no composer. He is a performer: a bridge between two worlds. His function is to bring into consciousness and give meaning to the streaming primordial forces, the ineffable feelings, and the abstract notions inhabiting the collective unconscious. Even when Habakuk's memory grows faulty (at times he skips some bars), he pursues his tonal renditions with joy, reverence, and enthusiasm, carried away, so to speak, by the sheer beauty of sound, which opens the door to the *other* undefinable infinite world beyond.

Still the boys wonder whether Habakuk is really a prophet. He must be, they reason, since prophecy demands discipline and Habakuk is a trained musician. Though his playing is not of the highest quality, it is structured, regulated, and directed. His foundations are solid. If he allowed his music to pursue its course unchanneled, his energies would be depleted, flowing here and there, with no focal point to structure his lyrical prayers and meditations. A centroid, a core, a nucleus is imperative for the artist and mystic alike, since each in his or her own way consolidates or federates what is disparate.[10]

Archetypal music, which activates contents in both the conscious and unconscious spheres, connects what has been severed or unrelated and brings into being new behavioral patterns that encourage a fruitful interaction between time and timelessness, space and spacelessness, the rational and the irrational. Communication between the ego and the collective unconscious is activated by melody and rhythm, as well as by astrological computations, triggering a panoply of fulgurant, autonomous energetic charges. The biblical prophets, invaded by archetypal images and their accompanying sonorities, paradoxically articulated, envisaged, and committed to writing nonverbal tones and audible silences. Once these forces were assimilated into consciousness, they enlarged the scope of their understanding, thus expanding their visionary capabilities. Similarly with the Habakuk of our story: the energy implicit in Habakuk's archetypal music does not divest him of his ego-consciousness; it does not lead to an eclipse of his ego—or to insanity. On the contrary, an increase in knowledge is effected in his case, paving the way for an apocalyptic revelation.[11]

One more factor is necessary for Habakuk's celestial visitation: the introduction of an *anima figure* (an autonomous psychic content within the male personality that can be alluded to as the inner woman). Psychologically and spiritually speaking, without the anima/soul, there would be no mystery of individuation, creation, or eternality. The anima/soul is the carrier of serenity, the harbinger of prayer, and the purveyor of comfort. Like Miriam, who sang, and Deborah, who proclaimed her song of thanksgiving and victory, so Naomi, a friend of the narrator in Habakuk's tale, will participate in making music of the spheres.

For the Kabbalist, Naomi may represent the Shekhinah, one of the Ten Divine Emanations of the Sefirotic Tree, which, for some, personifies the community of Israel under the banner of harmony, and for others is a symbol of God's feminine aspect. For the pious, the Shekhinah represents the mystery of faith, of inwardness, and of being.[12]

Naomi is the anima/soul for Habakuk and his group. A mother, sister, wife, mistress, and consoling force that reads into the hearts of young men, Naomi is associated with gentleness and tenderness, but not of the maudlin kind. Strong and heroic, feeling and thinking, she has the courage to love but not smother, to cradle but not pacify, and to give affection when needed. An enchantress of sorts (since she represents the eternal spring which exists within each living being), she activates the *imago Dei* in those who project upon her, reaffirming, symbolically speaking, human-kind's covenant with God: that dialectical relationship which warms and heals through joy and the wonderment of faith.

Naomi sits on the floor with the others and listens to Habakuk playing a Mozart sonata (the narrator does not mention which one). Silence reigns during the adagio movement; no one breathes. Habakuk continues on to the rondo and presto; and with "a flourish of his sword," sets out "to conquer that land unknown," pursuing sweeping tones which radiate outward as the rays of the sun do when breaking through the clouds. Then, suddenly, it is over. There is "a full great moment's silence, a withholding silence. Then the flame leaps up" (p. 101). It was *pure prayer:* "the prayer of a man weary unto death, a stricken man empty of everything, of all faith, all but: Out of the depths I cry unto thee, O Lord, hear me, O Lord, hear me—shine thy face upon me and give me peace" (p. 101).

Habakuk resumes his performance, speaking his song. The prophet Isaiah seems to have entered their midst, standing in the empty space—in the Center, the Light. Bach's *Sonata for Unaccompanied Violin* emanates from Habakuk's violin, its sonorities echoing about the room, swelling, expanding, and encouraging holy presences to penetrate the sacred circle. Jeremiah, Amos, and even the Nazarene penetrate where prayer and melody have become one and words have taken on the rhythmic quality of cosmic soundings.

Habakuk's playing takes on a different quality. As he lifts the bow that sweeps over the strings, a new force seems to have been released within him. Speaking as he plays, he projects a whole inner dimension into Bach's composition, which now fills the silent room with its unearthly sonances. His verbalizations—awesome and moving—are like visitations. "It all begins peacefully. . . . And soon the terror sets in. . . . Everything is tossed. Nothing keeps still, keeps fast. A fearful wind. . . . What will remain of all this . . ." (p. 103). Silence. Only the pounding of hearts can be heard. The forces of nature, chaotic, whirling, and confused, invade the sacred space prior to the prophetic visitation.

Habakuk utters Isaiah's apocalyptic words as he plays: "Behold the Lord rideth upon a swift cloud." The notes grow fervent, passionate, and fearful. Darkened clouds and blackness cover the world. "And he shall come into Egypt . . . and the idols of Egypt shall be moved at his presence" (19:1). Scales rise and descend in rapid sequences, as flame covers the earth. "And they shall fight everyone against his brother, and everyone against his neighbor; city against city and kingdom against kingdom" (19:2). The holocaust ravages. Life vanishes. "And the waters shall fail from the sea, and the river shall be wasted and dried up" (19:5). All withers; the earth is parched and bleak. Habakuk hurls out his notes, which twist and plunge, fall and cascade, in powerful spasmodic beats.

Habakuk questions: How can one survive these swiftest of currents? these most fearful of storms? these shattering, bruising, burning destructive forces? Is there hope of Salvation? (p. 104). Does Habakuk identify with Isaiah's prophecies? Does he *see* Nature's turmoil in Bach's music? Does the Spirit of God alight upon him as he plays? Is Habakuk describing the next war—the war of Liberation? Which of the young people in the room will perish?

Bach's archetypal tones, coupled with Isaiah's pronouncements, release shock waves throughout Habakuk's system. He has shed the weight of empirical domains, carving out new paths, discovering fresh outlets that lead him ever deeper into his mystical *Center,* to the source of all being or the God within. The *mystery of prophecy* has taken root. The tones emerging from Habakuk's violin—the instrument whose tones most resemble those of the human voice—are transmuted, like the patriarch Enoch, who walked with God, into a living fire. Words have become burning coals, alighting onto matter and then ascending to the firmament, spreading blocks of light throughout the blackness of the vaulted heavens—and throughout the *darkness* of the *glowing* cellar room.

Yizhar's Habakuk is a prophet and revealer who attains atemporal spheres through music and the word. A *nabi,* to use Martin Buber's expression, he bears God's message, becoming God's mouth and revealing His hidden mysteries through primordial sound: *the inaudible speech of inwardness.* When Habakuk plays, barriers vanish, impediments disappear, obstacles melt. Linguistically speaking, an association may be made between the words "prophecy" and "music"; the root of *nagen* (the Hebrew word for music) is *mug* ("to melt").[13] Music, then, is that power that melts or fluidifies elements and fractures rigid forces that prevent access to the feeling world. Music stirs the senses and the mind, forcing them to ascend or descend and dilate at their own pace. Habakuk has an epiphanic experience: Yahweh appears in a powerful storm and forces the clouds to darken and winds to shake the earth, seas to rise, and worlds to tremble—metaphors for the mystic's visitation and the poet's inspiration.

What has Habakuk read in the stars? the young people ask him. Habakuk continues to sing out Isaiah's words, to Bach's tonal modulations. "He shall smite and heal" (19:22), he intones, as upper and lower registers merge in a powerful harmony. The tones dim. Abrasive, searing dissonances shoot through the silent room. Color tones, ranging from the darkest of nights to the clarity of supernal spheres, flood the cellar. "Evil is not eternal," Habakuk chants (p. 106).

Habakuk's playing grows frenzied. Suddenly, as if God has communicated with him through sound, pace, and pitch, his prophecy commences: two of the youths in their midst, Yehiam and Ya'acov, will be killed; a stray shell will explode and kill Habakuk. Peace will then flow over the earth; clouds of war will no longer pursue humanity—blessings will be theirs. "I will rejoice in the Lord, I will joy in the God of my salvation" (Habakkuk 3:18).

Naomi, whose eyes shine like Sabbath candles, looks at each of the young people in turn, drawing them "into her goodness" and into her light. Guardian of the home, she stays the flood, points the way, and utters the prayer.

The concerts in Habakuk's cellar are over. War comes. The narrator and some of his friends join the Haganah and Palmach. Since Habakuk is too old to fight, he is sent to a kibbutz to dig trenches. One noontime, as he and some other laborers sit down to rest, they begin talking about the possibility of a cease-fire. A volley of shells bursts. Habakuk is killed, along with the others. He is buried on the slope of a hill, shaded by a pine grove. No memorial day has been allotted him. There is no ceremony; nor does anyone place a flower or a green branch on his tomb. No one ever knew Habakuk.

Lives converged momentarily in Yizhar's story, "like stars whose orbits cross once and part again, who knows if ever in eternity to meet again" (p. 108).

Habakuk, the patriarch and father figure, revealed the path of feeling, compassion, and love to those in need, through an intensification of consciousness brought about by a profound affinity with archetypal music. Tone became spirit (*ruach*). The violin, echoing and radiating its sonorities, activated transpersonal layers within Habakuk's unconscious, enriching and further strengthening an evolved ego. Habakuk has discovered his own inner light in God's radiance; he is a man whose faith is unassailable, like that of the biblical prophet who said: "The Lord God is my strength, and he will make my feet like hinds' feet, and he will make me to walk upon mine high places. To the chief singer on my stringed instruments" (Habakkuk 3:19).

10 Bhasa's *Dream of Vasavadatta:* Archetypal Music, a Sacred Ritual

Sanskrit theatre, of which Bhasa's *Dream of Vasavadatta* is a paradigm, fuses music, song, dance, action, and iconography. Whether in hymnal chantings, songs, orchestral compositions, or accompaniments during dance sequences, music in classical Indian theatre is archetypal. As Ananda Coomaraswamy wrote: "Indian music is essentially impersonal. It reflects an emotion and an experience, which are deeper and wider and older than the emotion or wisdom of any single individual. Its sorrow is without tears, its joy without exaltation, and it is passionate without any loss of serenity."[1]

Dramatists living in the first centuries A.D., such as Bhasa, were knowledgeable in musical systems, acting styles, and technical aspects of theatre—requirements in approaching the complex, concrete and abstract, worldly and metaphysical rules and regulations governing Sanskrit theatre. The instrumental and vocal music contained in the dramas was archetypal in nature because it was designed to convey eternal truths. As for the text, it was not merely spoken; dialogue, which alternated between prose and verse, was chanted, sung, or articulated in multiple meters. Costume, make-up, dance, body movements (legs, feet, toes, torso, and so forth), facial expressions (eye, eyebrow, cheek, chin movements), and the whole gestural language involving the physical person were metaphors for the mysteries of the invisible cosmic experience.

The aim of Sanskrit theatrical performance (which differs completely from Western concepts) is to create in the spectator a feeling of aesthetic delight (*rasa*), expressed not through words exclusively, but via suggestion and the combination of art forms: music, action, and gesture. An abstract, transpersonal perception, *rasa* comes into being via songs, symbols, and audibility. What is crucial in Sanskrit theatre are the *emotions* conveyed by the dramatist—not the story line or the characters. The protagonists are not considered real; they are prototypes, or idealizations, portraying certain basic human feelings (*bhava*) as concretized in specific situations.

Sacred Music: Cosmic Breath and Chantings

The various art forms are viewed as a unified whole during the theatrical spectacle in classical Indian drama because music, dance, and drama are considered sacred. Music, an earthly transposition of harmonies sung by the Gandharvas (celestial musicians), was believed to have been given to humankind by the gods. The Gandharvas were the husbands of the Apsarases, the heavenly nymphs who danced at Indra's court. It is said that the sage Narada, Spiritual Son of Brahma, the Creator, was the first musician. He brought into being the *Saraswati Veena*—the oldest Indian stringed instrument—which the goddess of learning, Saraswati, loved best.

The human voice is basic to Indian classical music, being used for recitation, humming, and vocalization of the Vedas, the holy books of the Aryans who invaded the Indus Valley (c. 1500 B.C.). The chanting of lyrical stanzas around three tones (tonic and the two whole tones on either side) in Sanskrit meters creates, so it is believed, a link between humankind and immortal beings.[2] The *brahman*—a title in later times identified with a member of the priestly cast—recited prayer, in which the breathing techniques used were in time personified and deified (Vayu became the god of wind or air). Human "breath" was associated with prayer, thereby identifying the *brahman* with a *universal principle*. Rituals based on the repetition of mystical syllables and phrases (*mantra*), such as *om mani padme hum*, were considered replete with psychic energy, or libido. The chanting of these sonorities, inwardly and in silence or exteriorized in tonal modulations, enabled the believer to evoke the gods or a transpersonal principle. We learn in the *Rig-Veda* that the power of sound as enunciated in certain formulas discloses cosmic principles and a whole secret initiatory language empowered to awaken various inner dimensions within the initiate.[3] Since sounds applied to prayer are holy, like a hierophany, they are emotionally charged. The universality of the feeling aroused within the practitioner depends upon the succession of notes created, their harmonies, and their rhythmical modes. Such soundings are archetypal; they are objective and subjective, detached and attached, paving the way for the individual to communicate with the Absolute or the All. The *Rig-Veda* and the *Yajurveda* contain certain musical formulas capable of arousing specific states of being or levels of consciousness. Instruments are also mentioned in these sacred texts: the alteration of their pitches, their rhythms and intensities, as well as the player's emotional and spiritual involvement in the musical phrases, heighten and sharpen the transpersonal experience.

Melody in classical Hindu musical systems is based on *ragas*. The word has its root in *ranj*, "to color." Figuratively, it means "to tinge with emotion." *Ragas* are intricate musical or harmonic phrases which govern the entire pattern of a piece. There are approximately 54,831 *ragas*, each possessing its own name and performance instructions. Certain *ragas* are sung at specific times of day or during specific months or seasons; others are associated with temperaments or emotions (love, fear, peace, serenity, etc.). They are aɪ hetypal in that they connect the individual with the collective and the temporal with the atemporal. The performer (or singer) who plays the specific *ragas*, adhering to the rules and regulations attached to this impersonal melody, improvises and embellishes by adding nuances and colorations of his own, thereby realizing his own talent and creativity and the intensity of his feelings, while also leading audiences into their own depths.

Bharata's Natyasastra

The rules and conventions for the arts in India were laid down by the legendary sage Bharata (dates ranging anywhere from the second century B.C. to the second century A.D.) in his thirty-six-chapter work *Natyasastra* (*The Art of the Theatre*). The word *natya* in Sanskrit means theatre, and *bharata* is defined as actor; the three syllables in his name are believed to refer to drama, music, and the dance. Theatre, which is a composite art, rests on the evocation of melody, emotion, rhythm, and an iconographical language.[4] The visual image, then, is interrelated with sound and movement; each must be balanced and in harmony with the other before *rasa*, or an aesthetic and spiritual relationship between the stage happenings and the spectator's psyche, can come about.

For Bharata, drama means "the imitation or representation of conditions and situations." As such, it is antipodal to Aristotelian notions of pity and terror, since these require *mimesis* of action.[5] Action is not the *sine qua non* for Sanskrit theatre; as we have already suggested, *rasa*, or enlightenment, is: that is, the awakening and participation of the cosmic experience via the performance. Dramatic action comes into being when certain factors disturb the previous condition of spiritual and emotional equilibrium, when desire, be it material or psychological, is aroused and the longing to fulfill it requires the overcoming of obstacles. The factor that has displaced the previous harmony and unity is looked upon with fear; to restore the plenitude of Oneness is the goal of Sanskrit theatre in general, and *The Dream of Vasavadatta* in particular.

Bhasa's Dream of Vasavadatta

We know virtually nothing about Bhasa, the author of *The Dream of Vasavadatta*. Scholars have placed his dates anywhere from the fourth century B.C. to the first century A.D. His birthplace is given as somewhere in northern India. The story narrated in *The Dream of Vasavadatta* is based on a legend from the *Ramayana*, embellished by the dramatist. The play's theme conveys *rasa*—that is, aesthetic delight—which is born with harmony, and *bhava*, emotionality dealing basically with human feelings.

The play is included in the *heroic* category of Sanskrit theatre and dramatizes a power struggle: the Raja Udayana of the Vatsa kingdom is vying against the ruler of a neighboring kingdom. Because a love motif is interwoven into *The Dream of Vasavadatta*, it also falls into the category of *lyrical* Sanskrit plays. Its two main *rasas*, then, are heroic and lyrical.

When notions such as heroism and love predetermine a play's action, the musical accompaniments—songs, chantings, and instrumentation—are not to be considered in their specificity, but rather in universal terms. Emotions such as love and heroism transcend the tearful individual situations according to Bharata (and this is true for Bhasa's play), abstracting protagonists and audiences from their immediate environment. Whatever their nature, emotions (*bhava*), as we have suggested, take on a collective or *supramundane* quality. They are not, therefore, exclusively empirical; rather, they convey "a unique category of experience unlike anything that is known to result from ordinary worldly pleasure."[6]

Archetypal in nature, *bhava* require a dissociation from the ordinary mortal or empirical emotion, allowing the emergence of aesthetic enlightenment, or *rasa*. The aim of such a transpersonal experience is to arouse a sense of serenity within the spectators, divesting them of the restlessness they might have known during their daily activities. To inundate them with feelings of bliss is to enable them to glimpse Supreme Beatitude.

Because emotions and the music accompanying these affective experiences are archetypal in nature, Bharata divided them into *major universal* and *accessory unstable* feelings. There are eight listed in the first category (desire, laughter, anger, sadness, pride, fear, aversion, wonder) and thirty-three in the second (discouragement, weakness, apprehension, weariness, etc.). Because the unstable emotions are ephemeral, they can become involved with the eight stable ones, producing dramatic situations. In *The Dream of Vasavadatta*, the combination of universal and personal, unstable emotions leads to the progressive development of the drama.

Technical Factors

The stages upon which *The Dream of Vasavadatta* may have been performed in earlier days were—in keeping with Bharata's dicta—either rectangular, square, or triangular. They were not overly large, so that the text, song, and body language conveyed by the performers could be heard and viewed at close range by the spectators. Sections of the theatre, divided into orchestra and stage areas, were not separated by any curtain. A greenroom was located in the rear of the performing space: its two entrances were separated from the stage by a curtain. The stage proper was divided into two parts: an elevated section and an acting area in front.[7]

At the outset of a classical Hindu dramatic performance, the orchestra enters first. Its members sit down between the two entrances leading to the greenroom; they face the stage and the audience. Since the drums are the most important instruments, the timpani is placed in the center; vocalists stand or sit on the right, with string instrumentalists to their left and flutists to their right; a female singer sits opposite the male singer.[8] Instruments are tuned, scales are played, drumbeats are heard, and clapping to keep time is also rehearsed.

Music is the groundwork of the play. Bharata wrote: "Songs based on *rasa* and context make the drama dazzle as the heaven with the stars. As without colors, a drawing is not beautiful, so is drama not attractive without music."[9] The singers may sing their *ragas* with words or in pure vowels. Nonverbal sonorities are believed to prove better the performer's virtuosity and to create increasingly pleasing combinations of tones and rhythms. The appropriate *ragas* are determined by locale, situation, season, and hour of the day, each paralleling to a great extent the protagonists psychological conditions, the intensity of their spiritual and physical involvements.[10]

The Performance

Since classical Hindu theatre is an offering to the gods, the locale where the play is performed is a virtual *temenos*. Everything connected with the theatrical ritual is sacred: the gods are watching, and for this reason, prior to the performance, water is sprinkled about the stage to purify it; oil lamps are lit near the pillars placed onstage; and incense is burned to cleanse the air. The female protagonist enters, makes an offering of flowers to the deity of the stage, and bows to the musicians and to their instruments. The Stage Manager enters. His two assistants carry an earthen pot filled with water, and the flag of Indra: this god was the protector of drama and those who participated in the aesthetic event.

The Stage Manager gives his benediction and also invokes the blessings of the audience. He then introduces the theme of the play by chanting some of its verses: "This is bad. The servants of the king turning out the people of the ashrama—I know their duty is to protect the princess, but—."[11] Two guards enter: "Make way, you. Make way." The audience knows immediately that some spiritual force or attitude has been transgressed and that *dharma* (virtue) has been spurned.

The two people who were pushed aside are Yaugandharayana, King Udayana's prime minister, who is disguised as a Brahman, and Vasavadatta, impersonating his sister Avantika, but who is in reality the monarch's wife. We learn that Yaugandharayana, ambitious for his king, has used every method, including the prophecy of holy men, to further the plans he has for his sovereign. The prophecy suggests that Padmavati, the daughter of the Raja of Magadha, with whom Udayana seeks to ally himself, will become his queen. Yaugandharayana has explained the situation only in part to Vasavadatta. She does not know about the marriage plans. Vasavadatta has agreed, therefore, to follow Yaugandharayana's suggestions and disappear from the king's life, making believe she has perished so as to enable Udayana to marry again. During a hunting expedition (prior to the happenings in the play), Udayana's camp at Lavanaka, a town near Magadha, was burned to the ground by agents of Yaugandharayana. Upon the monarch's return, he was told that his wife, along with his prime minister, who attempted to rescue her, has perished in the fire. It is at this point that Yaugandharayana and Vasavadatta, both wearing disguises, enter the ashram where the play's opening scene is located.

The audience is aware of the fact that Yaugandharayana and Vasavadatta are being turned away from the ashram and treated roughly by the guards. The Hindus are believers in the "Four Ends of Man," which must be obeyed at all times: *dharma*, which orders people to live righteously and virtuously by keeping to ethical works and standards, *artha*, which encourages individuals to live active lives, seeking to gain what they can materially through heroic and chivalrous means, but always in harmony with the social welfare of the state and the family unit; *kama*, which suggests that one enjoy the fruits of love and pleasure, but never become enslaved by them; and *moksa*, which encourages one to withdraw from the active world into the ascetic sphere after one has experienced fulfillment in the empirical sphere.

By fulfilling his plans, Yaugandharayana has acted unethically. He has not obeyed the rules of *dharma* virtue: *artha* (social good) is in conflict with *kama* (love). He has evaded his moral obligations, which are the very foundation of custom and religious law. To achieve his end he has set fire to the royal camp and has lied about the queen's demise. Yet, it may be argued that, since *dharma* implies a code of rules ensuring the well-being of the community, to enhance the king's power further is a valid excuse for such conduct.

The action in the opening scene is set in an ashram, indicating the sacred nature of the play. A retreat for ascetics, holy people, gurus, and students of Hindu religious works, the ashram is required for all those adhering to the "Four Ends of Man." Youths of Brahman class are taken into the forest to live in an ashram at the age of eight (the ages vary for other castes); there they are initiated into Brahmanic ideals. The knowledge gleaned by probing sacred texts constitutes a second, or spiritual, birth (the first being physical birth). After having undergone the spiritual disciplines required, the initiates' intuitive and intellectual faculties have been tested and they are able to reach various levels of understanding.

Ashrams are usually located in wooded or secluded areas embedded deep in natural surroundings. Living close to the world of nature, the initiate is predisposed to communicate with the Absolute in a domain where time and space become non-existent. The phenomenological world for the Hindu—the ashram in this case—is not merely a place or an object, but a manifestation of an emotional and spiritual condition.

The stage directions indicate that a Lady Hermit enters the ashram—this impersonal sacred area. She enters, paradoxically, seated. Since body language is of such import in Sanskrit theatre, and since neither decors nor virtually any accessories are used, body language is the medium by which she conveys her stilled movements. The actress manipulates her legs, thighs, hands, and arms, and details other emotions by means of facial expressions—all accomplished in a sitting position.[12]

The Lady Hermit welcomes Padmavati. Greeting her in endearing terms, the princess reveals her sensitivity and gentleness. She chants her feelings: "And your sweet words make the place even more pleasant" (p. 262). Vasavadatta, who is also present, is impressed by Padmavati's beauty and graciousness; she expresses her reactions in an aside accompanied by specific hand movements, postures, and tonal emanations. To guard the very close relationship that exists among word, music, and gesture, each flowing in and out of the other, Vasavadatta's iconographic movements and vocal modulations are precisely synchronized.

Both Padmavati and Vasavadatta may convey their feelings in song, expressing their personal emotions aesthetically and transpersonally, thereby exteriorizing and perhaps becalming the tumult within them. Choosing the *raga* appropriate to the mood, they may raise the pitch and intensity of the moment by means of semitones. The grace implicit in the actresses' improvisations also indicates the sweetness of their characters. Singing, as has already been suggested, is the product of great discipline; indeed, like yogic exercise, it requires concentration and breath control.

Padmavati's maid, addressing the Lady Hermit, talks of the princess's forthcoming marriage. Vasavadatta believes, erroneously, that Padmavati is to be betrothed to her brother and is delighted. When Yaugandharayana learns that Padmavati wishes to grant presents to those in the ashram, he approaches her and asks her to care for his sister (the disguised Vasavadatta), whose husband has gone abroad. Unaware of Yaugandharayana's plan, Vasavadatta expresses her surprise in precise body language, facial expressions, and vocalizations. She agrees to remain in the ashram, believing Yaugandharayana must have good reasons for suggesting it. When Padmavati agrees to care for her, the prime minister concludes that "Fate has an answer to everything" (p. 264).

A young Student enters, then looks toward the sky. He is tired, he murmurs. Eye movements and hand gestures convey the extreme heat of the day; they also express the time and the season. When he crosses his palms, for example, then moves one hand over the other and points to the sky, pausing in so doing, he is informing his audience that the sun is directly above. His description of the locale, accompanied by an appropriate *raga*, conveys the spirituality of his feelings. He may begin his recitative slowly, sustaining his awe and wonder at nature's bounty: "The deer wander about freely, breathing the harmless air. No cultivated fields nearby. The fat brown cows, the trees thick with fruit and flower, and of course the thick smoke from the huts climbing up into the sky" (p. 264). As he gestures, displaying a loose fist and first finger, pointing to the trees and other dazzling earthly works, he creates visual patterns in space. For the Student—and the audience—all is alive, mobile, and inviting in this ashram. A mood has been set, and a spiritual outlook conveyed in sequences of verbal and visual images and nuanced sonorities.

When Vasavadatta sees the Student, she immediately veils her face, impressing Padmavati by her extreme modesty. Welcomed into the holy place and given some water to sip to refresh him and dispel his fatigue, the Student reacts to this kindness. He tells Yaugandharayana, who asks him where he came from, all about the fire in Lavanaka which destroyed an entire town. Then he begins describing the king's reaction to the queen's demise: he is inconsolable and has covered himself with ashes. He does nothing but weep.

At this juncture, we learn of the king's undying love for Vasavadatta, underscoring one of the play's main motifs. On stage, Vasavadatta transmutes through song her feelings of joy at being so deeply loved. Her tones vibrate with emotion and flow forth virtually automatically, merging her specific feelings of love and longing with the infinite source from which they emanate. For the Hindu, such love is viewed archetypally as an earthly replica of divine union between Shiva and Shakti (female energy), the *linga* (sacred phallus) and the *yoni* (sacred womb). Emotion here, as before, is accompanied by specific movements of the torso, legs, face, hip, foot, and toe.[13]

Vasavadatta, listening to the Student's words, is reassured of Udayana's love; she reinforces her feelings of joy in corresponding verbal modulations, thereby conveying her longing to see him and her fear of the difficulties which she must undergo to reach her ends. The tempo also reveals her pain and discomfiture at the separation, evoking a responsive feeling in the spectator.

The mood is further accentuated when the Student repeats the King's lamentations: "O Vasavadatta, my queen, my wife! O Vasavadatta, my beloved!" These verbal abstractions, when coupled with instrumental music and hand and body gestures, are concretized for Vasavadatta and the audience. Love is no longer a mere abstraction; concretized, it heightens the universal emotional states conjured up: restlessness, longing, bashfulness, doubt, and other such complex ephemeral feelings. As the Student pursues his description of the King's tearfulness, recapitulating the real incidents, he informs those present that Udayana's ministers finally convinced him to leave the village of Lavanaka, and when he did so, "the stars and moon left too. The village lay in darkness" (p. 266). It was then that the Student also left.

Udayana's character has been conveyed in word and music. Integrity, love, and compassion are his motivating forces. It is no wonder that Vasavadatta is so enamored of him and willing to sacrifice her own joy for his well-being.

Evening has descended on the ashram: "The birds are now in their nests, the hermits have gone to the pool. How brilliantly the sacred fire gleams! The wayworn sun turns his chariot into the mountain cave" (p. 267). The close relationship between human and natural worlds is underscored by the tonalities sung by the performers and droned by the orchestra, which are based on on nature's own audible patterns: the cries of animals, the chirping of birds, the cow calling for its calf, or the bleating of a goat. The *tonic* notes of nature emerge. Because of the elemental factor in Hindu music, feelings long dormant or simply buried deep within the human being are awakened by orchestration.

Act II takes place in the palace grounds at Magadha. A servant circles onstage and may speak in high vocal registers, since she is shouting from a distance, informing all present that Padmavati and her retinue are in the garden playing ball. Vasavadatta has also joined in the merrymaking. Flowering plants surround these young girls at play. Padmavati's face is moist from the heat and dampness of the day, but this serves only to embellish her beauty. As for the game, it is an excuse to introduce song and dance into the happenings, thus underscoring the mood of fun and frolic. The *raga* for this sequence is spirited, with overtones of tenderness and pain. The graceful play of these girls, the short and staccato-like rhythmic patterns of their jumps and falls, interwoven in pleasing verbal and vocal motifs, offer both audience and divinities a most charming and alluring spectacle.

Padmavati soon tires. She chats with Vasavadatta, informing her of her desire to marry Udayana. Surprised and dismayed (though she dissimulates her reactions), Vasavadatta experiences acute distress. When she learns that the King has not instituted this marriage, but that it had been suggested by his ministers for political reasons, she considers Udayana blameless. Then, when Padmavati begins to declare her love for Udayana, because he is a "gentle man," and is handsome as well, Vasavadatta agrees with her, nearly giving away her identity. Quickly, however, she explains that someone has told her of his good looks. Vasavadatta's mood has altered from one of regret and longing to one of surprise and dismay. Tears of bitterness had been Udayana's after her supposed demise, she notes; now, however, since a marriage has been announced, "Darkness descends on my heart," she confesses, withdrawing still further into her loneliness and pain.

A disconsolate Vasavadatta is featured in Act III. She walks about the stage—now the palace garden—as though she existed in a transpersonal realm. She finally sits on the only accessory on stage: a bench. As she meditates, song emanates from the very depths of her being, blending inner vibrations with cosmic tones and rhythms. Everything pulsates. Her lamentations, conveyed in whispers, mental images, and in barely audible musical sequences, impose a mood.

While the others are preparing for the marriage festivities, Vasavadatta probes her own fate. "But I will live, I will cling to sad life, in the hope that I can see my husband again" (p. 269). Love and anxiety fill her world; these emotions, carried over to the visual domain, are expressed in body and hand gestures and eye and head movements. Her entire being becomes a metaphor for the deeply moving sensations which fill her world.

A maid sees her sitting ever so gracefully under an arbor: she is "high-born, loving, and intelligent" (p. 270). When Vasavadatta is told that she is to be chosen to make Padmavati's marriage garland, she is torn by excoriating pain: "The gods are cruel, making this a part of my duties," she tells herself, highlighting her speech with facial gestures which further suggest the pathos of her situation (p. 270). The fact that she has placed duty above love, and the good of society over her own personal welfare, suggests her strength and heroism and the greatness of her sacrifice.

Yet, Vasavadatta is human. The greater the Maid's admiration for

Udayana's person, the angrier Vasavadatta grows. She does, nevertheless, carry out her obligations. She takes the basket of flowers handed to her, empties its contents, and examines each of nature's wonders, one by one. The Maid informs her that the avidhava-karana flower prevents widowhood. Vasavadatta, then, will place many of these in her garland—for Padmavati and for herself. When she comes to the flower that "stops the arrival of another wife," she decides to reject it (p. 270). As she picks and plucks the right flowers for the garland, miming each of the gestures with appropriate movements, instrumentalists may also add their soft and lyrical modes. Eyebrows, nostrils, lips, cheeks, and chin all work together in Vasavadatta's face to create an image of both poignant sadness and permanent love for nature as well as for Udayana. Enriched by sound and the visual experience, the specificity of the feelings experienced is universalized, encouraging all those participating in the spectacle to identify with her situation.

The King has just entered the inner palace, the Maid tells Vasavadatta, who had completed the garland. The Jester enters, laughing. Reminiscent of Shakespeare's clowns, he introduces comic relief into a dismal situation. A *raga* may accompany the Jester's spoken words, reinforcing the spirit of merriment which sets in. He speaks or sings in syncopated rhythmic patterns. Times have changed, we learn; the king, who had been so despondent over Vasavadatta's death, has sought out a new wife. Paralleling this situation is the Jester's own discomfort: he has eaten too much during the festivities and complains of indigestion. His banter, subtle repartee, and lightness of foot, though humorous, point up an unsettled condition and the undefined direction of events.

Padmavati and Vasavadatta enter the pleasure garden. Padmavati wants to see the sephalika flower in bloom; its redness brings out the greenness of the other plants, she says. A *raga* ushers in the gladness of spring, with its intoxicating aroma of flowers, which fills the heart with glee and a certain melancholia as well. Just as music, dance, and bodily movements are significant to the text of Sanskrit drama, so, too, are colors. Red, as used here in referring to flowers, signifies a life force. It replicates fire, the ardor of youth, and desire, as well as the sanctity and mystery of love. Green, a natural and subdued tone, represents the fullness and richness of nature, particularly when associated with royal lovers.

Padmavati wants only a few sephalika flowers to be plucked, in order not to spoil the vision of the beauty and charm of the garden as a whole—a replica of her inner world, which she seeks to disclose to her new husband. Padmavati loves Udayana and imparts her feelings to Vasavadatta, who declares that the king's first wife had loved him even more than the princess does. Vasavadatta once again nearly gives herself away. How does she know the former queen's feelings for Udayana when she never saw either of them, questions Padmavati. Covering up her error, Vasavadatta adds: "She [Vasavadatta] would not have left her family the way she did if her love had been ordinary" (p. 272).

Precise choreography is required in this sequence, which features Padmavati, Vasavadatta, and a Servant on one side of the stage and the King and Jester on the other. A sense of activity, fluidity, and communicability is underscored, establishing a variety of moods to be conveyed. Nature's luxuriance and greenness, without the use of representational decors, props, or lighting effects, may be conveyed through the *raga*, in which the soft lyrical tonalities of the instrumentalists serve as accompaniments to the rhythmically nuanced vocalizations of the protagonists.

The Jester waxes poetic in describing the locale and in setting the stage for the King's revelations: "soft breezes in the garden, the scent of flowers plucked and strewn on the ground." The colors of Udayana's costume disclose his heroic and artistic temperament: orange is identified with bravery and courage; purple, with love; gray, with sadness. His facial decorations suggest his lofty position. Udayana reminisces about his great love for Vasavadatta: "the god of love fired all his five arrows at me the moment I saw the beauty of Vasavadatta. Now he shoots at me again. Hasn't he only the five arrows, though? Where does he get the sixth?" (p. 273).

The Jester embroiders upon nature's beauty: "Look at the lovely cranes, sir, up in the autumn sky, flying in formation like the outstretched arm of a man." He points to these various marvels with his finger, with a variety of eye and hand movements. The King adds to the Jester's descriptions when speaking of their beauty: "Now straight, now curving, swinging up and down like a massive constellation. The sky is like the belly of a serpent, and the cranes are the line that runs its length" (p. 273). The *raga* now heard further reflects nature vibrating in the stillness of soft, plaintive tones.

The women, on the other side of the stage, take up this same motif. They look at the cranes, described metaphorically as "flying lotuses." Vasavadatta, however, is fearful. She must hide, she realizes. She invites Padmavati and the Maid to follow her behind a jasmine bush. There they can listen to the King's lamentations and learn about his newfound joy without being seen. But uneasiness tarnishes Vasavadatta's feelings of elation as the two men walk toward the jasmine bush. To dissuade them from approaching too closely, the Maid shakes the bush, arousing the bees, which will keep the King and the Jester away. The ruse succeeds. Udayana returns to the bench, and the Jester follows.

The syncopated conversation pursues its course. Vasavadatta's sorrow augments as she learns of Udayana's love for his new bride. The singsong quality of the monarch's feelings may be conveyed in vocal half tones: deep sorrow at the loss of his first wife, and feelings of elation after his marriage to Padmavati. Tears fill Vasavadatta's eyes. She explains this sudden emotional flow as a reaction to the pollen in the air due to the Maid's shaking of the jasmine bush.

The Jester questions Udayana: "Did you love Vasavadatta more than you love Padmavati?" (p. 274). The King refuses to answer. Padmavati is annoyed by the Jester's interrogation. He is hurting her husband. The Jester pursues his queries: "You're my prisoner, sire. If you don't answer, I won't let you budge from here" (p. 275). Udayana acquiesces: "Padmavati is the finest lady in the world—for her beauty, her character, her grace. But she cannot take my heart away from Vasavadatta." In an aside, Vasavadatta reveals her satisfaction. "I have suffered, but now I suffer no more" (p. 275). She sees that the King is deeply disturbed as he reveals his feelings: "Even if my grief departs, my love remains rooted in her. And so my memory brings back my grief . . . this is the way with ordinary people: they get relief by shedding tears" (p. 276).

Padmavati walks toward the King to comfort him. Meanwhile, the Jester brings him some water in a lotus leaf. Padmavati asks why. To wash out his eyes, he explains. Pollen got into them from the dust in the garden. The entire sequence parallels what had taken place moments before on the ladies' side of the stage. As Udayana washes out his eyes, brushing them lightly with drops of water, he asks Padmavati to sit with him. He won't tell her, however, the reason for his tears. It would be too upsetting to her.

Act IV begins with a servant rushing onstage and calling to another: Padmavati is in the Ocean Room and has a very bad headache. Such physical manifestations of a painful emotional condition are relatively frequent in Sanskrit theatre, enabling audiences to understand the depth of despair. Emotions make inroads into the body, triturating, bruising, hurting it until someone—or oneself—helps heal the wound. Vasavadatta is called upon to soothe Padmavati by telling her a beautiful story. A *raga*, which would elicit a calming and serene effect to still her torment, may be offered at this juncture. The attempt to cure illness through tonal vibrations is implicit in Hindu metaphysics. Music, as an elemental power, can bring about such changes and can ease tension in the human heart and mind.

The Jester enters the stage muttering to himself: "Even on his marriage day the King cannot forget Vasavadatta. Such is love!" (p. 278). Udayana's inner world is predominant: he seems to be living in another realm as he walks onstage, lamenting the loss of his great love: "tall and graceful . . .

my wife whom the flames killed as frost kills the lotus" (p. 278). The *raga* chosen for this interlude determines the intensity of his feelings as well as their colorations and nuances. Each note emerging from the single-toned instrument which is his heart will vibrate, tremble, and stir the stilled atmosphere.

The Jester asks Udayana to see Padmavati; his presence may relieve her headache. The King agrees, and together they walk toward the Ocean Room (another stage area), only to find it empty. The Jester decides to entertain Udayana until Padmavati's return. (A parallel situation will be enacted between the princess and Vasavadatta.) As the Jester begins his humorous interlude, inadvertently or perhaps with premeditation, he mentions Vasavadatta's homeland, which instantly triggers the king's memory as a segment of the past floods his present. "Such memories . . . of her at her music lesson," he murmurs, while his fingers grow limp suddenly, then begin "strumming the soundless air" (p. 280). Droning tones emanating from the orchestra may replicate the delicacy of Udayana's feelings as he evokes his tender love. Interestingly, it is here that his artistic temperament comes to the fore; his understanding of music and his probing of natural phenomena reveal the universality of his feelings.

The Jester now will tell him another story, repeating some of the words over and over again—like a mantra. Udayana, now lying on the bed, is captivated by the Jester's prolonged tones; he seems hypnotized by the richness of their tonalities. The King falls asleep and the Jester leaves. Moments later, Vasavadatta enters. It is dark, and she thinks that Padmavati is in bed, alone, untended, and unloved. She lies down beside her (him) to keep her (him) company. Soon, the King begins to dream and talks in his sleep. Dreams, for the Hindu, are considered more authentic than the waking condition; bathing the individual in spaceless and timeless dimensions, they enable him to immerse himself in a transpersonal domain, abstract himself from worldly attachments and individual situations, and see things and people atemporally.

Vasavadatta listens to her name being pronounced by Udayana in his dream. Music seems to emanate from each of its syllables. Her joy, however, is short-lived. Fear intervenes. If she should be discovered, Yaugandharayana's plan will fail. Yet, "How sweet to listen to him!" Udayana implores Vasavadatta to speak to him.

> KING: My dearest, speak to me.
> VASAVADATTA: I will, I will.
> KING: Dearest, are you angry?
> VASAVADATTA: No, not angry, unhappy.
> KING: Come to me, dearest. (p. 281)

As Udayana stretches out his arms to embrace Vasavadatta, she realizes she must withdraw immediately, and she does.

The entire dream sequence, rendered in stylized movements, with minimal gestures and in softly vocalized tones, emphasizes the transpersonal quality of the entire scene. Dreams flow into reality at this point, fusing two worlds into an indissoluble unity, which is a manifestation of the Absolute. Even the tones of their voices may blend and the rhythms of their modulations pulsate in a newfound unity. This blending emphasizes the passionate nature of their feelings and metamorphoses the cosmic patterns of love episodes between divine beings—Shiva and Shakti.

The spirit of integration, so sensitively revealed in the dream interlude, comes to an end with Vasavadatta's departure and the Jester's entry. Udayana awakens. He is in a good mood, knowing that Vasavadatta is alive. But she is not, the Jester tells him. The King was dreaming; his vision was a mere illusion. "Let me dream forever, if it is a dream," Udayana pleads; "let it stay with me forever" (p. 281). Despite the Jester's negative replies, Udayana is convinced he saw his wife. "I saw Vasavadatta's face, her long hair, her dark eyes—I saw the lady of chastity. She touched me here: my arm still trembles with love of her" (p. 281).

The mood suddenly alters. The Chamberlain enters and announces that Udayana's army is ready for battle. Elephants, horses, chariots, and a vast array of soldiers are prepared to crush the enemy. Udayana's presence alone is needed to begin the struggle. A heroic *raga* should be played at this point to reinforce the martial mood. Love, lamentations, mirth, and tenderness have receded from the stage happenings. The soldier in the King has been awakened. Fierce struggle and intense combat lie ahead, as suggested by clear vocal tones, and also by the instrumentalists' loud and powerful drummings and their rhythmic and continuously accelerating beats. Udayana's fighting spirit has altered his countenance: the lovesick man has been transformed into the fiery leader. "Our arrows shall fall like waves on his ranks, and the elephants and horses shall march triumphantly on the ocean of his sins" (p. 282).

At the outset of Act V, we learn that Udayana has won back his lost kingdom and that Magadha has become an important buffer state for him through his marriage with Padmavati. As the military man's energetic spirit diminishes (his battle is over), the lovesick widower's pained expression returns. We are informed that the King had heard a man playing the lute that very morning and that he went up to him and asked him where he had found the instrument. "Near the banks of the river Narmada" is the answer. Udayana takes the instrument, places it on his lap, and then faints. When he returns to consciousness, tears flow uncontrollably, so deeply moved is he by the presence of the lute, which he associates with Vasavadatta. It was she who had taught him to play it. The instrument is alive for Udayana; it breathes, feels, acts, and responds to his loving words. "Once you rested in the arms of my queen, Vasavadatta—how did you find your way into the lonely and musty forest? . . . You don't remember the love she showered on you, how she embraced you when we were together, smiled at you and stroked you softly" (p. 283).

The lute kindles the King's past love to even greater proportions. His memories cascade forth, enunciated in micro-intervals and in tender modulations, accompanied perhaps by a *raga* which elaborates on the theme, imposing its personal imprint on the archetypal musical structure. Mythical consciousness is aroused by the *raga*, which leads Udayana into the timeless and spaceless dimension of his inner world. Then, as he begins plucking the strings of the instrument, stretching them almost to the breaking point, the sharpened tones conjure forth a whole new world.[14]

The Chamberlain from Vasavadatta's clan is announced. Udayana is embarrassed. His conscience is not clear. He wonders how Vasavadatta's parents, the King and Queen of Ujjain, will feel toward him. After all, he had eloped with their daughter and never legally married her. "And I couldn't even give her the protection she needed" (p. 284). Udayana is guilt-ridden. The Chamberlain, however, dispels his fears. The monarchs of Ujjain admire Udayana's bravery and respect his victory. "Fortune was always on the side of the courageous and never smiles on the weak and the hesitant." Udayana, in turn, wants the envoy to convey his gratitude toward his parents-in-law, who had brought him up like a son. He also wants them to know that Vasavadatta will never die. She lives in his heart as well as in the instrument which he holds so closely to him. The Chamberlain further reassures Udayana by informing him that Vasavadatta's parents had wanted her to marry him and that is why they asked her to teach him to play the lute. "But you were rash and ran away with her." After their departure, however, the wise monarchs of Ujjain had a plate made on which they had the portraits of Udayana and Vasavadatta etched; they also performed a wedding ceremony for the couple *in absentia*.

The Chamberlain hands the plate to Udayana, whose joy knows no bounds because he feels himself loved and forgiven. That he has a visible likeness of his beloved makes her presence still more real for him. Padmavati, sitting beside him during the interview, recognizes the woman in the portrait as Yaugandharayana's sister. Let her be brought here at once, Udayana orders. Vasavadatta enters and is asked to remove her veil; her reunion with the King is deeply moving. The *raga* that may be played at this moment, supplemented with facial movements and body language, heightens the intensity of the emotions. What makes the meeting that much more noble is the fact that only now does Udayana realize the depths of Vasavadatta's love for him. Her sacrifice is the manifestation of this great harmony of feeling.

Since polygamy was practiced in India, it is not surprising that at the conclusion of the play Udayana, Vasavadatta, and Padmavati unite in deep love. Harmony and balance have been restored where there had formerly been friction. A *raga* suggesting serenity in love and heroism leads to the condition of *dharma*. Virtue has now been restored. The drama—disruption—has ended.

The Dream of Vasavadatta may be considered a kind of initiation ritual of deprivation and ensuing pain, required for an understanding of the fullness and meaningfulness of a love experience. As in any creative work, the spectator experiences Bhasa's play according to the level of his or her understanding, spiritual insights, and sensitivity. For some, *The Dream of Vasavadatta* may reveal transcendental knowledge of primordial unity in the Brahmanic tradition. For others, it may disclose the importance of the "Four Ends of Man," the ancient and still ongoing Hindu metaphysical belief in *dharma, artha, kama,* and *moksa.* Still others may come away with a new understanding of the fusion of the arts (text, music, dance, body and gestural language, etc.) needed to bring about a harmonious interlude—a paradigmatic way of understanding cosmic unity as viewed in the Vedic and Upanishadic hymns. The archetypal music which governs the play reinforces the sacred nature of the stage happenings, leading the protagonists—and spectators as well—along their path to Salvation. The *ragas* used in *The Dream of Vasavadatta* are replete with potential and psychological and spiritual nuances. Their modulations disclose subtle and sometimes brash hymnal qualities, while their rhythms and pitches reverberate in a variety of complex soundings, affecting the psyches and senses of the protagonists and spectators, stimulating one set of emotions as they deliberately play down another. The human voice may take on the power of a *mantra*, reinforcing mood and mode, while the orchestral accompaniment parallels and reinforces the dramatic atmosphere of the moment, heightening the heartbeats and accentuating what is distressing, but having a calming effect as well.

Throughout the dramatic sequences, the aesthetic experience has been deepened and perceptions have gone beyond the personal drama of two individuals. The vastness of a cosmic happening is embraced. *Rasa* has brought enlightenment to protagonist and spectator, through participation in a living and breathing aesthetic ritual—*The Dream of Vasavadatta.*

O Mind! drink and revel in the ambrosia of melody; it gives one the fruit of sacrifice and contemplation, renunciation as well as enjoyment . . . they who are proficient in sound, the mystic syllable *OM*, and the music notes—which are all the form of the Lord himself—are liberated souls.[15]

11 Guan Hanqing's *Jade Mirror-Stand:* Archetypal Music as Multiplicity in Oneness

Music in *The Jade Mirror-Stand,* by the Chinese dramatist Guan Hanqing (Kuan Hanch'ing, 1280–1368), is archetypal in that it illustrates multiplicity in oneness, a concept in keeping with Chuang-tzu's (369–286 B.C.) view of music as an all-encompassing force with infinite reverberations.

> Perhaps you only know the music of Man, and not that of Earth. Or even if you have heard the music of Earth, you have not heard the music of Heaven. . . . Perfect music first shapes itself according to a human standard; then it follows the lines of the divine; then it proceeds in harmony with the five virtues; then it passes into spontaneity. The four seasons are then blended, and all creation is brought into accord. As the seasons come forth in turn, so are all things produced. Now fullness, now decay, now soft and loud in turn, now clear, now muffled, the harmony of Yin and Yang. Like a flash was the sound which roused you as the insect world is roused. . . . By the warm breath of spring . . . followed by a thundering peal, without end and without beginning, now dying, now living, now sinking, now rising, on and on without a moment's break.[1]

Archetypal music, metaphysically speaking, is crystallized emotion or distilled feeling, thoughtfully coordinated in reflection and rigorously disciplined in sequences. It may be said to center and stabilize a spectacle, to further and build action, while at the same time disclosing mysteries of human nature hidden in a great silent world of potential.[2]

In Chinese theatre in general, and in *The Jade Mirror-Stand* in particular, music is not merely entertainment or embellishment. It is part of a worldview, as well as a religious and social approach to life. Confucius, considering musical theory in his work *The Book of Rites*, states:

> Music is produced by tones and based upon the response of the human heart to external things. Thus when the heart is moved to contentment, its sound is broad and slow; when to joy, it is ebullient and free; when to anger, coarse and shrill; when to reverence, direct and austere; and when to love, harmonious and gentle.
>
> Music is the harmony of Heaven and earth, rites are the order. Through harmony all things are transformed; through order are distinguished. Music arises from heaven; rites are patterned after earth. . . . Therefore the sage creates music in response to Heaven, sets up rites to match earth. When music and rites are fully realized, heaven and earth function in perfect order.[3]

Music in *The Jade Mirror-Stand* is archetypal in that it exists transpersonally as energy, which has the potential of actuating a whole symbolic and poetic universe. In Guan Hanqing's play, as we shall see, it also acts as a linking device, connecting an overvalued thinking function to a repressed and undervalued feeling side of a personality.

Archetypal music, as implicit in *The Jade Mirror-Stand*, is introspective, as opposed to Aristotelian *catharsis*. Rather than being expressed externally, the libido it arouses is withdrawn from the outside world and driven into the psyche. Contents within the unconscious are aroused, to be sure, by the music's timbre and cadence; when, however, they emerge into the phenomenal world, they take on, paradoxically, fixity: love, hate, jealousy, fear, and so forth, are rigid and unyielding in all ways.[4]

In classical Chinese theatre, and *The Jade Mirror-Stand* is no exception, passages that are sung are more important than spoken ones. They support, sustain, and flesh out a play's meaning and mood. An orchestra, seated on the bare stage, controls the actors' timing, gestures, and choreographed sequences; it also accompanies the performers' songs. Although melody in vocal music is restricted, since melodic inflection alters the meaning of words, it is, nevertheless, crucial to a play's pace, suspense, climax, and denouement. Poetic images in a Chinese play also evoke lyrical soundings which echo and re-echo onstage, each conveying the drama of a situation. When juxtaposed to other figures of speech, they may increase or decrease their dynamism, intensity, and emotional impact.

For the Taoist Chuang-tzu, as previously mentioned, music sustains harmony between earth and heaven; it is the outcome of a blending of male (*yang*) and female (*yin*) cosmic principles. When in harmony, music reveals inward purity and truth and leads to the proper functioning of an empire. For the moralist/rationalist Confucius, "right music" furthers social order: "Music is simple enough. First the instruments are tuned. Then the piece is played to completion in harmony, the notes all clear, and without interruption."[5]

Because of Confucius's emphasis on morality, music and poetry were closely affiliated in China. Each had to be "perfectly beautiful and perfectly good." Only then could transcendent joy be experienced: "I never dreamt that the joys of music could reach such heights," he wrote. Nor is it surprising to learn that Confucius advocated the banishing of certain types of music: wanton, corrupt, and clever tunes were ugly, and therefore not moral; nor could they develop the thinking process or lead to a country's growth.[6]

Guan Hanqing

Guan Hanqing lived in a turbulent era, when China was under the rule of the Mongols. Genghis Khan's grandson, Kublai Khan, had united northern and southern China and founded the Yüan Empire (1276–1368). Culturally, it was a cosmopolitan period: the route through central Asia, which had been closed for so long, was reopened; Muslim and Christian traders, including Marco Polo, ventured to the Orient. Military expeditions to Burma, Java, Japan, and other areas were undertaken. Towns grew; rural areas suffered economic hardships. As to be expected, the Mongols significantly altered traditional Chinese social patterns, particularly among intellectuals, the scholar-official class, and artists.

Cambaluc (now Beijing) became the political, economic, and cultural center of China, where a plethora of writers, storytellers, singers, and entertainers of all types gathered. These creative individuals, referred to as "talented men," formed guilds and book societies and in time held theatrical competitions. Such was the environment in which Guan Hanqing lived.

Although we know relatively little about Guan Hanqing's life, we do know that he wrote more than sixty dramas, only eighteen of which are extant. When still relatively young, he earned a reputation as a poet and songwriter. He was also educated in the arts of dance and music; he had a subtle sense of humor and was a fine foot-ball player. Later, he created his own theatre company and even acted from time to time. A man of the theatre in the true sense of the word, he knew every aspect of his art thoroughly.

Guan Hanqing was also proficient in music. Ballad-singing and opera, one of the most popular forms of entertainment during the Yüan period, were performed to a great extent in parks and in brothels by "singsong girls," entertainers/prostitutes. Guan Hanqing, who befriended these women, grew to know them, their ways, thoughts, and feelings—and their art. From the several hundred popular songs in vogue he selected certain melodies, then wrote suitable poetry for them, after which he would incorporate both verse and lyrics into his play.

Important, too, was the fact that Guan Hanqing's association with the "singsong girls" had made him privy to their hardships, needs, and sorrows. No one better than he understood their cant, their beliefs, their attitudes toward life, and their singing techniques. Such exposure to *real* life was crucial in his growth as a dramatist and lent variety to his theatrical themes: *Snow in Midsummer* and *The Wife-Snatcher* deal with the system of justice and corruption in the courts; *Rescued by a Coquette, The Riverside Pavilion*, and *The Jade Mirror-Stand* focus on love and marriage; *Lord Guan Goes to the Feast* and *Death of the Winged-Tiger* are historical plays.[7]

The Jade Mirror-Stand is based on a conventional story: the young girl who marries an old husband. Although Guan Hanqing was sensitive to the economic, social, and emotional needs of women, he nevertheless favored such alliances. Let us recall that polygamy was practiced in China at this period, that marriages were arranged, and that the plight of the young girl marrying into a noble, wealthy, or even bourgeois family was not enviable. Her husband might seek her out during the first few months or even years of their marriage, but soon she was replaced by others—many others, including concubines. Much of the time, she remained alone and despaired. As wife to an old man, on the other hand, she would receive all his love and be the center of his world.

The Jade Mirror-Stand

Act I

An empty stage greets the audience, unlike in Western theatre, where one or more actors are in view as the curtain rises. Mrs. Liu, a widow, steps out onto the platform, recites four lines of poetry, then delivers a prologue in prose that serves to introduce the characters and underscore the theme of the play. Although women's parts were traditionally played by men, seasoned actors sang with such ease in falsetto tones and in high registers as to deceive the most trained of ears.

> Flowers may bloom again,
> But youth will never return.
> Do not count gold a treasure:
> Happiness is more precious. (p. 136)

As a widow in a Confucius-oriented society, Mrs. Liu follows rigid moral, ethical, and political codes. She dresses as befits an older person, in muted tones, and wears flesh-colored powder rather than the reddish-blue of the younger woman. Her gestures are subdued, underplaying rather than displaying her feelings. Emotions, as experienced by Mrs. Liu, are condensed, revealing only the essence of feeling.

We learn that Mrs. Liu's husband died when still young, leaving her with a daughter, Qianying, now eighteen years old. It was he who had taught her the important arts of calligraphy and the lyre. Mrs. Liu is now looking for someone to continue the young lady's instruction. The mere mention of calligraphy and the lyre situates the family culturally and socially. Learning, let us note, was encouraged by Confucius. He held that it led to positive conduct, helping people to live good lives and thereby serving both the individual and the state.

Mrs. Liu's voice takes on amplitude at this juncture; her spirits are rising because on this very morning she heard the cries of magpies. For the Taoist, the magpie augurs well. This bird, daughter of the King of Fire, who ascended to heaven after her nest had become inflamed, is considered to be a good-luck fairy (*chien-niu*). Anyone who dreams of the magpie or sees it flying about is sure to know happiness.

After the death of Mrs. Liu's husband, her nephew, Wen Jio, a member of the Hanlin Academy, invited mother and daughter to move into his home in the capital. The invitation was declined, however, and Wen Jio's visit was scheduled at an appropriate time, preparing his entrance into the stage area. In his opening remarks, sung and spoken, he explains that he is a scholar and a public servant who works in the capital. "Now that we have a wise ruler, men of talent are promoted, and wealth and official rank seem easy to win" (p. 137).

The role of the "scholar-official" in China was of utmost significance. As we know, Confucius accorded great importance to learning, which he equated with wisdom, virtue, benevolence, courage, and reverence. Every man had to go to school, whatever his class. Those who were intellectually inclined studied for years and years to prepare for the government examinations. If they passed them, they were assured of highly prized official posts. Although many failed, they kept right on studying, taking their exams over and over again. Since society was tightly knit and functioned with order and morality, each person—the scholar-official in particular—was responsible for maintaining institutions and codes of ethics and for promoting the well-being of the nation as a whole. Let us not forget that China looked upon itself as a single family, ruled by a supreme sovereign, the Emperor, who was the Son of Heaven. He set the example; everyone else was expected to follow his lead.

That Wen was no longer young was relatively unimportant in terms of matchmaking, as we have already remarked. Although his shoulders may have been bent, or slightly rounded, or even stooped, and his hair gray or white, what counted was the fact that he was a scholar-official and hence a highly desirable party. To take a bride at a late age was not uncommon for one who had risen to the heights of his civil-service post. According to Confucius: "At fifteen, I thought only of study; at thirty, I began playing my role; at forty I was sure of myself; at fifty I was conscious of my position in the universe; at sixty I was no longer argumentative; and now at seventy I can follow my heart's desire without violating custom."[8] Wen had made his mark in society; therefore, he now had time to become involved in "affairs of the heart."[9] Upon delivering his expository song-poem, in which he gives an account of his character, he confesses his solitude in a poignant lyrical interlude.

According to the Chinese musical system, based on twelve notes (*lu*)—six male and six female tones—a foundation note (*hunag chung*) was sung at the beginning of the solo. It was considered of such importance that it was revered as an eternal principle. The foundation note had the power to further (or not) the individual's well-being as well as that of the nation. Absolute pitch, therefore, was crucial. It had been carefully determined as far back as the first century B.C., when an imperial office of music was founded to standardize pitch and to oversee the musical life of the empire. It is no wonder, then, that years of training were required by the actor to study instrumentation, pitch, tonal quality, and breath control, as well as all the mystical associations elicited by note and number.

Juxtaposed to the sorrows of loneliness, which Wen describes in perfectly rational and objective terms, is the economic, social, and cultural situation of government officials in general. They are, indeed, famous, wealthy, and powerful, resulting in constant bombardment by favor-seekers wanting to discuss personal affairs and also problems of state. Their authority and influence are such that when they frown they make a "tiger cringe"; when they smile, "sparrows flaunt like phoenixes." As for their writings, they take on "the brilliance of the stars in heaven" (p. 138). Wen pursues his learned discourse with great formality, mentioning Confucius, teacher of kings and guide of men, who had been shunned and neglected during his lifetime and who nearly starved to death.

> Confucius was a king without a throne,
> Whose teachings influenced the entire world.
> From him his disciples learned
> The rule of morality. (p. 138)

Wen mentions his heritage: his eminent clan and his ethical ancestors who were wealthy men and court officials. Despite his worldly success, however, his life is empty; his heart is a void.

> But my gilded chamber and painted hall are empty,
> I was lonely after drinking
> And pass the spring day in boredom,
> Saddened by the breeze and the moon.
> Shall I never hold a bride in my arms,
> And drown all my cares in the pleasures
> Of the curtained wedding bed? (p. 139)

Although he sings with emotion, a Confucian restraint marks Wen's demeanor. Metaphorizing, he suggests that as water flows down a mountain it gains in momentum and may trigger dangerous landslides. So emotion must constantly be checked, arrested, purified, and disciplined. His gestures follow the metaphorical thought: his hands move with definition and polish, and always with dignity.

The integration of intellectual and abstract concepts with poetry and music conveys a sense of unity not uncommon in the Chinese theatrical spectacle and also reflects a psychological condition. Wen, who has spent his life acquiring status so as to be worthy of his ancestors, has developed his intellect at the expense of his feelings. Whatever was related to his emotional life was repressed and undeveloped and held down to a primitive level. Emotionally vulnerable on occasion, Wen might act irrationally, allowing his sentiments to gush forth unexpectedly. Such outbursts could sometimes have detrimental results, as we shall see.

The archetypal tonal and imagistic qualities in Wen's song-poem flesh out his needs and deficiencies. The "gilded chamber" in the above passage implies an overlay: unnecessary ornamentation which covers something beautiful in its own right. His life, we may suggest, until now has been involved in decors, veneers, peripheral matters, and sham. He goes on to state that the "painted hall," colored on the outside for all to see and admire, is empty. Even when drinking with his friends, he is filled with loneliness. To combat his utter hopelessness, he has recourse, as does the Taoist, who believes that one must live *in* nature, to images of grass, trees, water, celestial bodies, and spring, representative of renewal and happiness. Although the summer months display their luxurious growth and their array of vibrant colors, they sadden Wen. He sees them as leading into the coldness and bleakness of an oncoming winter. His lyrical interlude grows increasingly energetic and even shrill in quality, as he confesses his pain and desperation. Aesthetically sophisticated, the tones he sings are inspired by nature's own sonances, as were the twelve *lu* of Chinese music, which were said to have originated from bird songs. Peppered with sequences of single tones, Wen's aria replicates the wind in the leaves and the fluttering of wings.

After circling the stage, indicating that he has been traveling, Wen stops in front of Mrs. Liu's house. He is invited to enter and is offered a cup of wine. Qianying is asked to meet the guest. She is reluctant to do so, sensing what her mother may have in mind. Obedient, nevertheless, as demanded by protocol, she enters in a way befitting a demure young girl: her knees are slightly bent, the weight of her torso resting on one leg, her top half turned away from the lower part of her body. Her arms, working as a unit in parallel gestures, move with naturalness and grace. Although her foot movement may go unnoticed because of the length of her gown, her steps are minuscule: she puts her heels down first, then her toes, which are turned outward, like those of a duck. Although she may take many steps, she covers only a small area onstage.[10]

In keeping with the complex protocol expected of the higher classes in a Confucian-oriented society, the musical, choreographed sequence follows a specific ritual. Mrs. Liu asks her nephew to sit in her husband's chair, according him the honor befitting his status as scholar-official. Wen hesitates, however. It would be too presumptuous to occupy such an august position, he replies in soft, pleasant, and well-modulated tones. His gestures, as skilled as his vocal nuances, are stylized, creating their spatial designs with precision and in perfect timing with the music and tenor of the moment.[11]

Mrs. Liu grows visibly impatient at Wen's hesitation and insists he sit in her husband's chair. He acquiesces. Qianying curtseys, in compliance with her mother's order to pay her respects to her cousin. Though she may move her pupils from side to side as she welcomes her cousin, her eyes, in keeping with her role as obedient daughter, are cast downward.

No sooner does Wen gaze upon Qianying than he is smitten with her appearance. Conveying his feelings in pantomime, he may lift his sleeve, partially hiding his face. He expresses his newborn passion in subtle, mellifluous song—languorous but controlled.

> My soul is taking flight,
> My eyes are dazzled!
> She is an angel from heaven,
> Powdered, rouged and scented,
> With tinkling pendants of jade,
> And gauzy, new, heavenly garments,
> Yet her charm is still her own.

. . . .

I devour her with my eyes—
Flowers are not so lovely as her cheeks,
Jade not so fair as her skin. (p. 140)

The rhythms alter as Wen's tones grow increasingly tender, in keeping
with the images accompanying his song-poem. The soul "taking flight" in
the above passage may be identified with a bird soaring to unimaginable
heights and sweeping into heavenly abodes. Like the bird, Wen sees himself as overpowered, blinded, stupefied by the energy of his catapulting
emotions. His eyes are "dazzled" by the light that radiates from this
perfect, sublime, ethereal "angel." The extreme motility of the ascending/
descending imagery, coupled with the metaphysical and psycholorlgical
impact of the tones themselves, increases his agitation. It must be noted
here that Chinese composers did not use the twelve-note scale chromati-
cally, but rather they chose from among the pitches to create a pentatonic
scale, suitable to the moment, mood, and character. When combined with
the five modes in Chinese music, the twelve notes produced as many as
sixty different tones.[12] To add to the complexities of the musical piece in
question, each of the five modes symbolized not only tone but also the
elements (earth, metal, wood, fire, and water), and social classes as well
(the prince, minister, people, and so forth). The vocal strain that such a
physical and spiritual range placed on the singer/actor was indeed great.

Juxtaposed to the tonal flights of Wen's song-poem, generating for him
flame, heat, and excitement, were the evanescent and erotic visions he
associated with Qianying. To concretize his feelings, he makes mention of
his beloved's earthly coordinates, such as powder, rouge, perfume, and
pendants of jade, which "tinkle" as she walks. For some, the red of the
rouge, the odors emanating from the perfume, and the jewelry which
rings out in clear, bell-like tones may seem mundane. Not so for the
Chinese, for whom they are transformed into "gauzy" and "heavenly"
garments, evoking lofty, but equally sensual, spheres. The rouge of
Qianying's cheeks, the blackness of her brows, and the smoothness of her
hair all enhance her beauty, but they are also sexually inflammatory,
particularly for Wen, whose feeling side has been so undervalued. More-
over, since virtually no decor was used in Chinese theatre, kimonos and
robes made of silks, satins, and brocades, and embroidered with silver and
golden threads, interwoven with brilliant greens, reds, turquoises, yellows,
and other colors, served to heighten the vibrant atmosphere. (Indeed, so
gorgeous and so highly prized were these costumes that they were handed
down from one generation to the next.)

That Wen should have mentioned jade in his song-poem not only relates to the play's title, but it also takes on metaphysical significance. Like gold, jade represents the sun's energetic power and its healing and nourishing qualities. Deep green jade—the most highly prized by the Chinese—is associated with earthly growth and fecundity. Taoists were convinced that the properties of jade assured immortality; accordingly, they filled the apertures of their dead with jade and gold in order to prevent putrefaction. Jade's beauty spells perfection. It embodies the five virtues—goodness, transparency, sonority, immutability, and purity—as well as the moral qualities of prudence, justice, harmony, and sincerity. No greater compliment could have been paid by Wen than to compare Qianying with jade.

Mrs. Liu asks her daughter to bring her cousin some wine; she does so with utmost grace and with subtle gestures, rarely displaying her hands, instead using her sleeves to convey her feelings. Though her lids cover part of her eyes, what remains visible is bright and expressive. All else in her demeanor is hidden, veiled, and mysterious.

Wen sees her glide along and responds to his tempestuous emotions in another rapturous song-poem. No matter how moved he may be, his performance, in keeping with theatrical conventions, is not a matter of inspiration or impulse but is rigorously disciplined. He focuses on her "slender fingers," which hold the cup of wine, and seems intoxicated by the very sight of them. A vessel of abundance, the wine cup dazzles him because his love's hands clasp it. A marvelously irrational domain comes to the fore; a virtually unknown world beckons to him. Not only is he aroused by erotic sensations, however; the heart is making him increasingly vulnerable to Qianying's beauty.

An *anima* figure, Qianying is a projection of the autonomous force that lives in Wen's unconscious: that soul image which kindles the flame of love within him. The energy that had been repressed, stifled, and sealed in that inner space is about to surface.

Qianying, holding the cup of wine between her fingers, determines the fate of the man for whom it is destined. She hands it to him, and so titillated are his senses by her proximity that he spills some of the wine on his robe. Psychologically, his feelings can no longer be contained; they overflow and overwhelm him. The richly sensual tones of his song-poem may increase in amplitude as timbre and single tones rather than melody dominate.[13] Unlike Western music, which is based to a great extent on harmony, Chinese music acquires its richness from the multiplicity of timbres and their upper harmonic counterparts.[14]

The mood of love and romance is brought to a halt when Mrs. Liu asks her nephew to teach her daughter calligraphy and the lyre.[15] Wen cannot teach these arts to Qianying, he confesses in another recitative. He does not have the expertise needed. Psychologically, he is uttering a truth, because proficiency in the lyre indicates, symbolically, mastership in the emotional domain. As for calligraphy, associated with the domain of beauty, also sorely neglected by him throughout the years, he affirms his incapacity to teach her an art in which line, texture, and form must be laid out in exquisite patternings.

Mrs. Liu insists. Wen must begin instruction the following day. Unable to contain his feelings at such a prospect, his tones vibrate in song as he compares his beloved to "a spray of cherry blossoms" that fills his heart with sorrow, but also with longing and wonderment.

> Just now the setting sun hung over the willows,
> Now dark clouds cover the sky;
> We shall sit together by the green gauze window,
> But when night falls I shall lie alone in the gloom;
> And rain dripping from the leaves
> Will only increase my despair. (p. 142)

Moisture pervades his imagery. Tears inundate the musical tones, which now take on transparency and a crystalline quality. Such a mood is antithetical to that created by cherry blossoms, which announce the birth of spring; by the sun, which creates the glorious day; and by the willow, associated with divine law and immortality. Wen sees only their melancholy side—vestiges of a world from which he has cut himself off. Although wrapped in bleakness, he dreams of the "green gauze window" which allows him to look outside his world/room upon nature. In so doing, he feels a sense of release, a burgeoning of hope, and an invitation to love.

Act II

Rather than go to his office, Wen returns to Mrs. Liu's home the following day to offer his services as teacher of calligraphy and the lyre. He watches Qianying arrive on the scene: her sculpturesque form, sharply delineated against a bare stage, is comparable to that of a goddess, he muses. The metaphors and similes used to highlight the beauty of her flowing gown, with its "water" sleeves and V-shaped neck, its satin and silk embroidery, not overly ornate, but elegant in its simplicity, are conveyed in song.

> Her lotus skirt is flecked with kingfisher blue
> Her soft neck is white as jade. . . .
> She is an angel who scatters lovesickness,
> And could I see this fair vision in my dreams
> I should not dread even the approach of dawn;

> The moon might sink and the lamp burn low,
> But I should sleep on till the sun
> Shone through my eastern window. (p. 143)

Song and image are resplendent in their linearity and consistency, replicating the Taoist's identification with nature, the various times of day, and the cardinal points.[16] Such a rapport with the manifest world expands consciousness—so necessary for Wen, the rational, thinking type. The array of luminescent tones in the concrete depictions ("kingfisher blue") and their melodic equivalents in the bird songs encourage him to look through his "eastern window" onto life, joy, and physical pleasures. The rounded image of the sun, indicating a concentration of energy and fire tones, takes on a luminous and strong *yang* quality; then, focusing on a dependent moon, or *yin*, counterpart, Wen discloses a desire to link what had formerly been severed: the feeling and the thinking functions.

The "lotus," though universal in application, is particularly significant for Buddhists and Taoists. Representative of purity of being, it rises above the stagnant and mud-filled waters of life; its immaculate nature opens up intact to the spiritually and morally deserving. Rectitude and sobriety, as well as wisdom, are identified with this plant, upon which Buddha sat when meditating. Like a mantra, it brings peace and quietude to those who focus on its eight petals. Sexual connotations are also inherent in the lotus: its rigid stem connotes virility; its leaves and luxurious growth are identified with the vulva, that is, with abundance and prosperity.

Qianying's "lotus skirt . . . flecked with kingfisher blue" is an allusion to her as an ascending *anima* figure. Rising to spiritual climes, heady with a sense of release as she penetrates aerated regions, she parallels the colorful bird in Wen's song. A soul image, Qianying lives in Wen's unconscious as a dream or vision would, dispelling his fears of the approaching dawn, which brings increasing loneliness. In contrast to his opening song, Wen now welcomes the new day, which has taken on fresh meaning and luster, shining through his "eastern window."

Qianying is asked to play the lyre and does so with the grace and charm expected of this cultured girl. It must be noted here that Chinese performers are not only trained to play one or more character types (the ingenue and the singsong girl, for example), but they are also expected to be fine musicians. While the tones emanating from Qianying's instrument reveal her talent, they also disclose cosmic harmonies and mystical amplitudes. The manner in which she holds her instrument, and the virtuosity of her fingers as they make their way up and down the strings in complex patternings, are arresting. She is modest but not passive. Nor is she fearful. Having studied the Confucian code, she knows what is expected of her; she is intelligent and well-read, strong, and perhaps even willful.

Plaintive tones fill the air as Qianying performs, causing feelings to vibrate in Wen, who transforms them into another song-poem. Verbal and tonal paintings now cascade in animated resonances onstage: "embroidered silk curtains," a "gilded chamber" with screens "inlaid with silver." These brilliant colorations increase the lavish sparkle of the scene.

> What delight to listen to the seven strings
> As they echo joy and sorrow!
> This stately, unearthly music
> Sweeps away all worldly thoughts
> And banishes mundane cares;
> Her touch is light, and the music
> Is like the cry of wild storks in northern lands.
> Resonance ripples from the golden stop-key,
> Sweet harmonies from the chilly strings,
> And the touch of her slender fingers is exquisite
> In this art she has mastered superbly.
> Most subtle in perception,
> Pretty as cherry blossom,
> Pure as orchid,
> She embodies the rare virtues
> Of earth and heaven! (p. 144)

The archetypal music emanating from Qianying's lyre carries Wen's ego (center of consciousness) into suprapersonal spheres. His emotions have found a semblance of release, for there he experiences his *anima* in projection. He no longer feels alone and neglected, but instead feels related to this beatific figure. The tones of the seven-string harp which reverberate in his song reinforce his feelings of sublimity. His heart dances to the "unearthly music" which flows into his being. As her graceful fingers glide over those taut strings, they sweep "away all worldly thoughts."

The imagery is in keeping with Wen's incandescent sensations. "The cry of the wild storks in northern lands" is an omen of good fortune and filial piety: this bird is believed to nourish its aging father. It is said in China that if the stork just looks at a woman she conceives. No more positive and productive vision could inundate Wen's inner world at this time. Even the image of the "chilly strings," although bringing to mind cold and barren climes, is followed by that of the "cherry blossom." No longer does it presage a desolate winter, as it had prior to Wen's meeting with Qianying; now it spells hope and joy. Images of immateriality are evoked by the music: she is as "pure as orchid," Wen sings out, referring to a much-prized flower associated in China with spring renewal and generative qualities. Many species of orchids, it may be noted, grow in the air and not in the earth, drawing their sustenance from invisible sources. So, too, does Qianying exist within Wen as an ethereal, weightless being who floats about incorporeally. She is *anima* in all respects; to project upon her, as he does, permits him to relate to the feminine within himself and bring harmony to his own being.

The mood suddenly changes, as Mrs. Liu brings the concert to a conclusion. Wen must now teach her daughter calligraphy. Just as musicianship necessitates extreme discipline, so, too, does calligraphy. A sense of abstraction and definition is required to form and shape; to draw a picture in a few strokes demands a knowledge of perspective. Line, for the Taoist, is tantamount to the life principle: it is energy given meaning. The world outside, therefore, must be observed, digested, and interiorized; each character, in perfect clarity and accord with the next, must be placed in balance by the calligrapher.

Wen begins his instruction, and, as he tells Qianying to keep her wrist down and hold her pen straight, he squeezes her hand. The young girl grows angry. How dare he touch her hand! Taken aback, Wen apologizes. Despite Mrs. Liu's reprimands, Qianying has a mind of her own and quotes from *The Book of Rites:* "after the age of seven, boys and girls should not share one seat" (p. 145). Her mother accuses her of showing off her book learning. Nevertheless, Qianying's fortitude, her apparent stubbornness, and her wit and intelligence serve to tantalize Wen still more.

The lesson pursues its course to the accompaniment of archetypal music, which arouses increasing rounds of sensations in Wen, filling him still further with the warmth of belonging to the world around him—her world. The calligrapher, like the musician, although using the language of the brush, reveals content and mood through his figurations. In Wen's inspirational vision, he virtually apostrophizes the brush that Qianying holds:[17]

> O lucky brush
> Of rabbit's hair and bamboo,
> Caressed by such tender fingers! (p. 145)

The painter's brush had special significance for the Chinese, who believed it was endowed with a livingness and an energy of its own. Like an amulet, it had magic power, that of reproducing on paper what existed in an amorphous state in the mind. Usually made of rabbit's hair, the brush had an erotic nature that was underscored by its tapering shape and its soft resiliency. That Wen longs to caress and fondle what Qianying holds in her exquisite hands is obvious. Furthermore, the brush's handle of bamboo—a metaphor for rectitude—also denotes the phallus.

Soon, Mrs. Liu concludes the lesson, and Qianying curtseys and leaves. To Wen's great delight, her "footprints in the sand" remain (p. 145). Women's footprints and feet were fetishes in China. In high society, the feet of female children were bound, resulting in their deformation. Women could hardly walk and preferred to remain in seclusion, wholly dependent upon the man. Mutilation of the foot increased the man's power over the woman; psychologically speaking, it heightened his sexual pleasure, since he looked upon her as a child, to be cared for, adored, and desired. Slippers, usually silk or satin and exquisitely embroidered in various colors, also played a part in the foot cult; where they are viewed as an erotic image symbolizing the vagina, into which the phallus/foot was placed.

> Most slippers hide some lack of symmetry,
> The candid sand shows no mercy;
> But her footprints are flawless—
> Slender, well-formed and bewitching.
> She is charming in a passion,
> When she stamps her feet in anger. (p. 146)

As Wen observes Qianying's feet, he enumerates her many virtues in high-pitched tones, with generous use of tremolos to convey his rapture.

His song goes on to say that he is bewitched by her "white teeth," associated with aggressivity since they incise and masticate matter from the outside world. He grows excited by these energetic principles. Because teeth also protect and prevent intrusion into the body by unwanted forces, they mesmerize him. The battle is on: he is the hunter, and she the hunted. Qianying's "bright eyes" and her playful manner charm him still further. As he ends his song-poem, he may prolong the last words, emphasizing mood and also indicating to the orchestra that a change of pace and pitch is in order.

A plan matures in Wen's mind as Mrs. Liu suggests he find a suitable match for her daughter. To show the pleasurable nature of his thoughts, he rubs his hands together. His tones take on added vigor, but they always remain within the bounds of the code befitting a perfect gentleman. No need of a dowry, he informs Mrs. Liu: a gift of a "jade mirror-stand" from the husband to the wife, however, should be given (p. 147). Although his fingers and hands may flutter about when he sings at this point, revealing his nervousness, once his course is decided upon he conveys his sense of well-being by hitting the palm of one hand against the other, forcefully, so that the audience may hear the impact.

That the wedding gift is to be a jade mirror-stand is understandable, since jade, as we know, represents the highest of virtues: physical, moral, and spiritual. The mirror permits the observer to see herself as an individual and as part of the collective (heaven, earth, high, low). In China, the mirror, associated with the moon, is a yin force—a queen—as contrasted to the sun, the yang or emperor, who casts his brilliant rays upon the moon, injecting it with life and luminosity. The stand is the structure that keeps these two cosmic forces in balance, endowing the world with cosmos rather than chaos. It is the ideal wedding gift.

Act III

Wen enters the stage at a leisurely pace; Qianying, in slow and graceful steps; and the Matchmaker, called in for the occasion, walks relatively swiftly. Drums and flutes accompany the procession in discordant and shrill, but also mellifluous, tones.

The Chinese flute, a high-pitched wind instrument, conveys a thoughtful pensiveness and even feelings of melancholy. The Taoist believed that this instrument had supernatural qualities: the ability to generate light, to cut rocks, to create thunder and produce rain, to fecundate the earth. Because the sound waves emanating from the flute fill the cosmos, they can alter weather patterns and determine destinies.

As for the drum, it, too, is endowed with incredible potency. Varying in size, type, and material (wood, bronze, or jade), drums generate sonances that are equated with primordial sound. Loud or soft, strong or sentimental, the drumbeat underscores the emotional climate. Metaphysically, percussion instruments are associated with cosmic rhythms. Instrumental in directing the course of the sun and its ascension, the rhythm of these instruments indicates the growth of yang power in the play.

Drums and flutes convey Wen's attitude.

> If the player won't have me,
> Then I must take her by force. (p. 149)

Wen realizes that Qianying is still angry with him and intends to reject his advances, but he is so certain as to how to proceed that he is no longer concerned about her negative attitude. To the accompaniment of harsh, hammering drums, Wen sings out in forceful tones, but never wildly, as the drama's tension rises. He knows that reason must take precedence; to be objective and to think rationally is Wen's forte. Should he yield to his feelings, he would curry favor neither with Qianying nor with himself. To take a stand and to inspire his future bride with admiration is the honorable way, he concludes, his voice sounding in slow, stylized sonorities. Confucian training has taught Wen to evaluate his situation and then to act accordingly. He must banish, momentarily, that primitive feminine aspect of his personality which he had plumbed when giving way to his feelings.

Qianying's temper rises during this interlude, and her body trembles ever so slightly. Although her scorn for him is obvious, her feelings are internalized in keeping with Confucian tradition. Still, in a strong aside, she promises herself that should he step closer to her she will scratch his face. Although sensing her rejection of him, Wen sings out his confidence now that he has decided to resort to his thinking function. He enumerates what he believes will captivate her, the wonderful material things that will be hers when she becomes his wife: servants, "rare dainties," chests "crammed with silk embroideries," jade of all types, and so forth.

Moments later, Qianying is asked to drink the wine that will solidify her union with Wen. This time she purposely spills the elixir, indicating symbolically her contempt for such a loveless marriage. Qianying, the anima figure, refuses to be sacrificed to custom. Independent, perhaps even revolutionary for her time, she rejects the subservient role to which women have been relegated.

The Matchmaker, however, informs Qianying that should she not relent she would be "disobeying His Majesty's decree" (p. 152). Such threats and pressures, Wen believes, can only worsen the situation and encourage the young lady's wrath. He kneels before the Matchmaker, begging him to be gentle and understanding, after which he breaks into song.

> For I look on you as my goddess and guiding star . . .
> As my young and pretty wife,
> You will not use your needle
> Except to show your skill by stringing pearls;
> You will not wet your hands
> Except to wash them in warm, scented water.
> Married to a minister,
> You will have all the food and clothes you need. (p. 153)

To treat her like a "goddess," which is Wen's approach, is to encourage worship and, by the same token, distance and remoteness. This way, he remains psychologically uninvolved. But the mention of "stringing pearls" leads to the creation of a continuous living pattern and the perfecting and solidifying of relationships. A luna yin symbol comes into being with the mention of the pearl. Such an image spells perfection, since this iridescent form grows in watery regions, where it takes on its translucent colorations and its concentric layerings, perfecting itself during the maturation process.

Wen also promises her a carriage, horses, and driver:

> Your equipage is handsomely turned out
> With green tassels, gilded axle, silver nails,
> And brightly painted wheels,
> And no one else will share
> Your smart, distinguished carriage. (p. 153)

The flute and drums may speed up their rhythms in this interlude, paralleling an increase in agitation. The image of the carriage, a complex symbol, represents both heavenly and earthly spheres: heavenly, because of its square floor; earthly, because of its round wheels. The mast, holding the disparate parts together, is a kind of world axis or a mediating force between divine and terrestrial spheres. A vehicle, speeding through time and space, also carries one through the life/death experience. Buddhists equate the driver's course, which has such great significance, with *intellect*. It is not the speed of the chariot that is of import in this parable, but the driver, who must steer his fiery steeds, keeping them on the straight road, within the law of the land and not beyond the limitations of his personality. Identified with the ego, the carriage exists only through its parts as it makes its way into the vast expanse of the Self.

Master of his destiny, or so he intimates, and in perfect control of the shading of his musical phrasing, Wen informs Qianying that if she should marry a younger man she would be treated like a toy—"rubbish to be tossed aside"—once the honeymoon was over. Neglected and lonely, gazing upon her husband as he dispenses his favors to his concubines, she would pine away. He, on the other hand, would forever be true to her. "Even if fairies came down from the moon," he assures her, he would never look at them. It is finally agreed that Qianying will marry Wen.

Act IV

The action takes place in the dragon and phoenix pavilions in the capital. Prefect Wang, with all the pomp and ceremony befitting his station in life, enters with his attendants to the accompaniment of clappers, drums, and cymbals, thereby emphasizing the significance of the occasion.

It was customary in China for halls to be named after animals. The dragon, one of the most popular images, represented yang power, vigorous enough to infiltrate the universe. A guardian force as well, it protected the inhabitants of a palace from evil. Thus the dragon became the symbol of the emperor. Let us recall that as the head of state the emperor was its supreme functioning agent, responsible for its continuity. Prince among Men, he was revered and held virtually sacred power. As Confucius wrote, "he sets the good example, then he invites others to follow it."[18] Psychologically, the dragon may stand for potential force, the non-manifested contents of a psyche, which also protects it by keeping it within the bounds of a safe course.

As for the phoenix, though it soars to heavenly spheres, it is born of the earth and stands for that communicative energy and reciprocal force which encourages metaphysical, empirical, or psychological activity between polarities. The phoenix is androgynous—an emblem of conjugal bliss. The Taoist views the phoenix as the cinnabar bird, bringing from the south the flame of summer—like blood, a creative, fecundating, and energizing force. In that it dies in fire and is reborn from its own ashes, it represents the eternal life/death process.

The prefect tells Wen and Qianying that a feast has been prepared. The accompanying music, molded into sequences of patterns, is perfectly integrated with the gestures and movements befitting the occasion. Before partaking of the food and wine of their wedding celebration, Wen must write a poem. If it is well received, he shall drink wine from a golden goblet and his lady fair shall wear a gold phoenix pin in her hair and powder on her face. If his verses are not worthy, he shall be given water to imbibe from an earthenware pitcher; as for his wife, she shall put straw in her hair and paint her face black.

Gold, the purest of metals, indicates spirituality and solar force. As the royal emblem, it also endows humankind with intelligence and perception, and vegetation with the luminosity and warmth needed to grow. As for the chalice which contains the wine, an emblem here for the human heart, it is seen as a protective force, identified with the uterus that nurtures the fetus.

To wear a golden phoenix in her hair would not only enhance her beauty, but it would also endow Qianying with supreme virtues: yang would be added to her yin, permitting her to fulfill her role in life as wife and future mother. If, on the other hand, she must put straw in her hair, she would fall, socially and psychologically, from her previous high condition. As for the black paint, it would not only mar her beauty and besmirch her physically, but this chthonian hue, identified with the lower strata of society, befits one who performs inferior tasks. A countercolor, black is considered a negative essence associated with the *prima materia*, or undifferentiated nature. Her face blackened, Qianying would be unable to attain celestial heights and instead would remain embedded in the abysmal depths of humid darkness.

Wen knows he has the upper hand and decides to alarm Qianying by stating that he lacks confidence, not having written any verse since he passed his examinations many years ago. The parrying between Wen and Qianying in this scene, accompanied undoubtedly by music shifting from high to low registers, increases the excitement. Qianying is fearful; she trembles, always in stylized and restrained manner; she may frown as she begs Wen to write his poem. To paint her face black and to drink water from an earthenware cup would be too great a humiliation to bear. She must address him as "husband," he tells her, and no longer as "Sir." She concedes and asks him to concentrate on his work.

Wen is delighted with the turn of events. He will write the poem—a symbolic rite of passage—to finalize the nuptials. And so he does, singing out his pleasures in sequences of fifths, signifying the yielding of the woman.

The poem is well received, the gifts are awarded, the congratulatory feast is prepared, and "joy is complete" (p. 157). Wen bows to the prefect, as the golden goblets from which they all drink add glitter and resplendence to the pleasurable occasion. Woodwinds, strings, and percussion instruments enliven the banquet. Wen takes pride in his creative capacities as poet, in his character, which binds him to love and fidelity, and in his intellect, since he planned the entire venture—rationally.

> Now our marriage is a true one,
> The sorrows of love are ended,
> We shall take delight in each other—
>
> . . . .
> From now on we shall live in harmony—
> By my own exertions I have won my love. (p. 159)

Archetypal music, an important factor in Guan Hanqing's play and in Chinese theatre in general, not only adds to its richness and texture but replicates an ideological as well as a psychological condition. The song-poems floating about in the air, and the images which take on contour and shape, emerge from the oneness of the subliminal realm. The drama's audibility blends in shrill or melodious tones and a variety of timbres and cadences. Woodwinds, strings, and timpani are crucial in fleshing out the moods of the protagonists, the climaxes, and the moments of uneasiness, as well as the full-fledged eroticism running through the entire piece. The vocal images contained in spoken or sung words (ascending birds, tinkling jade, the wheels of a carriage, and so forth) take part, each in its own way, in the collective symphony which is the theatrical experience and the distillation of the drama of life. The shrill, clicking, twanging, piercing, resonant, mellow, soft, and mystical emanations of the instrumentalists, and the various vocal styles and modes of the performers, might not always be audible to the human ear. The overtones, resonating at such intense amplitudes, might evade the human capacity for hearing. As the poet T'ao Yuan (365–427 A.D.) wrote: "Only a zither without strings can express final stirrings of the heart."[19]

Archetypal music, as implicit in *The Jade Mirror-Stand*, reflects a behavioral pattern which works in secret and sometimes in silence on soma and psyche, coordinating feeling and thought in a world that exists beyond the visible and audible domain. It is a composite of opposites, which makes the unique act of creation possible. As Chuang-tzu wrote:

> When I played again, it was the harmony of the Yin and Yang, lighted by the glory of sun and moon; now broken, now prolonged, now gentle, now severe, in one unbroken, unfathomable volume of sound, filling valley and gorge, stopping the wars and dominating the senses, adapting itself to the capacities of things,—the sound whirled around on all sides, with shrill note and clear. The spirits of darkness kept to their domain. Sun, moon, and stars, pursued their appointed course. When the melody was exhausted I stopped; if the melody did not stop, I went on. The music was naturally what it was, independently of the player.[20]

12 Mishima's *Damask Drum:* Audible and Inaudible Archetypal Soundings

Yukio Mishima's Noh drama *The Damask Drum* (1955) discloses new concepts in archetypal sound: inwardly as well as outwardly heard pitches sounded on a unique and mysterious drum. In the religious and egoless world of Noh, the tones of the ritualistic beatings on this instrument create a network of silent as well as rhythmified patterns, leading protagonists and viewers into an undifferentiated aesthetic continuum: the fourth dimension. Whether audible or not, these archetypal reverberations spin their web about all those involved, thereby determining the drama's mood, plot, and choreographed sequences. The archetypal drumbeat *is* power and energy; it *is* concrete phenomenon. As such, it shapes not only events but the protagonists' fantasy images as well. At the same time, it lifts the veil which covers a haunting and terrifying inner world.

Yukio Mishima (1925–70), novelist, poet, dramatist, film director, and head of a personal army of approximately one hundred men, wrote successful Noh plays. Expanding their focus beyond traditional Japanese philosophy, history, and culture, Mishima's Noh dramas are transpositions into modern terms that answer contemporary spiritual needs. Past and present are blended into one symbolic dramatic ritual in *The Damask Drum:* image, texture, color, and tonality lure and allure the viewer into a complex of mysterious elements.

The product of a samurai upbringing, Mishima was educated according to the tenets of his class. The code of strength was of utmost importance, and courage, will, and loyalty to the Emperor had been impressed upon him since his earliest days. Spartan in his ways, honorable in his views, humble in his attitudes, Mishima was also a specialist in the martial arts of *kendo* (dueling with bamboo staves) and karate. There was, however, another side to this man of iron: he was a poet. Endowed with extraordinary sensitivity, Mishima understood and reacted to the exquisitely delicate aspects of Japanese art. Entering into complicity with nature in its most elemental ramifications, he felt the *livingness* of the Oriental's nuanced universe. As a student at Tokyo Imperial University in 1944, he set down his thoughts and feelings in a collection of short stories. The future Nobel Prize winner Kawabata, who became Mishima's mentor, encouraged him to pursue a literary career, and his advice was accepted by the acolyte. The author of 257 books (including fifteen novels, some of which have been translated into English), Mishima emphasized Japan's rich heritage and the poignancy of the confrontation which his culture had to undergo in modern times. At the age of forty-five, Mishima committed *seppuku* (ritual suicide), thus effecting in the real world what had been imagistically and symbolically portrayed in his premonitory work *Runaway Horses*.

Noh Theatre

Noh theatre came into being as a result of the extraordinary creativity of Kan'ami Kiyotsugu (1333–1384) and his son, Zeami Motokiyo (1368–1444), and the protection given them by the Ashikaga shogun, Yoshimitsu. Like this ancient art form, *The Damask Drum* also combines dance, music, and poetic recitation. Unlike Noh, however, there is no singsong declamation in Mishima's play; nor is there a chorus seated on the left side of the stage under a porchlike protrusion, chanting, speaking, or engaging in dialogue with the main character. The orchestra, comprising a flute, a stick drum, and two hand drums and seated to the right upstage, is also abolished in *The Damask Drum*. What Mishima does retain, however, is a single drum, which takes on supernatural and magical power. Nevertheless, the drum featured in this modern Noh play differs from the ancient ones, which were made of skins or horsehides with laced silk cords connected to two discs. When the discs were tightened or slackened, they yielded tones ranging from soft, rich soundings to high-pitched and almost metallic emanations. The instrument used in *The Damask Drum* is different: it is covered with damask and not hide. Sound, therefore, cannot possibly spring from its fibers, no matter how hard or how long someone beats it. Yet, it *does* sound at a specific point in the play—but not all ears are capable of hearing it.

Mishima abolished many of the sculptural and ritualistic effects of Noh, such as the alternating immobilized stances of the actors, their dances, the stomping of feet during certain interludes, and the sliding or shuffling walk. He did, however, introduce audiences to a Japanese dance master, who becomes the play's catalyst. Mishima also transposed situations. The medieval version of *The Damask Drum* featured an old gardener who worked on the grounds of a palace and fell in love with a Chinese princess. To show her contempt for him, she sent him a drum made of damask—not skin—promising him that if he could hear sounds emanating from the drum when he struck it his love for her would be requited. The naive gardener believed her and began beating the drum, which remained mute until he died of exhaustion. In keeping with the conventional two-part Noh structure, the gardener's ghost returns and extracts a terrifying vengeance from the princess, forcing her to expend her energy performing the same fruitless task until her end.

Mishima's *Damask Drum* introduces audiences to an old janitor, Iwakichi, whose job is to clean and maintain a law office. As the play begins he is talking to Kayoko, a pretty young clerk, who complains about the difficulties involved in earning a living and her problems with her boyfriend. During the course of the conversation, we learn that Iwakichi has fallen in love with one of the clients, Hanako, of the fashionable dressmaker shop on the other side of the street, whom he has observed only through the window. Kayoko derides the old man for his passion. Suddenly the lights are switched off in the law office, only to be turned on in the dressmaking establishment. We now listen to the conversation of four persons: a heartless dance master, an unfeeling young man, an arrogant member of the Ministry of Foreign Affairs, and the self-satisfied owner of the business enterprise. Irony and satire mark their discourse. We are informed of Iwakichi's love letters, which Kayoko has been delivering daily to the dressmaker's establishment. In an act of supreme derision, the dance master thinks up a plan to teach this old man a lesson. He takes one of his props, a drum, and attaches a note to it informing Iwakichi that if he beats the drum his ladylove will hear the sound and be forever his. The drum is thrown through the open window into the law office opposite. Iwakichi receives it, reads the note, and is thrilled at the prospect. What he does not know is that the drum is made not of skin but of damask. No matter how hard he pounds, no sound is emitted. His despair drives him to suicide.

The second part of *The Damask Drum* features Iwakichi's return as a ghost. His ladylove, Hanako, is no longer the pure idealized image he had believed her to be but is a "whore." Unrequited in her love experiences, she longs for Iwakichi's "real" love, as he does for hers. He beats the drum again and again, a hundred times, passionately, fervently. Both he and the audience hear the sounds. As a punishment for the woman's heartlessness throughout her life, however, she is doomed to remain deaf to the sound.

Iwakichi's despairing ghost finally vanishes. As for Hanako, she is alone, her face fixed in a vacant gaze.

Not only are the plot and characters modern in Mishima's play, but so are the sets and the entire theatrical structure. The traditional Noh stage was built on a level with the audience, giving the impression of being outdoors. White gravel spread in front of the stage separated audience and actor; it also functioned as a natural reflection for stage lights or sunlight. A new spatial arrangement is introduced in the contemporary work. No longer do asymmetrical forms and subtle colors occupy the attention of audiences; now there are three centers of interest and composition: the third floor of an office building in downtown Tokyo; a law office on the right side of the acting area, described as a "room in good faith"; and, on the left, a couturiere's establishment, "a room in bad faith." Center stage is occupied by virtually empty space: a street with neon signs flashing on and off, injecting brash elements of contemporary life.

The Damask Drum is a play in which the unexpressed is more important than the revealed. Silence predominates over the articulated word; the void prevails rather than the filled; and the amorphous is preferred to the formed. That the inaudible and audible drumbeats create a new time image in sound injects an arresting and intriguing sense of mystery, but it is also frightening. The unheard tones in the first part of Mishima's play are certainly plausible, since, no matter how hard one beats on a damask drum, the human ear cannot hear the sound. In the last part of Mishima's work, however, the situation changes. Because the variety of pitches heard by both Iwakichi and the audience cannot be heard by Hanako, feelings of malaise are created. The stage happenings have become illogical and incomprehensible. A world of imponderables has taken over.

Taoism, Shinto, and Zen Buddhism in Noh

For the Oriental, the world of soundlessness (really a misnomer, for the frequency of sound waves may be too high or too low for the human ear to apprehend) ushers in a mystical dimension in keeping with the religiously oriented traditional Noh drama. As in the ancient art form, *The Damask Drum* is imbued with the three most important Japanese philosophical traditions: Taoism, Shintoism, and Zen Buddhism. According to the tenets of these traditions, the transcendental rather than the individual sphere, the eternal and not the mortal, the life force (cosmic energy or breath) and not the concrete deity are to be experienced. Noh plays, therefore, bathe not in linear time but in cyclical arrangements. Accordingly, although *The Damask Drum* takes place in April, events could unfold in the burgeoning spring season after the arid winter of any year and in any place in the world. Although the decor is representational, it is also vague, indefinite, and symbolic, reflecting a mood, a vision, and an idealized love. Powerful emotions lead directly into a whole range of feelings and pain, which is controlled but burns inwardly, altering continuously in accordance with the cosmic life force. The visible elements—the law office on the one side and the dressmaking establishment on the other—reflect not merely the exterior world but an inner mystical and psychological climate. Because of the profoundly spiritual focus, viewers apprehend Noh drama in general and *The Damask Drum* in particular intuitively. Insights are released and enlightenment is experienced. The mystery of matter and sound becomes discernible, not, perhaps, in the phenomenological or audible world, but rather in the deeply spiritual universe of the Japanese soul.[1]

The Damask Drum, then, has maintained the formulas of Noh theatre in its spiritual outlook, themes, characters, and tonal qualities. Although it brings to the stage specific situations and individual beings, an ambiguous condition is experienced. The characters are archetypal in nature; they bathe in a mythical world beyond the space-time continuum. Like weight-less entities, they articulate their tensions, and grief grips them in spas-modic progressions. Like Zen Buddhism and Taoism, Mishima's play is meditative, introspective, slow-paced, subtle, and suggestive. The depth and meaning of Iwakichi's love may be apprehended in sudden flashes of illumination; it is not brash or aggressive, but turned inward. It is sensed. Like conventional Noh drama, *The Damask Drum* has no real plot. For a Westerner, an infinite amount of patience is required to understand the series of complex images which make up its song-and-dance sequences, its tonalities, and the inflections included paradoxically in the muted and sounded dialogue. All aspects of Iwakichi's sensations (the feelings evoked during the course of the performance; the tensions aroused by the images implicit in his discourse, poses, gestures, and pace; the timing, for exam-ple, between the sweeping sequences and the poetic apostrophe to the potted laurel tree in the office which he personifies and cares for with love and affection) are stylized and predetermined.

Nature and Noh

Important in *The Damask Drum*, as it had been in ancient Noh theatre, is the relationship between the stage proceedings and nature. Although the play takes place in two office buildings, there is a symbolic correlation between Iwakichi's feelings and attitudes and nature in general, reflecting a correspondence between the cosmic domain and the individual's phe-nomenological world.

In the collective and cosmic world of Noh theatre, nature is neither crushed nor violated, nor is it used exclusively for man's benefit, as is so frequently the case in the Western world. In *The Damask Drum*, nature is experienced as part of a whole; it is loved and appreciated spiritually, aesthetically, and physically. Iwakichi looks at the potted laurel tree in the office, for example, caring for it, loving it, personifying and apostrophizing it. He grasps its spirit and its superworldliness; he understands its beauty, its mobility, and its pulsations.

In accordance with the close correspondence between man and nature characteristic of Noh drama, natural forces are alive in *The Damask Drum:* wind, for example, to which Iwakichi alludes when he opens the window, enters into the stage ritual as a turbulent force and a catalyst. Iwakichi sometimes describes his feelings in terms of the wind, thus emphasizing their transpersonal nature: "I can't stand that dusty wind that blows at the beginning of spring." He longs for "the calm of the evening" with its "beautiful sunset." Spring, although specific, takes on universality because of the death/rebirth cycle of which it is a part. It reflects the rhythms of life as well as the lives of the society and civilization to which the protagonist belongs. Spring is the symbol of eternal renewal. It mirrors the notion of perpetual becoming and of love forever burgeoning and vanishing.

Iwakichi fears inner chaos, of which the wind, as it hums, is an outer manifestation. "The dusty wind" forces up the dross and earthiness of life as well as its spiritual counterpart. He rejects the frightening and sinister character of a wind which alters nature's seeming stability, and he longs for the stillness of the clouds, which endows the world with serenity. As the wind dies down, images of softness and tenderness appear in Iwakichi's mind, immersing him in the tranquil climate of his own being: "The wind's died down since evening" (p. 39).

In keeping with Shinto belief, everything in nature, whether animate or inanimate, is alive. Birds, for example, speak out their song iconographically to Iwakichi, and he responds to these energetic and melodious principles: "Those are pigeons from the newspaper office. Look at them scatter. Now they've formed a circle again . . ." (p. 40). Birds represent a link between celestial and terrestrial spheres and between superior spiritual and psychic states. That Iwakichi's birds are scattered indicates their lightness and their feelings of liberation from matter, so weighty and distasteful to those who seek to soar free and unfettered in airy realms. That they form a circle symbolizes a leveling of what had been hierarchized and therefore the need for an absence of distinction between peoples and classes. Iwakichi no longer feels socially subservient to his beloved; nor does he see a dichotomy between their ages. Diversity, then, has become unity. A longing for completion is also implied by the circle image—a continuous round, without beginning or end, encompassing time as well as space. Time, in this case, is viewed as a succession of continuous, invariable, and identical instants—rounds of sorts, associated, paradoxically, with the impermanence of everything in the manifest and unmanifest world.

Shinto deities (*kami*), in the form of spirits of trees, mountains, flowers, ancestors, heroes, sun, and moon, breathe, act, and react in the existential sphere. Man approaches the *kami* without fear and in friendship. In Mishima's play, a force, or *kami*, inhabits the essence of both the drum and the laurel tree. When Iwakichi receives the drum through the window, his hopes immediately dilate. He hangs it on the laurel tree, thereby bringing together what had been separated (the wood of the drum and that of the living tree). In ritualistic fashion, the primordial sound made by the magic drum, though unheard by human ears, fills the room, its rhythm and timbre replicating a whole hidden world of feeling:

> Laurel, lovely, dear, laurel, forgive me. I'm going to hang the drum on your green hair. Heavy, is it? Just be patient for a while. It becomes you. It becomes you very well, like a big beautiful ornament that has fallen from heaven into your hair. . . . It's all right, isn't it? Even when I begin to beat the drum, I won't shake your leaves. I've never before been so happy before you. Whenever I've seen you I've thought: My unhappiness has made you more beautiful, has made you put forth your leaves more abundantly. And it's true, my laurel, it's true. (p. 66)

Although the drum does not respond to Iwakichi's pleadings, the laurel tree does. It has been transformed in his fantasy into a princess, who takes on life in a garden inhabited by the moon: "She's the princess of the laurel, the tree that grows in the garden of the moon" (p. 40). All the poetry, sensitivity, and creative impact of his feelings emerge in this one symbol. Its beauty and gentleness become consoling forces for Iwakichi, who feels his loneliness with such desperation. His ladylove is compared to this celestial body: "If I tried to describe to you how beautiful her face was—It was like the moon, and everything around it was shining . . ." (p. 42). Fujima, the dance master, also uses the moon as metaphor: "Shading under a woman's eyes is a lovely thing, isn't it? Like clouds hovering under the moon, you might say" (p. 45).

The laurel and the moon, recurrent images in Iwakichi's world, also usher in a mood of melancholy. The moon, symbol of transformation, represents biological rhythms and cyclicality. Frequently evoked by Japanese poets, the moon is associated with indirect rather than direct experience and knowledge, as well as with passivity, receptivity, and the dream. As it makes its way in the night world of Iwakichi's unconscious, this celestial force conjures up a domain inhabited by spirits, ghosts, and images which would allow him to embrace his beloved. At the drama's conclusion, Iwakichi alludes to the moon as "covered with mud and fallen to earth" (p. 69). His sublime vision of the pure being he had loved has been defiled; his ethereal image, weighted with dross, has become sullied.

The Japanese have always been "moon lovers."[2] Iwakichi is no exception. The eerie and mysterious light which emanates from the moon suggests a dim, insinuating, and shaded domain. It is never brilliant or filled with glaring lights; rather it is remote, distant. Objects illuminated by moonlight are not individualized but blend into the environment—hazy, essentially obscure, hiding through the branches of the laurel, stirring the feelings of the onlooker. The moon's soft rays fall lovingly on the complex designs and forms of the stage. A shadowy world emerges, paving the way for the ghostly encounter in the second part of *The Damask Drum*.

The moon and the laurel are one for Iwakichi. Each injects a sense of belonging or participation mystique, and each endows the events with painful feeling-tones, underscoring the bleakness of Iwakichi's temporal existence and the beauty of his idealization. Yet, when Iwakichi's spirit returns, his beloved is no longer that chaste being he had created in his mind's eye, but rather a "whore" who longs for the purity of an unborn—unmanifested—love. As he beats the drum once again, hoping this time to bridge the gap—to link dichotomies between the invisible and visible spheres—the cold rays of an unfeeling moon envelop the atmosphere, divesting the world of all its warmth and leading to another painful demise.[3]

The notion of timelessness and eternal becoming, mentioned previously in the image of the circling pigeons, is clearly discernible in traditional Noh drama, as it is in *The Damask Drum*. Iwakichi experiences the three-dimensional and the four-dimensional worlds interchangeably. In the phenomenological domain, matter and spirit only *seem* to operate antithetically; in "reality," they are manifestations of the Taoist's yin/yang principles: a single universal cosmic force. Since matter and spirit are one in the atemporal sphere, death and life coincide, as do image and reality, fiction and fact, sound and soundlessness. Duality and multiplicity exist only in the existential domain, that is, in Iwakichi's empirical world. The conflicts which arise are stressed by Mishima throughout *The Damask Drum* not only for dramatic purposes, but also for metaphysical reasons. Age as opposed to youth, inanimateness and animateness, life and death, outer and inner domains, solitude and society, business and poetry, silence and noise are forever intruding one upon the other. As Iwakichi says, "They've switched off the light. Every day at the same time. . . . When this room dies that one comes to life again. And in the morning when this room returns to life, that one dies" (p. 42). The continuity of this duality expresses the eternal play of conflicting forces which must be endured in life.

Stage Setting in Noh

That Mishima has situated his drama on the third floor of two office buildings is in keeping with the important factor of verticality in Noh drama. The height of the office buildings corresponds to the mountains which figure so prominently in early Noh theatre. Motionless and awesome, mountains represent ethereal spirit and light circulating about the universe. So the office buildings in *The Damask Drum* reveal Iwakichi's idealized vision: his love, which is too absolute, and his desire, overly encompassing. The dichotomy between the purity of this image—that is, his ladylove (height)—and the earthiness of the woman of reality (ground) is too great to take on existence in the empirical world. It can only come to life in the imagination. Iwakichi's earthly fall in suicide at the conclusion of the first part of *The Damask Drum* compels him to take stock of the polarities between fantasy and reality and to rework his vision. Only in death does divergency vanish and oneness prevail.

Characters in Noh

Inasmuch as Noh theatre is archetypal and bathes in the collective domain, specifics such as characters and sets, as previously mentioned, are considered symbolically. Characters in traditional Noh theatre are generally fixed, as they are in Mishima's play. Iwakichi, the Old Man, corresponds to the *shite*, the main actor. Although he does not wear a mask, his face remains immobile and expressionless. It virtually becomes a mask, standing out in sharp contrast to his bodily movements, vocal tones, and the sculptured spatial forms which he weaves onstage as he sweeps the room, tends to the laurel tree, and writes his letters. Iwakichi's expressionless face severs him from the outside world, forcing him to look inward. "Emotional coloring" is injected by means of a variety of poses of the head and neck and by downward and upward glances and intricate gestures. The ensemble of accessories used by Iwakichi, such as his broom, the laurel plant to which he talks, the letter-writing ceremony, and his nuanced vocal emissions, is integrated into a new unity, thus making for a total effect. The individual character takes part in a cosmic drama.[4]

Iwakichi in many respects is reminiscent of a Zen Buddhist priest, who is detached from the material world, which he considers meaningless. He has swept it all away, symbolically speaking, and has rid himself of the dross and the material encumbrances which tie him to life. His inner riches—his fantasy world, his dream, the realm of the absolute—are of higher value to him. Only in the spiritual sphere does he feel the pulsations, breath, and cosmic rhythms of the universe about him; only in this domain does he experience the dynamism of life and feelings of belonging. The opposite world of artifice, materialism, arrogance, and cruelty is expressed in the dressmaking establishment across the way and represents forces with which Iwakichi must contend.

Kayoko, the young letter-carrying clerk, may be considered a kind of contemporary *waki*, a wanderer in the temporal and atemporal realms. She sets up the dialogue or chemical interchange between the two views of life. Although specific, the repetition of her activity takes on cyclical import: that of a perpetual death/rebirth ritual. Hope is injected into Iwakichi's life when she delivers the letters, and despair when no answer is forthcoming. Not only does Kayoko act as a link between Iwakichi's world and society at large, but she herself also straddles two civilizations: past and present. Beset by economic difficulties, she, too, is a victim of spiritual crisis: that of the individual who has not yet discovered her groundbed.

The dance master, the young man, the government official, and the owner of the dressmaking establishment are ironic, satiric, and humorous in a rather grotesque and even cruel manner. They are modern counterparts of the *kyogen*, those ancient clowns who kept audiences amused by their farces and jesting. Anonymous beings who emerge from nowhere and vanish into darkness, they serve to heighten tension and to explain the stage happenings in less than poetic language. They infuse comedy as well as cruelty into Iwakichi's poignant love situation by sketching vignettes through which are revealed unusual incidents associated with letters delivered by Kayoko.

The Sounded/Soundless Damask Drum

Although only a stage prop, the damask drum, as a symbol, is steeped in tradition. It is representational and yet remains functionless. Comparable to the *koan*, a device used by the Zen Buddhist to banish rational and syllogistic reasoning (techniques so dear to Western mentality), it serves as a basis for experience.[5] It allows Iwakichi to become exposed to the mysteries of existence, to intuit undreamed-of truths, and to transcend individual understanding. The drum causes Iwakichi's sudden awakening to the realization of his situation and its impossibility—hence his suicide. When he first takes hold of the drum after it has been tossed out of the office window into his own, he thinks he can win his beloved by pounding on it. He has not yet been initiated into the atemporal sphere of the *koan* and so is incapable of entering into that dimension which would allow him to understand the "foolishness" of his passion.

Iwakichi's drum-beating is doomed to failure. As a *koan*, it bathes in its own logic; it participates in cosmic consciousness, which is incompatible with that of worldly spheres. Iwakichi strikes the drum again, but it makes no sound; and again he pounds on it, in highly stylized gestures, his passion rendered that much more powerful by the very discipline of his gestures. "I'm going to beat it now, so listen! It doesn't make a noise. They've given me a drum that doesn't make a noise! I've been made a fool of. I've been played with. (*He sinks to the floor and weeps.*) What shall I do? What shall I do?" (p. 67). Had Iwakichi been trained by a Zen master, his comprehension of the meaning and focus of the object would have been deeper. As stage property, the drum belongs to the logical, rational, and intellectual sphere and is not part of the archetypal realm. In that it was sent to Iwakichi by those living in the temporal world, the drum represents formalism, convention, and geometrical, causal reality. The dimensionless universe sought by Iwakichi, and implicit in Zen Buddhism and Taoism, implies a world *in potentia*—the notion of perpetual becoming. The drum which Iwakichi beats but which remains soundless because of its material is as alive as the potted laurel tree.

Bells and chimes also fill Mishima's tonal and atonal world: the owner of the dressmaking shop rings a bell to stop the argument over how best to punish Iwakichi for his presumptuous love for one of her clients. The sound jars, disrupts, and cuts the interchange, paving the way for a pause and a change in course. When "delicate chimes" ring out, at the outset of the ghost sequence, another suspension of action is indicated, with the introduction of an atemporal sequence. Bells and chimes are important factors in Shinto ritual: their tones may indicate the presence of *kami*. In Zen Buddhist tradition, where prayer is inwardly oriented, bells, gongs, and drums play a significant role in the religious service. These acoustical intrusions are not heard by the practitioner's intellect, but by his belly, the center of consciousness. Because Zen Buddhist services are pursued in silence and meditation, interspersed with chantings and recitations, such metallic and tympanic sounds stir that much more forcefully. Like the blows given by the Zen master to his student when preparing him to receive the *koan*, these sounds cut the atmosphere and sear the protagonist, working on his flesh and nerves and shocking him into a new state of awareness.

When Iwakichi's ghost pounds on the drum at the end of the play, he hears it resonate, as does the audience. "My love will make a damask drum thunder." And the drum yields its full sound. "It sounded! It sounded! You heard it, didn't you?" (p. 75). But Hanako hears nothing. She is as insensitive to the pulsating of a real heart as she is to the drum roll. Again Iwakichi strikes the instrument in choreographed patterns: one beat for each of the letters he wrote. She is deaf to his efforts. Two worlds; two ways; two responses to the stimuli of music. Tension mounts as Iwakichi counts the beats: one, two, three—the sharp, penetrating primordial sounds hitting the ear as the drum discharges its agitated vibrations into the atmosphere. "Thirty, thirty-one, thirty-two. . . . You can't say you don't hear it. The drum is beating," Iwakichi cries out. "A drum that never should have sounded is sounding." Stillness; silence. "Ah, hurry and sound it," she begs. "My ears are longing to hear the drum." He sets himself to the task once again. "Sixty-six, sixty-seven. . . . Could it possibly be that only my ears can hear the drum?" (p. 76).

The archetypal soundless drum of the first part has now burst into song. Its utterings, delicate and faint at the beginning of the drumming sequence, grow harsh, brash, fierce, rousing, unyielding, brutal, and exasperated; feelings become distorted, passionate, enraged. Each beat mirrors an atemporal condition of emotion and spirituality.

Hanako begins to despair. "I can't hear it. I still can't hear it," she bursts out. Weakened by his efforts and still counting the beats, Iwakichi cries out: "Eighty-nine, ninety, ninety-one. . . . It will soon be over. Have I only imagined I heard the sound of the drum?" But the drum goes on sounding. Iwakichi almost yields to fatigue and despair. "It's useless. A waste of time. The drum won't sound at all, will it? Beat it and beat it as I may. It's a damask drum" (p. 76).

Hanako compels him to go on and on. "Hurry, strike it so I can hear. Don't give up. Hurry, so it strikes my ears," she pleads. Iwakichi, growing steadily more feeble, nevertheless continues his heroic task, as tension reaches lancinating levels.

> Ninety-four, ninety-five. . . . Completely useless. The drum doesn't make a sound. What's the use of beating a drum that is silent. . . . Ninety-six, ninety-seven. . . . Farewell, my laurel princess, farewell. . . . Ninety-eight, ninety-nine. . . . Farewell, I've ended the hundred strokes. . . . Farewell. (p. 77)

Silence. Iwakichi vanishes. Hanako, as in a dream vision, speaks: "I would have heard it if he had only struck it once more" (p. 77).

In contrast to Western theatre, in which actors attempt to mark character roles with individuality, the Noh actor focuses his efforts on the creation of emotion—love, anger, revenge, hate—in order to go beyond the individual personality. The facts of the drama are stated at the outset; the atmosphere, mood, and poetry must be portrayed by the role itself during the course of the spectacle. For the Westerner, *The Damask Drum* may lack action and conflict. For the Oriental, tension is concentrated and distilled in the images, poetry, gesture, and plastic forms which move about the stage as well as in the archetypal music which absorbs and imposes its energetic patterns on the happenings as a whole. The spatial compositions as well as their audible and silent counterparts work as a whole to create the mood and develop the single emotion, which is basic to Noh theatre.

The Damask Drum reflects the Taoist's and Zen Buddhist's calmness of mind and oneness with nature. It is a manifestation of the Shintoist's animistic beliefs, which endow inanimate objects with a *livingness*, thereby enlarging the scope and depth of the dramatic spectacle. Noh theatre, whether ancient or as re-created by Mishima, is unique. It differs from other forms of performing arts, such as song, mime, dance, verse, and drama, yet it includes them all. It is the intensity of the sustained emotion in *The Damask Drum*, and not the realistic portrayals, which moves audiences. Sublimated passion, with its exquisitely nuanced poetry and its cosmic purpose and design, indelibly forces its impress upon the viewer of the drama.

The various intensities of the vibrations of primal sound in *The Damask Drum* take on tangibility for some, but for others their oscillations remain outside the range of audibility. Those who live locked in the circumscribed mundane world are unable to *hear* and to achieve the sought-for egoless state, blocked as they are by the limitations of their own personalities. They can neither perceive archetypal tone, nor experience subliminal levels of being, nor leap into cosmic spheres—into the unknown. Sound, silent or not, is a barometer for measuring the depth of one's understanding and feeling. Music, in Noh theatre and in Mishima's stage piece, is the raw material, the concrete phenomenon, and the self-originating archetypal power which gave birth to *The Damask Drum*.

Conclusion

Archetypal music infiltrated the minds and psyches of the authors whose writings we have explored in *Music, Archetype, and the Writer*. While tone, diapason, and rhythm affected their inner ear, thereby arousing the deepest layers of their unconscious, these resonances also stimulated and heightened their imaginations and creative élan, thereby determining and channeling their drive and performance.

Hoffmann, Balzac, Baudelaire, Tolstoy, Kandinsky, Joyce, Proust, Sartre, Yizhar, Bhasa, Hanqing, and Mishima listened to their inner voices, to those melodies arising from the deep—sometimes in harmonious sequences, at other instances in stridently and searingly cacophonous amplitudes. The science and/or art of ordering tones and sounds in successions and combinations was instrumental in amplifying the vision and sensibilities of these twelve authors and thereby adding a new dimension to their verbal language.

The interaction of archetypal music and the written word in the works discussed here contributed to the process of transforming the not yet created into the created, the subjective into the objective, and the personal into the impersonal. Sonance and tempo, as catalysts, were ancillary factors in the development of the novels, plays, poems, and essays under scrutiny. These audible factors received by the brain and psyche helped to universalize ideas and images, dynamize symbols and associations, and actuate rhythms, overtones, and volume, thus preparing the writer for the *giant awakening*: that is, the birth of the event—the work of art.

How archetypal music imposed its modulations and reverberations on the brains and psyches of these authors is a mystery. How tone succeeds in affecting a writer's vocabulary, phrasing, thematic development, metric progressions, and choices of phonemes, ideas, and vocabulary is equally hermetic.

Inward hearing is as cryptic and enigmatic a concept as the memory of the tonal sequences in general and their effect upon a writer's nervous system and his creative process. How does that "electrochemical pulse that beats in our neurons with a rhythm that is no less than the language of the brain" function?[1] No one as yet knows. Still more questions emerge. What are the "engrams" in which our collective memories reside and to which Jung refers in his writings? How do the body's sensory organs funnel signals in the brain from one neuron to the next? How did the writers of "Kreisleriana," "Gambara," "Richard Wagner and 'Tannhäuser,' " *The Kreutzer Sonata, Sounds,* "Eveline," *Remembrance of Things Past, Nausea,* "Habakuk," *The Dream of Vasavadatta, The Jade Mirror-Stand,* and *The Damask Drum* respond to the electrical pulsations emanating from the tonal sequences impacted on their brains and psyches and register the event in their writings?

The unknown still reigns in this field. As Beethoven suggested, "every true creation of art is independent, mightier than the artist himself. . . . Music gives the mind a relation to the [total] harmony. Any single, separate idea has in it the feeling of the harmony, which is Unity."[2]

Archetypal music is involved in giving tangibility to word, intensity to situation, and depth to feeling. The energy charge alive in the audible sequences buried within the word, image, and rhythm of the novel, poem, essay or play may also affect, and in equally enigmatic ways, the nervous system of the reader. The magnetic powers the author passes on to the reader may dynamize in him or her a fresh flow of vibrations, tempi, and diapasons which may foment a plethora of feelings and ideations.

Archetypal music, as inherent in and conveyed by the word, may arouse sense impressions in those who come within its orbit, and it may do so in a variety of ways: giving birth for some to a *new* aesthetic, to a variety of intellectual, visceral, and psychological experiences. It may be suggested that the reader, when listening to the tonalities embedded in the configurations imprinted on the page, experiences them as primary utterances, as germinal colorations, as embryonic beats. The mysterious interconnectedness of word and music, then, reaches beyond the known into the unknown—endowing the participant with a gift of great magnitude.

Archetypal music, as we have seen, implies the emergence of a primal force which conveys the fruit of an inner experience of soma and psyche, of the cerebral and the instinctual. It may be viewed as a *revelation* of the imaginative capacities of the creative individual. Once the catalytic event has been encountered, however, rational, disciplined, and ideational factors must take over so that the raw material swept into consciousness may be distilled, as technique refines and polishes the work of art. Pierre Boulez wrote:

> "Technique" is not, in fact, a dead weight to be dragged around as a guarantee of immortality. It is an exalted mirror which the imagination forges for itself, and in which its discoveries are reflected; the imagination cannot, without running the risk of weakness, rely on "instinct" alone, as Baudelaire emphasizes. Over-reliance on this instinct has led it, like the cuckoo, to lay its eggs in the nests of others. Imagination must stimulate intelligence and intelligence must anchor imagination; without this reciprocal action, any investigation is likely to be chimerical. . . . It has been said that music is as much a science as an art; how could these two entities be fired in the same crucible, except by the Imagination, that "queen of faculties"?[3]

Archetypal music—with all of its unanswered questions—may open up the reader to new perspectives, amplify consciousness, deepen the process of coding and encoding, of computerizing phenomena and orchestrating the variety of encounters into fresh verbal harmonies or cacophonies. It may also displace the reader's responses: shock, obliterate, and/or illuminate heretofore darkened areas within the unconscious, excite to passion or anguish, anticipate desired future developments, or encourage a yearning for the past—the joys of childhood.

Just as the vocalizing power heard inwardly by the writers discussed affected their creations, so, too, is the reader's soma and psyche influenced by these same tonal qualities, tempi, amplitudes, and abstract or concrete visualizations inherent in the written word.

Like a mantra or a prayer, archetypal music encourages author and reader to move about in infinite spaces, in dazzling auralities, in tonal distillations existing in four-dimensional climes. No longer tyrannized by the phenomenological world with its certitudes and structures, liberated from the bondage of genre, categories, and preconceived ideations, the author's and reader's only authority is the inner need that drives them to realize their enterprise—the fusion between melody and word.

Is it any wonder that shortly before Jung's death he had wanted to construct—but died before he was able to complete the project—an "Aeolian harp" on his land in Bollingen? This stringed instrument, to be hung from a tree, would have, when caressed by the wind, produced a *music of the spheres*: archetypal and primordial. Its cacophonies and/or harmonies filtering throughout the universe could be transliterated by those who could *hear* them into the written word. As Chuang-tzu wrote:

Great Nature exhales, one calls it wind. Just now it is not blowing; but when it blows then all the hollows of the earth are filled with sound. Have you never heard the blowing of this wind? The hanging steeps of the mountain woods, the hollows and holes of age-old trees; they are like noses, mouths, ears, like choir-stalls, like rings, mortars, pools, like laughing water. Now it hisses, now it buzzes, now it scolds and now it snorts; now it calls, now it whines, hums, cracks. At first it sounds strident, but afterwards panting sounds follow it. When the wind blows softly, there are gentle harmonies, when a cyclone blows up, there are violent harmonies. When the cruel storm calms down, all the stops are out. Have you never noticed how everything stirs and trembles then? And the harmonies of heaven's organ: They resound in a thousand different ways. But behind them is a driving force which causes those sounds to cease and causes them to come to life again. This driving force— who is it?[24]

Music is soul, Word is Logos; their interaction creates the Work of Art— the giant feast of *Creation*.

Notes

Introduction

1. Jung, *Speaking Interviews and Encounters*, p. 275.
2. Jung, *Dream Analysis*, p. 440.
3. Jacobi, *Complex Archetype Symbol in the Psychology of C. G. Jung*, p. 36.
4. Jung, *The Visions Seminars*, I, p. 4.
5. Jung, *Collected Works*, II, par. 222.
6. Ibid.
7. Edinger, "An Outline of Analytical Psychology," p. 5.
8. Jacobi, *Complex Archetype Symbol in the Psychology of C. G. Jung*, pp. 36–48.
9. Ibid., pp. 48–49.
10. Ibid., p. 43. From the Introduction to Esther Harding, *Woman's Mysteries*, p. ix.
11. Edinger, "An Outline of Analytical Psychology," p. 6.
12. Jacobi, *Complex Archetype Symbol in the Psychology of C. G. Jung*, p. 109. (Quoted from Kerenyi, "Prolegomena" to *Essays on a Science of Mythology*, p. 4.)
13. Ibid., p. 110.
14. Ibid.
15. Ibid., p. 52.
16. Clarkson, "Creative Listening: An Archetypal Attitude to Musical Experience."
17. Wethered, *Drama and Movement in Therapy*, pp. 113–14.
18. *The Upanishads*, p. 113.
19. *Popul Vuh*, p. 82.
20. *The Works of Plato*, Book III, *The Republic*, p. 108.
21. Kaegi, "The Transformation of the Spirit in the Renaissance," *Eranos Yearbooks*, I, p. 280. From Lucien Lefèbvre's "Le Problème de l'incroyance au XVIème siècle."
22. Bonny and Savary, *Music and Your Mind*, p. 47.
23. Schopenhauer, *The World as Will and Representation*, I, p. 269.
24. Jung, *Speaking Interviews and Encounters*, p. 275.

Chapter 1

1. *Romantiques Allemands*, I, p. 615. Translated by Albert Béguin. Paris: Pléiade, 1963. All references to "Kreisleriana" come from this edition.

2. Marie-Louise von Franz, in the Introduction to Hannah, *Encounters with the Soul: Active Imagination*, p. 1.

3. *Romantiques Allemands*, I, "Premiers lundis." From *Le Globe*, p. 7.

4. Watts, *Music: The Medium of the Metaphysical in E. T. A. Hoffman*, p. 22.

5. Jung, *Psychological Types*, p. 544.

6. Schopenhauer, *The World as Will and Representation*, I, p. 261.

7. Watts, *Music: The Medium of the Metaphysical in E. T. A. Hoffmann*, p. 37. From Plato's *Timaeus*.

8. Jung, *The Visions Seminars*, II, p. 464.

9. *The Larousse Encyclopedia of Music*, p. 544.

10. Zuckerkandl, *The Sense of Music*, p. 22.

11. Ellenberger, *The Discovery of the Unconscious*, p. 202.

12. Darnton, *You and Music*, p. 7.

13. Cannon, Johnson, and Waite, *The Art of Music*, p. 318. See also Daemmrich, *The Shattered Self*.

Chapter 2

1. Zuckerkandl, *Sound and Symbol: Music and the External World*, p. 2.

2. Balzac, *La Comédie Humaine*, IV, p. 597.

3. Jung, *Psychological Types*, p. 565, and *Collected Works*, vol. 3, pp. 40, 240, 56, 87.

4. Ernest Neumann, *The Unconscious Beethoven*, pp. 72, 115.

5. Cannon, Johnson, and Waite, *The Art of Music*, p. 6.

6. Jung, *Psychological Types*, p. 47.

7. Ibid.

Chapter 3

1. Baudelaire, *Oeuvres complètes*, p. 1205.

2. Jung, *Collected Works*, vol. 9[1], p. 5.

3. Jacobi, *Complex Archetype Symbol in the Psychology of C. G. Jung*, p. 48.

4. Ibid., p. 66.

5. Jung, *Collected Works*, vol. 15, p. 96.

6. Donington, *Wagner's Ring and Its Symbols*, p. 380.

7. Cannon, Johnson, and Waite, *The Art of Music*, p. 380.

8. Eliade, *Myths, Dreams, and Mysteries*, p. 15.

9. Cannon, Johnson, and Waite, *The Art of Music*, pp. 382–84.

10. Donington, *Wagner's Ring and Its Symbols*, p. 19.

11. Ibid. Letter to Roeckel, Nov. 25, 1850.

12. *The International Cyclopedia of Music and Musicians*, pp. 2006–8.

13. Ibid., pp. 2007–8.

14. Jung, *Collected Works*, vol. 15, p. 96.

15. Poulet, *Les Métamorphoses du cercle*, p. 46.

16. *The International Cyclopedia of Music and Musicians*, p. 2006.

17. *Tannhäuser*. Angel Record brochure.

18. *The International Cyclopedia of Music and Musicians*, p. 2006.

19. Ibid., p. 2008.

20. Donington, *Wagner's Ring and Its Symbols*, p. 260.

21. Harding, *Psychic Energy*, p. 155.

22. Jung, *Collected Works*, vol. 9[1], p. 252.

23. Edinger, *Melville's Moby-Dick*, p. 148.

24. Mohr, "Redemption through Love," p. 4.

25. "Correspondence with My Friends," 1851. *Tannhäuser*. Angel Record brochure.

26. "On the Performance of *Tannhäuser*," 1852. Angel Record brochure.

27. Richard Wagner, "A Communication to My Friends." *Lohengrin* brochure. Deutsche Grammophon Records.

28. Jacobi, *Complex Archetype Symbol in the Psychology of C. G. Jung* p. 20. See Ernest Neumann, *Wagner as Man and Artist*, and Galand, *Baudelaire poétique et poésie*.

Chapter 4

1. Tolstoi, *Master and Man: The Kreutzer Sonata Dramas*, p. 131.

2. Christian, *Tolstoy: A Critical Introduction*, p. 86. From Nekrasov's letter to Tolstoy, Dec. 16, 1857.

3. Ibid.

4. Greenwood, *Tolstoy: The Comprehensive Vision*, p. 55.

5. *The New Grove Dictionary of Music and Musicians*, pp. 260–61.

6. Jung, *Collected Works*, vol. 4, p. 130.

7. Ibid., p. 98.

8. Franz, *On Divination and Synchronicity*, pp. 53–55.

9. Jung, *Collected Works*, vol. 14, p. 79.

10. Greenwood, *Tolstoy: The Comprehensive Vision*, p. 139.

11. Ibid., p. 247. Quoted in Derrick Leon's *Tolstoy: His Life and Work* (London: 1944), p. 247.

12. Jung, *Collected Works*, vol. 3, p. 56.

Chapter 5

1. Kandinsky, *Concerning the Spiritual in Art*, p. 19.

2. Ibid., p. 20.

3. Herbert, "Reminiscences," in *Modern Artists on Art*, p. 20.

4. Ibid., p. 23.

5. Selz, *German Expressionist Painting*, p. 341.

6. Ibid., pp. 224, 184.

7. Weiss, *Kandinsky in Munich*, p. 15.

8. Neumeyer, *The Search for Meaning in Modern Art*, p. 86.

9. Franz and Hillman, *Lectures on Jung's Typology*, sect. 1, p. 7.

10. Herbert, "Reminiscences," in *Modern Artists on Art*, p. 22.

11. Jung, *Seminar on Dream Analysis*, pp. 178, 700; Franz and Hillman, *Lectures on Jung's Typology*, sect. 1, p. 18.

12. Jung, *Psychological Types*, p. 385; Overy, *Kandinsky*, p. 35.

13. Herbert, "Reminiscences," in *Modern Artists on Art*, p. 22.

14. Jung, *Psychological Types*, p. 586.

15. Arnheim, *Toward a Psychology of Art*, p. 104.

16. Kandinsky, *Concerning the Spiritual in Art*, p. 17.

17. Weiss, *Kandinsky in Munich*, p. 85.

18. Cannon, Johnson, and Waite, *The Art of Music*, p. 431.

19. Kandinsky, *Concerning the Spiritual in Art*, p. 20.

20. Jung, *Psychological Types*, p. 522.

21. Kandinsky, *Concerning the Spiritual in Art*, p. 15.

22. Ibid.

23. Ibid.

24. Ibid., p. 25.

25. Ibid., p. 38.

26. Ibid., pp. 24, 38.

27. Erich Neumann, *Depth Psychology and a New Ethic*, p. 30; Herbert, "Reminiscences," in *Modern Artists on Art*, p. 27.

28. Herbert, "Reminiscences," in *Modern Artists on Art*, pp. 27–34.

29. Ibid., p. 34.
30. Kandinsky, *Concerning the Spiritual in Art*, pp. 24–26.
31. Ibid., pp. 25, 39, 36, 24.
32. Ibid., pp. 3–45.
33. Kandinsky, *Point and Line to Plane*, p. 38.
34. Brun, *Héraclite*, p. 126.

Chapter 6

1. Joyce, *The Dubliners* (New York: Penguin, 1983). Edited by Robert Scholes. All quotations are taken from this edition.
2. Dolch, "Eveline," in *James Joyce's Dubliners*, p. 3.
3. Healy, *The Complete Dublin Diary of Stanislaus Joyce*, p. 6.
4. Ellmann, *James Joyce*, pp. 144, 284.
5. Healy, *The Complete Dublin Diary of Stanislaus Joyce*, p. 58.
6. O'Brien, *The Conscience of James Joyce*, p. 20.
7. Ellmann, *James Joyce*, p. 18. From Stanislaus Joyce, *My Brother's Keeper*.
8. Ibid., pp. 103–4.

Chapter 7

1. All quotations from Proust are taken from *A la recherche du temps perdu*, I and III, except for those indicated by *SW* preceding the page number, which are taken from C. K. Scott Montcrieff's translation of *Swann's Way*.
2. See Proust, "Essais et articles," *Contre Sainte-Beuve*, p. 565.
3. Capra, *The Tao of Physics*, pp. 55, 62.
4. Ibid., pp. 63–64.
5. Franz, "Archetypes Surrounding Death," p. 20. Quoted from C. G. Jung, *Letters*, II, 45ff. (February 29, 1952).
6. Ibid.

Chapter 8

1. Sartre, *Nausea*, p. 176.
2. Jacobi, *Complex Archetype Symbol in the Psychology of C. G. Jung*, p. 110.
3. Ibid., p. 32.
4. Bouville was modeled after Le Havre, where Sartre taught at the lycée.
5. Greene, *Jean-Paul Sartre: The Existentialist Ethic*, p. 21. See Caws, *Sartre*.
6. Greene, *Jean-Paul Sartre: The Existentialist Ethic*, p. 25.
7. Jung, *Seminar on Dream Analysis*, p. 273.
8. Fell, *Emotions in the Thought of Sartre*, p. 14. See Sartre, *The Emotions: Outline of a Theory*, p. 51.
9. Lafarge, *Jean-Paul Sartre*, p. 26.
10. Capra, *The Tao of Physics*, p. 55.
11. Jung, *Psychological Types*, p. 534.
12. Manster, *Sartre: A Philosophic Study*, p. 129.
13. Jung, *Seminar on Dream Analysis*, p. 269.
14. Ibid., p. 270.

Chapter 9

1. A similar process of mythologizing is evident in two of Yizhar's other works, namely, *Ephram Goes Back to Alfalfa* (1938) and *Days of Ziklag* (1958).
2. Yizhar, *The Midnight Convoy*, p. 78.
3. Ficino, *The Book of Life*, p. 162.

4. Kaplan, *Meditation and the Bible*, p. 7.

5. Halevi, *A Kabbalistic Universe*, pp. 128–30.

6. Scholem, *Major Trends in Jewish Mysticism*, pp. 75, 77.

7. Halevi, *A Kabbalistic Universe*, p. 12.

8. Jung, *The Visions Seminars*, I, p. 44.

9. Halevi, *A Kabbalistic Universe*, p. 129.

10. Kaplan, *Meditation and the Bible*, p. 103.

11. Adler, *The Living Symbol*, p. 39.

12. Scholem, *Major Trends in Jewish Mysticism*, p. 229.

13. Kaplan, *Meditation and the Bible*, pp. 63–64.

Chapter 10

1. Bhavnani, *The Dance in India*. From Ananda Coomaraswamy, *Dance of Shiva and Fourteen Other Essays* (New York: 1918).

2. *Sources of Indian Tradition*, I, p. 269. From *Skanda Purana. Suta Samhita*, 4.2.3, pp. 114–16.

3. Ibid., p. 190.

4. Baumer and Brandon, *Sanskrit Drama in Performance*. From Raghavan, "Sanskrit Drama in Performance," p. 17.

5. *Great Sanskrit Plays in Modern Translation*, pp. xv–xvii.

6. Sources of Indian Tradition, pp. 253–70.

7. Raghavan, "Sanskrit Drama in Performance," pp. 9–43.

8. Ibid., p. 24.

9. Ibid., p. 39.

10. Ibid., p. 52. From Vatsyayan, "Dance or Movement Techniques in Sanskrit Theater."

11. All quotations from *The Dream of Vasavadatta* come from *Great Sanskrit Plays in Modern Translation* (p. 261).

12. Vatsyayan, "Dance or Movement Techniques in Sanskrit Theater," p. 62.

13. Raghavan, "Sanskrit Drama in Performance," p. 39. See Shanta Gandhi's "A Sanskrit Play in Performance: *The Vision of Vasavadatta*," Christopher Byrski's "Sanskrit Drama as an Aggregate of Model Situations,"and Eliot Deutsch's "Reflections on Some Aspects of the Theory of *Rasa*," all in the same volume as Raghavan's essay.

14. Hamel, *Through Music to the Self*, p. 51.

15. From Ragasudharasa, "Melody *Andolika*," in *Sources of Indian Tradition*, p. 270.

Chapter 11

1. *Chuang-tzu*, p. 34.

2. Wilhelm, *Lectures on the I Ching*, p. 60.

3. *Sources of Chinese Tradition*, I, pp. 168–69.

4. Zuang, Zuolin, and Shaowu, *Peking Opera and Mei Lanfang*, pp. 28–29.

5. *The Sayings of Confucius*, p. 33.

6. *Confucius: The Analects*, pp. 46–47.

7. *Selected Plays of Guan Hanqing*, Foreword by Wang Jisi, pp. 1–11.

8. *Confucius: The Analects*, Introduction, p. 37.

9. Ibid.

10. Halson, *Peking Opera*, pp. 12, 49.

11. *The Sayings of Confucius*, p. 18.

12. *The Larousse Encyclopedia of Music*, pp. 26–27.

13. Ibid., p. 26.

14. The instruments used by the orchestra not only sustain mood but flesh it out. The *cheng*, for example, an ancient type of reed organ (2600 B.C.), is one of the few instruments to produce harmonious tones. From the Chinese flute, made of bamboo, copper, marble, or jade, emanate pleasant sounds, somewhat similar to its Western counterpart. The four-

stringed Chinese violin, with its cylindrical soundbox made of bamboo, wood, or coconut shell, and covered in the front with snakeskin, is tuned in two unisons a fifth apart, while lower tones dominate the higher two-stringed instrument. Gongs, clappers, drums, cymbals, lutes, and other musical apparatus add to the aurality of the spectacle. See Halson, *Peking Opera*, pp. 39–46.

15. Beautiful handwriting for the Chinese is not only an exercise in form; it is an art. Painters, such as Chao Meng-fu, who lived in the Yuan period, as did Guan Hanqing, often were scholars and calligraphers before becoming painters. As for the lyre, a whole body of lore surrounded this seven-stringed harplike instrument, whose vibrations were believed to replicate those of the human heart. Highly sensitized, it conveyed emotion in subtle and muted sonances, its infinitely reverberating tones merging the individual with the transpersonal. See Tregear, *Chinese Art*, pp. 138ff.

16. Yuee, *The Chinees Eye*, pp. 49–52.

17. Ibid., pp. 76, 113–19.

18. *The Sayings of Confucius*, p. 27.

19. Wilhelm, *Lectures on the I Ching*, p. 59.

20. *Chuang-tzu*, p. 143.

Chapter 12

1. For information on Noh theatre, see Nakamura, *Noh*.

2. Suzuki, *Zen and the Japanese Culture*, p. 393.

3. Mishima, *Five Modern No Plays*.

4. Maruko and Yoshikoshi, *Noh*, p. 119.

5. A typical *koan* is: "When both hands are clapped listen to the sound of one hand. If you have heard the sound of one hand, can you make me hear it too?" The acolyte studying Zen is posed this question by his master. See Suzuki, *An Introduction to Zen Buddhism*, p. 59.

Conclusion

1. Langer, *Feeling and Form: A Theory of Art*, p. 131. From Ludwig van Beethoven, *Briefe und Gesprache*, p. 146.

2. Dlugoszewski, "What Is Sound to Music?"

3. Ibid.

4. Franz, *C. G. Jung: His Myth in Our Time*. Quoted from Chuang-tzu, *Das Wahre Buch vom sudlichen Blutenland*, p. 11. Translated by R. Wilhelm.

Bibliography

Adler, Gerhard. *The Living Symbol.* New York: Pantheon Books, 1961.

Arnheim, Rudolf. *Toward a Psychology of Art.* Berkeley: University of California Press, 1972.

Balzac, Honoré de. *La Comédie humaine.* VI. Paris: Editions du Seuil, 1966.

Baudelaire, Charles. *Oeuvres complètes.* Paris: Pléiade, 1961.

Bauer, George Howard. *Sartre and the Artist.* Chicago: University of Chicago Press, 1969.

Baumer, Rachel van, and James R. Brandon, eds. *Sanskrit Drama in Performance.* Honolulu: University of Hawaii, 1981.

Baynes, H. G. *Mythology of the Soul.* Baltimore: Williams and Wilkins Co., 1940.

Bhavnani, Enakashi. *The Dance in India.* Bombay: Taraporevala Sons and Co., 1979.

Bonny, Helen L., and Louis M. Savary. *Music and Your Mind.* New York: Harper and Row, 1973.

Brun, Jean. *Héraclite.* Paris: Seghers, 1969.

Byrski, Christopher. "Sanskrit Drama as an Aggregate of Model Situations." In *Sanskrit Drama in Performance.* Honolulu: University of Hawaii, 1981.

Cannon, Beekman C., Alvin H. Johnson, and William G. Waite. *The Art of Music.* New York: Thomas Y. Crowell, 1972.

Capra, Fritjof. *The Tao of Physics.* Berkeley: Shambhala, 1975.

Caws, Peter. *Sartre.* London: Routledge and Kegan Paul, 1979.

Christian, R. F. *Tolstoy: A Critical Introduction.* Cambridge: At the University Press, 1969.

Chuang-tzu. Translated by Herbert A. Giles. London: Mandala Books, 1961.

Clarkson, Austin. "Creative Listening: An Archetypal Attitude to Musical Experience." London, Ontario. Unpublished, 1978.

Confucius: The Analects. Translated and with an Introduction by D. C. Lau. New
    York: Penguin Books, 1955.
Daemmrich, Horst S. *The Shattered Self.* Detroit: Wayne State University Press,
    1973.
Darnton, Christian. *You and Music.* New York: Penguin Books, 1946.
Deutsch, Eliot. "Reflections on Some Aspects of the Theory of *Rasa.*" In *Sanskrit
    Drama in Performance.* Honolulu: University of Hawaii, 1981.
Dlugoszewski, Lucia. "What Is Sound to Music?" *Main Currents in Modern
    Thought* (Sept.–Oct. 1973).
Dolch, Martin. "Eveline." In *James Joyce's Dubliners.* Edited by James R. Baker and
    Thomas F. Staley. Belmont: Wardsworth Publishing Co., 1969.
Donington, Robert. *Wagner's Ring and Its Symbols.* London: Faber and Faber, 1963.
Edinger, Edward. *Melville's Moby-Dick.* New York: A New Directions Book, 1978.
———. "An Outline of Analytical Psychology." Unpublished.
Eliade, Mircea. *Myths, Dreams, and Mysteries.* New York: Harper Torchbooks,
    1960.
Ellenberger, Henri F. *The Discovery of the Unconscious.* New York: Basic Books,
    1970.
Ellmann, Richard. *James Joyce.* New York: Oxford University Press, 1982.
Fell, Joseph P., III. *Emotions in the Thought of Sartre.* New York: Columbia Univer-
    sity Press, 1966.
Ficino, Marsilio. *The Book of Life.* Translated by Charles Boer. Irving, Texas: Spring
    Publications, 1980.
Franz, Marie Louise von. *On Divination and Synchronicity.* Toronto: Inner City
    Books, 1980.
———. "Archetypes Surrounding Death." *Quadrant* (Summer 1979).
———. *C. G. Jung: His Myth in Our Time.* Translated by William H. Kennedy. New
    York: G. P. Putnam's Sons, 1975.
Franz, Marie Louise von, and James Hillman. *Lectures on Jung's Typology.* New
    York: Spring Publications, 1971.
Frey-Rohn, Liliane. "Evil from the Psychological Point of View." In *Evil.* Evanston:
    Northwestern University Press, 1967.
Galand, René. *Baudelaire poétique et poésie.* Paris: Nizet, 1969.
Gandhi, Shanta. "A Sanskrit Play in Performance: *The Vision of Vasavadatta.*" In
    Sanskrit Drama in Performance. Honolulu: University of Hawaii, 1981.
Great Sanskrit Plays in Modern Translation. Transcreations by P. Lal. New York: A
    New Directions Book, 1964.
Greene, Norman N. *Jean-Paul Sartre: The Existentialist Ethic.* Ann Arbor: Univer-
    sity of Michigan Press, 1963.
Greenwood, E. B. *Tolstoy: The Comprehensive Vision.* New York: St. Martin's Press,
    1975.
Halevi, Z'ev ben Shimon. *A Kabbalistic Universe.* New York: Samuel Weiser, 1977.
Halson, Elizabeth. *Peking Opera.* Hong Kong: Oxford University Press, 1982.
Hamel, Peter Michael. *Through Music to the Self.* Boulder: Shambhala, 1979.
Hannah, Barbara. *Encounters with the Soul: Active Imagination.* Santa Monica,
    California: Sigo Press, 1981.

Harding, Esther. *The I and the Not-I*. Princeton: Princeton University Press, 1973.

——. *Psychic Energy*. Princeton: Princeton University Press, 1973.

Healy, George H. *The Complete Dublin Diary of Stanislaus Joyce*. Ithaca: Cornell University Press, 1971.

Herbert, Robert, ed. "Reminiscences." In *Modern Artists on Art*. Englewood Cliffs: Prentice-Hall, 1964.

The International Cyclopedia of Music and Musicians. Edited by Oscar Thompson. Sixth edition edited by Nicolas Slonimsky. New York: Dodd, Mead and Co., 1952.

Jacobi, Yolande. *Complex Archetype Symbol in the Psychology of C. G. Jung*. Translated by Ralph Manheim. Princeton: Princeton University Press, 1959.

Joyce, James. *The Dubliners*. New York: Penguin, 1983.

Jung, C. G. *Collected Works*. Vol. 3, translated by R. F. C. Hull (New York: Pantheon Books, 1960). Vol. 4, translated by R. F. C. Hull (Princeton: Princeton University Press, 1970). Vol. 8, translated by R. F. C. Hull (Princeton: Princeton University Press, 1969). Vol. 9, translated by R. F. C. Hull (Princeton: Princeton University Press, 1968). Vol. 11, translated by R. F. C. Hull (New York: Pantheon Books, 1963). Vol. 12, translated by R. F. C. Hull (London: Routledge and Kegan Paul, 1953). Vol. 13, translated by R. F. C. Hull (Princeton: Princeton University Press, 1967). Vol. 14, translated by R. F. C. Hull (New York: Pantheon Books, 1963). Vol. 15, translated by R. F. C. Hull (New York: Pantheon Books, 1966). Vol. 17, translated by R. F. C. Hull (New York: Pantheon Books, 1954). Vol. 18, translated by R. F. C. Hull (Princeton: Princeton University Press, 1976).

——. *Psychological Types*. London: Pantheon, 1964.

——. *The Visions Seminars*. I and II. Zurich: Spring Publications, 1976.

——. *Seminar on Dream Analysis*. Edited by William McGuire. Princeton: Princeton University Press, 1984.

——. *Speaking Interviews and Encounters*. Edited by William McGuire and R. F. C. Hull. Princeton: Princeton University Press, 1977.

Kaegi, Werner. "The Transformation of the Spirit in the Renaissance." In *Eranos Yearbooks*. I. New York: Pantheon Books, 1954.

Kandinsky, Wassily. *Concerning the Spiritual in Art*. Translated by M. T. H. Sadler. New York: Dover Publications, 1977.

——. *Point and Line to Plane*. New York: Dover Publications, 1979.

Kaplan, Aryeh. *Meditation and the Bible*. New York: Samuel Weiser, 1978.

Lafarge, René. *Jean-Paul Sartre*. Translated by Marine Smyth-Kok. Notre Dame, Indiana: University of Notre Dame Press, 1970.

Langer, Suzanne K. *Feeling and Form: A Theory of Art*. New York: Charles Scribner's Sons, 1953.

The Larousse Encyclopedia of Music. Edited by Geoffrey Hindley. New York: Hamlyn, 1974.

Manster, Anthony. *Sartre: A Philosophic Study*. London: Athlone Press, 1966.

Maruko, Saiji, and Tatsuo Yoshikoshi. *Noh*. Translated by Don Kenny. Osaka: Joikusha, n.d.

Matore, Georges, and Irene Mecz. *Musique et structure romanesque dans La Recherche du temps perdu.* Paris: Edition Klincksieck, 1972.

Mishima, Yukio. *Five Modern No Plays.* Translated and edited by Donald Keene. New York: Vintage, 1973.

Morh, Richard. "Redemption through Love." R. C. A. Victor Recordings. Library of Congress catalog card numbers: R61-1104/R61-1105.

Nakamura, Yasuo. *Noh.* Tokyo: Weatherhill/Tankosha, 1971.

Neumann, Erich. *Depth Psychology and a New Ethic.* New York: G. P. Putnam's Sons, 1969.

Neumann, Ernest. *The Unconscious Beethoven.* New York: Alfred A. Knopf, 1927.

——. *Wagner as Man and Artist.* New York: Vintage Books, 1952.

Neumeyer, Alfred. *The Search for Meaning in Modern Art.* Englewood Cliffs: Prentice-Hall, 1964.

The New Grove Dictionary of Music and Musicians. London: Macmillan, 1980.

O'Brien, Darcey. *The Conscience of James Joyce.* Princeton: Princeton University Press, 1968.

"On the Performance of Tannhäuser, 1852." Angel Record brochure.

Overy, Paul. *Kandinsky.* New York: Praeger Publishers, 1969.

Plato's Timaeus. Translated by Francis M. Cornford. New York: Bobbs-Merrill Co., 1959.

Popul Vuh. English version by Delia Goetz and Sylvanus G. Morley, from a translation by Adrian Recinos. Norman: University of Oklahoma Press, 1953.

Poulet, Georges. *Les Métamorphoses du cercle.* Paris: Plon, 1961.

Proust, Marcel. *A la recherche du temps perdu.* I and III. Paris: Pléiade, 1954.

——. "Essais et articles." In *Contre Sainte-Beuve.* Paris: Gallimard, 1971.

Raghavan, Brandon V. "Sanskrit Drama in Performance." In *Sanskrit Drama in Performance.* Honolulu: University of Hawaii, 1981.

Romantiques Allemands. I. Translated into German by Albert Béguin. Paris: Pléiade, 1963.

Sartre, Jean-Paul. *Nausea.* Translated by Lloyd Alexander. New York: A New Directions Paperbook, 1964.

——. *The Emotions: Outline of a Theory.* Translated by Bernard Frechtman. New York: Philosophical Library, 1948.

The Sayings of Confucius. Translated by James R. Ware. New York: New American Library, 1955.

Scholem, Gershom. *Major Trends in Jewish Mysticism.* New York: Schocken Books, 1965.

Schopenhauer, Arthur. *The World as Will and Representation.* I. Translated by E. F. Payne. New York: Dover Publications, 1969.

Selected Plays of Guan Hanqing. Translated by Yang Zianyi and Gladys Yang. Beijing: Foreign Language Press, 1979.

Selz, Peter. *German Expressionist Painting.* Berkeley: University of California Press, 1974.

Simmons, Ernest J. *Introduction to Tolstoy's Writings.* Chicago: University of Chicago Press, 1968.

Sources of Chinese Tradition. I and II. Compiled by Wm. Theodore de Bary, Wing-Tsit Chan, and Burton Watson. New York: Columbia University Press, 1960.

Sources of Indian Tradition. I. Wm Theodore de Bary, general editor. New York: Columbia University Press, 1958.

Suzuki, Daisetz T. *An Introduction to Zen Buddhism.* New York: Grove Press, 1964.

———. *Zen and the Japanese Culture.* Princeton: Princeton University Press, 1973.

Tannhäuser. Angel Record brochure.

Tolstoi, Leo. N. *Master and Man: The Kreutzer Sonata Dramas.* New York: Thomas Y. Crowell, 1899.

Tregear, Mary. *Chinese Art.* New York: Oxford University Press, 1980.

The Upanishads. Translated from the Sanskrit by Juan Mascaro. New York: Penguin Books, 1983.

Vatsyayan, Kapila. "Dance or Movement Techniques in Sanskrit Theater." In *Sanskrit Drama in Performance.* Honolulu: University of Hawaii, 1981.

Wagner, Richard. "Correspondence with My Friends," 1851. *Tannhäuser.* Angel Record brochure, n.d.

———. "A Communication to My Friends." From Guy Ferchault's "L'ici-bas et l'au-dela." *Lohengrin* brochure. Printed in Germany by Gerhard Stalling AG, Oldenburg, Deutsche Grammophon Records, n.d.

Watts, Pauline. *Music: The Medium of the Metaphysical in E. T. A. Hoffmann.* Amsterdam: Rodopi, 1972.

Weiss, Peg. *Kandinsky in Munich.* Princeton: Princeton University Press, 1979.

Wethered, Audrey G. *Drama and Movement in Therapy.* London: MacDonald and Events, 1973.

Wilhelm, Richard. *Lectures on the I Ching.* Translated by Irene Eber. Princeton: Princeton University Press, 1979.

The Works of Plato. Book III. *The Republic.* Translated by B. J. Jowett. New York: Tudor Publishing Co., n.d.

Yizhar, Smilanski. *The Midnight Convoy.* Jerusalem: Jerusalem University Press, 1969.

Yuee, Chiang. *The Chinese Eye.* Bloomington: Indiana University Press, 1964.

Zuang, Wu, Huang Zuolin, and Mei Shaowu. *Peking Opera and Mei Lanfang.* Beijing: New World Press, 1981.

Zuckerkandl, Victor. *Sound and Symbol: Music and the External World.* New York: Pantheon Books, 1956.

———. *The Sense of Music.* Princeton: Princeton University Press, 1971.

Index